The Pie Lady of Winthrop

The Pie Lady of Winthrop
and Other Minnesota Tales

By Peg Meier and Dave Wood

Neighbors Publishing
P.O. Box 15071
Minneapolis, Minn.
55415

For the Ruths: Ruth Meier, Peg's mother, and Ruth Wood, Dave's wife.

Introduction

MOST reporters like to interview the governor in his executive office, or buttonhole high-powered businesspeople in their mahogany suites, or ask tough questions of legal eagles as they emerge from courtrooms. Most reporters assume that power and wealth are where it's at.

We aren't like most reporters.

We get our kicks talking with regular people. We enjoy sitting at their kitchen tables and in cafes on Minnesota main streets, drinking coffee, asking questions and listening to people pour out their tales.

As reporters for the Neighbors section of the Minneapolis Star and Tribune, we've talked with tradesmen, farmers, teachers, small-business owners, small-town mayors, housewives and entrepreneurs. We've talked with their kids and their parents. We've talked with a newspaper editor in Sauk Centre who didn't want to talk to us, but finally did. Now he talks to us all the time. We've talked with the Mountain Lake school bus driver, the teen-agers in Ada who hang around the swimming pool, the nurses at the Minneapolis blood bank. We were present at the closing of Central High School when one student told us that he hadn't realized until just then that "Central was a special place." We've been awestruck at a Lebanese Catholic church service. We've flown in a light plane with an arthritic 72-year-old woman.

We've laughed with our sources. Sometimes we've been close to crying with our sources. Often we've filled ourselves to the earlobes on coffee, on 3.2 beer, on banana cream pie, on Juicy Lucies.

Everyone has a story, but we prefer tales told by people unused to being media stars. They tell their stories in a more straightforward manner than do big shots. People have told us things about themselves that even their neighbors didn't know. (And, in some cases, still don't.)

The speech of our kind of people is unaffected. They use little jargon or hype. Their exaggerations are small, as are their egos. Some actually thank us for listening. One woman said, "It's as if I spent a lifetime preparing to tell you my story."

For this book, we've chosen some of our articles that originally appeared in the Minneapolis Star and Tribune. We think they capture the spirit of life in Minnesota. Here you'll find the Pie Lady of Winthrop, the funeral director of Kenyon, a telephone company executive turned preacher, a woman with a knack for winning contests, and a grandson of the last czar's tailor who landed in northeast Minneapolis to set up his own tailor shop.

The lives of some of our people have changed since last we wrote about them. You'll find follow-ups at the ends of those stories.

∾

We came to our jobs from different directions.

Dave tried to major in journalism in college but hated it so much he spent 20 years as a college English teacher and free-lance writer before succumbing to the temptations of employment at the Minneapolis Tribune in 1981. Now he is books editor of the Star and Tribune. He's also the author of "Wisconsin Life Trip," "Wisconsin Prairie Diary" and "Telling Tales Out of School."

Peg arrived at the Tribune in 1970 via a more traditional route: high-school newspaper, college newspaper, small-town newspaper, medium-city newspaper, big-city newspaper. She covered cops and courts, fires and funerals, press conferences and school board meetings — all the usual stuff, press pass in hand. All the time she liked writing feature stories best, and before she knew it she landed in the Neighbors section in 1982. After covering the state's history during Bicentennial, Peg couldn't let history alone, so she wrote "Bring Warm Clothes, Letters and Photos from Minnesota's Past," which has been a Minnesota best-seller.

This book would never have been written without the help and encouragement of a variety of people:

We want to thank Wallace Allen, who created the Neighbors section; Charles W. Bailey, who encouraged his people to publish books; Hal Quarfoth and Marilyn Becerra, two Neighbors editors for whom we have happily worked. Thanks also to the Star and Tribune editors who continue to encourage us to write the type of stories you'll find in this book: Linda Picone, Tim McGuire and Joel Kramer. Let's not forget Jack Goodwin, assistant news editor and wonderful man, who said he'd buy 10 copies of this book if we put his name in it. Also, thanks to Annie Henry of B. Dalton Bookseller and Helen Henton, a reader in Olivia, both of whom nagged us until we put together this book.

We gathered a fine team to produce "The Pie Lady of Winthrop." Michael Carroll designed it, Brian Cravens rode herd on the computers that spit it out, Todd Grande painted the cafe scene on the cover and drew the illustrations. Dorothy Meyer typed the manuscript, and Ingrid Sundstrom edited the manuscript and found our mistakes. If you find any more, please write to Ingrid, dear woman, at the newspaper. Linda James was our researcher and created an index that, believe it or not, has two entries entitled "Nice people."

Finally, we want to thank the hundreds of Minnesota people who have trusted us with their stories.

—*Peg Meier and Dave Wood*

Contents

Bill Anderson
The Loveable Priest

Mazeppa, Minnesota
1983

A VISITOR can't be in Mazeppa for more than a few hours without picking up stories about the town's Catholic priest, the Rev. William Anderson.

• About how he loves the Zumbro River Valley and calls himself "Billy of the Valley." He tells people his tombstone will read "B.V.D." for "Billy of the Valley — Dead." Not true. The stone already is in place but it says simply, "Bill Anderson, Minister."

• About how he drives away from downtown with a full bag of groceries balanced on the trunk of his car, on purpose, just so he can have the satisfaction of seeing a trail of people running after him to save his groceries. One time his eggs got smashed, but he said they were worth losing to see the concern people have for a fellow human being.

• How he makes special trips to a gourmet shop in Mantorville, Minn., to buy black jelly beans to hand out to children after mass. (He snitches a few himself. The only ones worth having are black, he says.)

• How the church bulletin he puts together is called "Pewsnews" one week and "Prayboy Magazine" the next.

• How he abolished the "crying room" for infants, welcomed babies to mass and announced that adults could use the crying room because they need it more.

• How he showed up in town one day wearing a clerical collar, greatly unusual for him, and announced he had caught fleas from his dog. "Oh, Father," they said in disbelief. He tore the collar off to reveal printing on the inside: "Hartz 2 in 1 Collar." (He has no dog. He has teddy bears.)

• How he has teen-agers enjoying church.

∽

With recommendations like those, we went to find the priest. The rectory door was covered with signs he made in his print shop. (Printing is his hobby.) For example: "Effective August 1, 1978, it will not be possible to find me here when I am away" and "To Jesus Christ: Walk Right In! To all others, open door first and walk right in!" and "Caution — No Smoking. No matches, no candles. Oxygen in use."

Oxygen was in use. Anderson, 63, has had lung problems since he was a boy. When he was 11, he spent the entire summer in bed. Last winter a bout with pneumonia sent him to a Rochester hospital for three weeks. He sleeps sitting up in a chair. His emphysema brings one advantage, he says; it keeps his sermons short.

"I try not to let it bother me. I do my leg work in the morning and if I feel good in the afternoon, I do my visiting at hospitals and nursing homes. Don't feel too sorry for me. I feel better than Christ did when he was on the cross."

Anderson has been serving St. Peter and Paul Church in Mazeppa for nine years. Before that, he taught biology, languages and religion in Catholic high schools in southern Minnesota — Wabasha, Wilmont and Adrian. He did parish work on the side.

He grew up in Easton, Minn. (south of Mankato), one of 13 children. He was the sixth child and the first boy. Did his parents assume their eldest son would be a priest? No, nothing like that, he said. "I became a priest because I wanted my own bathroom." He got it. He lives alone in a big old rectory that has three bathrooms.

He does have his serious moments. "My ministry," he said, "is trying to be a friend to people. I don't lay big burdens on them. I don't believe Christ wanted us to. If I'm an image of Christ — and I suppose I am, and they are, too — they need me to reach out and touch their lives. I use humor to get my point across because it works. Well, sometimes, it works. Actually I'm not so funny. I just look funny."

And he was back to being funny.

He pulled out a notebook of wise sayings, some his own, some stolen: "A bishop is a man who has not been able to find honest work." "A novena means no wine." "Some laws of the church have made it possible for an adult Christian to avoid making one personal decision." "God has a terrific sense of humor. Just study the world and all its creatures, and you'll laugh for ever and ever." "Don't be embarrassed to ask God for a miracle. He's good at them."

His parishioners, and others in town, tell about his innumerable kindnesses. Anderson is always working behind the scenes to help out, they say. When something good happens, it's likely that the priest was either the instigator or the inspiration. When someone's life takes a bad turn, he's there with comfort — and no jokes.

He's active in community work and in getting people together. He even gets the Catholics and Lutherans together. (He calls it "sectual intercourse" and adds, "That's a good one. That should get me national fame.") He speaks highly of Mazeppa's Lutheran pastor, Bill Ziebell, and gets a big kick out of Ziebell taking 30 people on a bus trip to Chicago to see, "of all things," an exhibit of Vatican art.

In Mazeppa, people worry about the priest's health. If he's not at the Coffee Cup in the morning, somebody makes sure he's OK. They ban smoking at after-mass coffees when Father Bill is around. If his lungs are too clogged up to enjoy performing a wedding ceremony, the family finds another priest to pinch-hit.

He occasionally drops the self-effacing humor and admits he has some friends in Mazeppa. When he got back from the hospital last winter, he related, "Probably a third of them gave me a hug and kiss. I'm not asking for that kind of treatment, but if it happens, it happens. I can hardly love myself and here they are, loving me."

—P.M.

Richard and Jeanne Coffey
Living on a Bog

Hinckley, Minnesota
1982

When we made our decision to move to the woods, we combined our ideas. Gone were the lofty windows, the microwave kitchen, the wall of electronic playthings, sunken tubs.... Our life, our home, would be dependent upon wood chips, not silicon.

—Richard A. Coffey, "Bogtrotter"

RICHARD and Jeanne Coffey used to live at the Towers condominium in downtown Minneapolis. Richard kissed Jeanne good-by amidst the diesel fumes from the MTC buses before she boarded one for work at a Wayzata bank and he went off to his job as a magazine editor. For amusement, they went to cocktail parties, they ate in fancy restaurants, they watched TV.

"We made a lot of money," says Richard, 41, "but we spent a lot of money. We were spending our lives earning our lives."

And so that's why they quit their jobs in December 1980 and went to live near a bog outside of Hinckley. They no longer watch TV because they don't have electricity. Gin and tonics in summer are out because they don't have a refrigerator to make ice cubes. Although there's a fancy restaurant 11 miles away in Hinckley, they prefer to eat the homespun food Jeanne cooks in the Atlanta wood cookstove and serves at an old oak table. For amusement, they read Balzac, modern Russian history and books about nature by the warm glow of kerosene lamps. Jeanne spins wool and sews all their clothes on a pre-1910 Singer and they both tend the garden Richard hewed out of the wilderness. They cut wood, lots of wood, wood to heat the 16- by 24-foot cabin they built for $1,100.

Jeanne carried pails of water into the cabin, and I pushed the wheelbarrow.... There were others with dreams in the city streets. But we walked in ours alone, we walked in the confidence that the day would come when the sounds of buses and airplanes and the crowds of booted feet would fade into the peeps and chirps of birds and squirrels. The smoke of engines would be caught up in a breeze, and the city would be gone.

It's warm and toasty in that cabin but the world outside is harsh, as the winter light sifts down through 60 acres of birch and aspen surrounding their tiny dwelling. Jeanne pours another cup of coffee, and Richard explains, "We didn't want a cabin on a lake with boats. We wanted a place that nobody else liked, a place where they wouldn't come in and build a Radisson Hotel. I was a budding naturalist in the mid-'70s and bogs intrigued me. First, I liked them because they were spooky, but later I learned they contained an incredible amount of animal life. This is the transition zone where north and south meet, where pheasant meet ruffed grouse, where deer meet bear." The Coffeys aren't hunters; they're watchers and admirers, and there is always something new to see and admire in the eerie bog, when that certain slant of light on winter afternoons bathes the harsh countryside with a threat of snow.

Without oxygen, the partially decayed vegetation ceased to break down and peat was formed. Over time the mat of vegetation thickened, and highly specialized plants found a home in the acid water. Thousands of years from now, the vegetable matter of our bog will compact and support meadowlands. . . .

Sure, the snow will come, but there's no threat of being jammed up on 35-W on the way to or from the airport, according to Richard. The cabin resounds with laughter as Richard and Jeanne tell of the period of adjustment, of the wonderful neighbors who helped them over the rough spots, of their past life in the Towers, the old life they spent getting and spending. "When we lived in Minneapolis, we'd spend our weekends on the bog," says Richard. "The weekends kept getting longer and longer and finally the opportunity arose and we came up here."

That opportunity came when the Pine County Historical Society offered the Coffeys jobs as co-curators of the fire museum, which is housed in the old train depot on Hwy. 23 in downtown Hinckley. A meticulously assembled memorial to the historic fire of 1894, it's open from May 1 to Oct. 31. It drew 25,000 guests last year, 20,000 this year, and customers at Ma's Cafe on Main St. give the Coffeys lots of credit for the museum's success.

The co-curator job pays $13,000 per year. Richard also writes "Coffey Break," a column for the Hinckley News, which pays $5 a week "when John Lyon [the publisher] remembers to pay me." He also writes magazine articles and recently published a book, "Bogtrotter" (Dorn Books, 1982). Jeanne fills in at the Farmers & Merchants State Bank and sells real estate.

How's that going?

"I don't know," she says, laughing and pouring coffee from the bottomless pot. "I started selling recently and now I've run out of relatives."

Nevertheless, they both agree that money is no problem. They just get by with less.

> *The older people in the community ... laughed when we asked how to get the toilet seat warm when it was twenty degrees below zero. "Take it in the house and hang it behind the stove, and when you go out, don't waste no time...."*

It's idyllic, sitting in the little cabin, heat radiating from the potbellied stove. There's good talk of books everyone means to read but doesn't, while Buckwheat, the golden retriever, lies on the rug. But it hasn't been easy for the Coffeys to adjust to bog life. "Sometimes," says Richard, "I'd kill for a Burger King." On their infrequent trips to the Twin Cities, Jeanne says, they load up on junk food and come back to the bog with bellyaches. "I'd bake all kinds of bread and we'd just eat and eat. We gained 30 pounds collectively the first year."

"If we ever leave," says Richard, "this will be known as our Eating Period."

"One night," recalls Richard, "we looked at each other. We dug the car out of a snowdrift, drove into Hinckley and took a room at Cassidy's Motel. Then we took a shower, the first shower we'd had since we arrived months before." Today, such ablutions are taken care of in the sauna Richard built out back.

Two concessions to modern life are a telephone, which the fire museum directors demanded, and a battery-operated radio. "That's our lifeline." It reminds them of traffic snarlups on 35-W. "If we'd have been in the city during the Iranian hostage thing or the space shuttle, it would have been just more news," says Richard. "But up here, we felt incredibly close to those people and kept turning the radio back on to get more news of them."

At first, the Coffeys thought of their idyll in the bog as a temporary adventure. Now they're confused. "Sometimes," Richard says, "we worry about our future and the need to acquire something material. Other times, we worry that we're not doing anything important for society." "But then," adds Jeanne, "we think that feeding the animals and writing about nature is purpose enough."

> *[The first summer] we spent our time like the new rich, squandering our hours of warm wealth wandering about the bog and woodland, looking in on the affairs of the wilderness around us.*

Writing about nature. Richard began the Hinckley News column because he wanted to communicate to the local folks his feelings about their arrival in the bog and to promote the fire museum. Before he knew it, he was writing "Bogtrotter," a philosophical treatment of nature, of fire and of ice. But it's much more than that. It treats of the Coffeys' first year in the cabin. It treats of his love affair with Jeanne, how they came to know and to love and to learn from their neighbors. How they fought mosquitoes that first summer, how they dug a well. And Thanksgiving. How they took a walk one night and got lost very near the cabin. How they built the out-house and how Richard ran from it toward the cabin, pulling his pants up as he went. Skunks.

"Bogtrotter" tells of their doubts and how they resolved them. Like the time when Richard found out that the chainsaw was a remarkable tool, but wondered if it was cheating to use it. Or when Jeanne was appalled at deer hunters. Finally, they figured out that the only way to avoid facing these problems was to return to the Towers, put a copy of Audubon magazine on the coffee table and talk about conservation and the environment at cocktail parties. They decided to face the problems.

> *Death in the woods is not tragic. The crack of a rifle is but a momentary interruption to the tapping of the woodpecker.... When the excited voices of men have died away, the chickadees sing and the blue jays scold and the woodpeckers tap their message on the rotted snag of the birch tree.*

And so there they sit in the cabin, waiting for the sun to set, the moon to rise and winter to come in all its harsh fury. "You know," says Richard, "I was never aware of the seasons back in Minneapolis, nor did I realize that the sun went down at 4:30." It's about time for the Coffeys to light the kero-sene lamps and make ready for supper and an evening with Balzac. Time for the reporter to hasten across the primitive road through the forest of birch to the highway where his car is parked. And to drive to Cassidy's Mo-tel for a good hot shower and all the other inconveniences of modern civili-zation.

> *The woodlot was a place of change, a stage of many different plays .... Presenting the birth, life and death of its actors ... There was ter-ror for some behind the brush pile, play for many in the clover, and conception in the leaves. The woodlot could be an elysian dream one moment and a blood-splattered nightmare the next. Winter was pure Brueghel the Elder. Our highland, surrounded by bog, was at once a sanctuary for the frightened and a table for the hungry.*

—D.W.

> *Jeanne Coffey wrote us at Christmas 1984 explaining that the lit-tle cabin now has electricity. "If you are ever in our neighborhood, stop in. We even have a Mr. Coffee! Electricity hasn't modernized us com-pletely. We still pump our water and we still have our outhouse ...."*

The Ganleys
Solving Neighborhood Burglaries
Minneapolis, Minnesota
1983

THE BURGLARS hit late at night. While residents slept, thieves crawled through windows and prowled through houses in north Minneapolis. In the morning, people realized their television sets and sterling silver and other valuables were gone. Change and billfolds were missing from nightstands; the burglars must have tiptoed around people in bed. Butcher knives were stolen from kitchens and tossed into back yards; the burglars apparently armed themselves with knives while in the house.

Break-ins came faster and faster. Almost every week, the neighborhood grapevine reported another. Almost all were between midnight and 5 a.m. Some homes were hit twice. Sometimes the thieves worked two nights in a row.

The once-secure neighborhood became nervous. Groggy neighbors told one another how they had tossed and turned in bed, listening for footsteps. At least one child was sent away to grandma's. People bought watchdogs and better locks for doors and windows.

Jerry Ganley at first suspected some kids from the neighborhood. He and his wife, Elizabeth Harris, watched from the window of their duplex at 1725 Girard Av. N. and spotted prowlers. These prowlers weren't kids.

Brian Lickness confirmed it. He woke up at 4:45 a.m. Oct. 15 and found a burglar in his bedroom. A shotgun — his own shotgun — was stuck in his face. His wife woke up, took one look and hid her face in the pillow. She didn't want to see more. The burglars took his car keys and billfold. They rummaged through the car and took two chrome chafing pans from the trunk.

Something had to be done, the neighbors decided. If this kept up, someone they knew would be hurt or dead or raped or God knows what.

Jerry Ganley called his brother, Mick, a Minneapolis police officer. The two had grown up in the neighborhood, delivered newspapers for years and knew almost every house. They still refer to houses by the names of owners in the 1950s, when they were boys. Their parents live in the house in which the boys grew up. Mick has moved four miles away, but the old neighborhood is home. He didn't like the idea of burglars at work there.

Mick Ganley pored over police reports. He found that in the course of three months, there had been more than 30 break-ins in the immediate neighborhood — about nine square blocks bounded by Golden Valley Rd. on the north, 16th Av. N. on the south, Girard Av. N. on the east and James Av. N. on the west. That's near the North High School football field.

The number of burglaries was, as Mick Ganley put it, an oddity for a neighborhood that usually has a burglary or two a year. "It just didn't happen before." He talked to his supervisors about getting the burglars. "Get cracking on this thing," said Capt. Tom Whelan and Lts. Fred Moen and Gary McGaughey. They asked for volunteers and they got good cops, Ganley said.

"We were dealing with trickier than your average burglars," he said. "You try not to think you're in a Charlie Chan movie every time you're on a case, but I swear, these guys were smarter than most. For one thing, they were more light-footed."

Neighbors and police agreed that the burglars were hitting so often that it stood to reason that a good surveillance plan would catch them. Every night, from a few strategically located houses, they watched. Citizens pulled two- or four-hour shifts. Some, like Jerry Ganley, occasionally watched all night. He's a fireman and spent big hunks of time at the living room window on his nights off. He could see much of the neighborhood from there.

In other houses, families went to bed and police officers stood watch from their windows. Mick Ganley said assignments got sticky because smoking officers had to go to smoking households. They were all *eating* households, however, and residents left treats for the officers. Patrolman Debi Farmer, Mick Ganley's partner, fondly remembers Jerry Ganley's homemade apple pie, complete with Haagen-Dazs ice cream. For the police, the watch meant long hours, double shifts, traded duties. Farmer missed her son's 5th-birthday party.

Jerry Ganley's house was communications central. Ganley and his wife would turn off all the lights and pretend to go to bed. Instead they took their places in dark rooms. They moved the telephone to the bathroom, turned down the volume and put on a tiny night-light. Several times every night, neighbors would call with information or just to say, "Keep up the good work."

They made a map of the neighborhood and listed residents' names and telephone numbers, in case they needed the police fast. They took notes on cars moving through the neighborhood. They knew who came and went from which houses at what times: "It's OK; that just so-and-so's brother." They knew what time which cat yawned.

Action was slow. The neighbors and police saw some prowlers but no break-ins. Residents realized that much police work is unworthy of television shows. Mick Ganley said, "It was so boring that when your nose started to run, it was great because it was something different."

Police superintendents couldn't continue to provide the manpower. Neighbors kept up. About 20 people took turns standing watch. Elizabeth Harris said, "We sat down one night and said, 'This is crazy and we hate it, but it's important and we have to do it.' "

She said she and other residents were more angry than afraid: "At least I didn't know I was terribly afraid until one night when the prowlers were in our front yard. I could see them, all dressed in black and staring at our house."

Her brother-in-law Mick added, "At times like that we were trying to decide if they were architecture students, studying our locks and windows. But you talk about fear. We had a block meeting about the break-ins, and there was raw fear on the surface."

The intense watch lasted a month. Police were put on and off the case, depending how close they were to catching the thieves.

They were learning quite a bit and began to zero in on a few suspicious characters. One prowler kept his hands in his pockets as he skulked around the neighborhood; he was known as "Pockets." Another was called "Shower Cap" because he usually wore one. The suspects lived in the neighborhood, just half a block from Jerry Ganley.

The Ganley brothers charted the prowling and learned that it was usually Mondays, Tuesdays and Wednesdays beginning between 2 and 3 a.m. One time the Ganleys guessed there was a burglary before the residents did.

Because it wasn't known if the suspects had a scanner radio to overhear police talking about the case, the officers and neighbors developed a code. "Home base" was Jerry Ganley's house, the "nest" the suspects' house. "Ho Chi Minh Trail" was a brush-lined trail that the suspects often took, "Spanky" the pit-bull dog the prowlers had with them. Their every movement between midnight and about 5 a.m. was recorded: "Pockets, no Spanky, eastbound toward home base."

At one point, the neighbors considered what they called the "Andy of Mayberry approach" — contacting Pockets and Shower Cap and telling them, "Shucks, there's been a rash of burglaries in the neighborhood. But don't worry, we'll all be watching from our windows every night and we'll get 'em." No one was especially eager to relay the message and, besides, the neighbors wanted not only an end to the break-ins but some arrests and convictions. They kept on watching.

They hit pay dirt early on Nov. 6. Elizabeth Harris saw Pockets on the Ho Chi Minh Trail with a television set in his arms at 3:45 a.m. She just about had a heart attack. Police were not in the neighborhood at the time, so she telephoned them. Two squad cars pulled up and put lights on the suspects' house. Pockets ran out the front door before police were able to arrest him. At 4:10 a.m., police got a call — burglary of an occupied house in the neighborhood. A 24-inch color TV set had been stolen.

The police put the detail back on the next day.

Four days later, a police officer spotted a wanted bulletin. The suspect in the bulletin was wanted for the assault of his girlfriend's sons, ages 3 months and 2 years. Police recognized the photograph as that of Pockets. From the bulletin, they learned the suspect's name and other pertinent information.

On Nov. 11, armed with a search warrant, Ganley and other officers arrested Robert Ed Johnson (known to the neighbors as "Pockets"), 25, at his residence, 1811 Girard Av. N. He was charged with burglary of occupied dwellings, second-degree assault and theft of property over $250. According to police records, Johnson's house was filled with stolen property from burglaries, including the two chafing pans stolen from the trunk of Brian Lickness's car.

He also has been charged with criminal sexual conduct and first-degree assault. Police allege in their complaint that Johnson sexually abused the 2-year-old, fractured his skull and caused other injuries. He also sexually abused the 3-month-old and broke his leg, the complaint alleges.

Robert Johnson has pleaded not guilty to all charges. Trial is set for Jan. 30.

His younger brother, Edward Earl Johnson ("Shower Cap"), 19, of the same address, was arrested Dec. 5 as he walked out the back door of a neighborhood house that police say he was burglarizing. He was charged with burglary. Both Johnsons are in the Hennepin County Jail.

Mick Ganley, Debi Farmer and five other officers have been recommended for police department commendations. So have 13 neighborhood residents.

The police are pleased. "We knew it would be a lot of work with the probability of few results," Mick Ganley said, "other than the satisfaction of putting someone in jail."

The neighbors are pleased. "We got them," Jerry Ganley said. He stressed that it was a neighborhood effort that did it: "At least 13 people were very diligent," he said. "It wasn't just us. We had the best vantage point." It didn't hurt to have a cop in the family who was vitally interested in the neighborhood, he said.

They would recommend their crime watch. Elizabeth Harris said, "We think it's a good lesson to people who think they can't fight crime."

—P.M.

Mina Peterson
The Pie Lady of Winthrop

Winthrop, Minnesota
1984

THEY CALL her Mina, but her real name is Martha Wilhelmina Peterson and she's "the pie lady of Winthrop." Folks in these parts like pie because it lays a good foundation for all the coffee they slosh down at Lyle's Cafe, which is open 24 hours a day, closing only on Saturday night and all day Sunday.

By 8:30 on a Wednesday morning, Mina already has two apple, one pumpkin and one custard pie in the oven in the long, galley-like kitchen. She's wearing slacks, blouse and red print apron. She flops down a wad of pie crust on the work table and *whiff-whiff-whiff*, the wad becomes a delicate circle you can almost see through. She picks it up gingerly and tosses it in a pie pan. It lands without need of adjustment. In go the blueberries. Then *whiff-whiff-whiff* and the top crust is rolled. She deftly slashes a design on the crust and lays it over the berries, crimps the edges, paints the top with cream, then turns her attention to sour cream and raisin. "That's quite a seller," she says, shooting a canny little sideways glance at you, as if to say what's a reporter doing here in this kitchen?

The reporter's in the kitchen with Mina because it isn't often he runs into a 93-year-old restaurant worker.

Yup. She took her job at this restaurant 40 years ago, two years after her husband, John Edgar Peterson, died. She's worked for current owner Marge Lindstrand since 1950 when Marge and her late husband, Lyle Saxton, took over the place. Marge, who picks up Mina at 7:30 three mornings a week, says it's strange the way things happen. "Years ago my husband, Lyle, would say that we'd have to think about getting a replacement for Mina because she wasn't going to live forever. Now Lyle has been dead for 14 years."

Mina *whiff-whiff-whiff*s with her rolling pin and talks about her life. She was born in Helsingland, Sweden, and was 3 years old when her parents took her to Illinois and later to the Winthrop area. "I didn't want to come [to Winthrop]. I was having too much fun in Illinois." Canny smile. *Whiff-whiff-whiff*.

She led the life of a farmer's wife, gave birth to five children, remembers the good times, the hard work. "At threshing, oh, how we cooked. People liked my beans. When I'd send lunch out to the field pitchers they always asked if I'd throw in a dish of beans. They liked my beans."

"Oh, yah, I guess. I like apple pie best. There's nothing like a good apple pie. But the sour cream and raisin is sure a seller here."

Do Scandinavians like sour cream? Is that it?

"They like cream *period!*"

Here comes the photographer.

"Oh, don't make the picture too big and show my wrinkles. I had my picture in the New Ulm paper. It was *terrible.*"

Mina has hit her stride by 9 a.m., as she takes the first pies out of the oven, puts new ones in, then walks briskly back to her station. She tears strips of cloth off the baked pies to reveal perfect flaky crusts. "I use the rags around the edges, that's my way. I guess I read about it in the paper."

A few years back, Lindstrand figured that Mina had baked upwards of 80,000 pies since she began work at the cafe. "Oh, yes, I used to bake more of them than I do now. That was when pie was cheap, not a dollar a slice." (Lyle's charges 90 cents for a hefty slice.) She shakes her head at inflation and begins to separate a dozen eggs, nestling the spent shells like spoons in her left palm. No motion is wasted. "Oh," she says, "it goes pretty easy when you do it all the time. I don't need a recipe to follow, you know."

Has it been tough being a widow for 42 years?

"You get used to anything," she says, opening a big can of shelled pecans. "These are easier than shelling them the old way." Canny smile.

When is she going to retire?

"Oh, I'm too dumb to retire, so I'll just keep on. No, really, I'm just so glad I can be around with these young people. I just like to be here. Do you know? In all these years, I've never had a fight with Marge. You can't get a boss better than she is," says Mina, jerking a floured thumb over her shoulder as Lindstrand passes behind her back.

Lindstrand says, "Mina's an inspiration to all of us. You don't dare come to work and say 'I'm so tired' or complain about aches and pains when Mina's standing there rolling out the pie crusts."

Mina bends from the waist and slides a heavy can of flour from under her work table and starts scooping flour into a bowl. Then she stands up in a flash and slops some milk in the bowl, starts to stir and says she's been lucky. She has a nice four-room house where she lives alone and "where the lawn isn't too big to worry about." Although her son died many years ago, her four daughters live in the area and see her often.

"And I'm very interested in church. I go to the Covenant Church every Sunday. There are only two of us old women left. The new generation has taken over. Pastor Larry Pennings is a very nice young man. I used to work here on Sundays until evening services. When I got to church, everyone knew that Mina was there because they could smell hamburger and onions."

She says that WCCO's Roger Erickson's family place adjoined the Peterson farm. "Oh, he [Roger] was always full of craziness." She shakes her head. "I heard him one day on the radio and he told about when he got kicked in the head by a horse. Someone said 'That must have hurt.' And Roger said 'You bet. That horse limped *for days.*'"

By 11:15, it's time for Mina to piece together her meal of roast beef and corn and sit down with dishwasher Lucille Johnson and two reporters. Waitress Margaret Draeger, who has worked at Lyle's for *only* 33 years, brings coffee. One reporter orders apple, the other raisin and sour cream pie. Mina watches carefully as they take their first bites. After the "oohs and ahs" have died down, she resumes her meal.

At the next table, Darrell and Irene Knudson of Walnut Grove are digging into pie, on their way to visit a daughter in River Falls, Wis. They like to time their trips so they can stop at Lyle's. How does the pie go down? Great, they say. "Only problem," Darrell says, "is the waitress wouldn't serve us the pie *first.*"

And then it's time for Martha Wilhelmina Peterson to go to her little home with the little yard and watch her favorite soap opera, "The Guiding Light."

—D.W.

Mina Peterson had cancer surgery in April 1984. She told her doctor if he could manage to get her back on her feet, she'd bake him a sour cream and raisin pie. As of January 1985, Mina, now 94 years old, was back baking pies one day a week at Lyle's.

Edith James
Returner of Lost Things

Minneapolis, Minnesota
1983

W HEN EDITH JAMES got back from lunch, she had no time for coffee
and a cigarette. The telephone was ringing and ringing and ringing. A young man stood impatiently at the door, wanting his lost
gloves and wanting them fast. No such gloves. She grabbed the phone.

*Lost and found. . . . A box of what, sir? . . . Where were you sitting
on the bus? . . . Was it northbound? . . . In a box or in a checkbook? . . .
Spell your last name. . . . Hold on, sir.*

James doesn't find it at all strange that someone would leave a box of
blank checks on a bus. As the lost-and-found clerk for the Metropolitan
Transit Commission (MTC), she hears "everything, absolutely everything."
Like the day before. A man called to say he had been taking his false teeth
to the dentist and left them behind on the bus seat.

*Sir, they did find your checks. . . . The driver won't be in until af-
ter I close. You'll have to come in tomorrow. . . . 3106 Nicollet Av.
S. . . . You're welcome.*

Books and canes. Eyeglasses and gym bags. Doctors' bags and lawyers'
briefcases. Keys enough to open a locksmith's shop. Bottles of booze, a few
unopened. An inflatable female doll, the kind not used by children.
Rarely does a driver complete a run without finding *something* left behind. Things go in streaks. Some rainy weeks, James gets 150 umbrellas.

*Is it a Tote, the fold-up kind? . . . What color? . . . Usually I don't
get the things until the next day. I'll have you call tomorrow, after
8:30. Umbrellas usually come in.*

Now it's Glove and Mitten Season. Don't call and tell her you left your brown gloves on the bus. She has dozens of brown gloves. Tell her you left your light brown gloves with dark brown leather fingers on Bus 16 west-bound at 2:17 p.m. Wednesday.

She holds gloves, mittens, umbrellas, books and other nonvaluables for two weeks. Valuables are kept a month. Every other week, James sends out 50 to 75 postcards to people whose names are in wallets and other posses-sions. Most items are claimed, but those that aren't picked up are returned to the finders — usually passengers and drivers. If the finders don't want the items, MTC employees, including James, get a crack at them. Libraries and schools get some books, and eyeglasses go to old folks' homes. If no-body wants the other stuff, James takes it to the Salvation Army.

Every winter James gets a couple of pairs of gloves and mittens for each of her six children, two grandchildren and a foster son. Not that there are a lot of gloves and mittens around the James house. Her kids lose them.

James keeps a supply of gloves and umbrellas as loaners for MTC peo-ple. Usually she keeps a spare umbrella or two in her car. One time she was nominated for sainthood by a woman walking umbrella-less in a thunder-storm; James shoved a loaner out the window to her without bothering to explain that umbrellas are her business.

She makes some exceptions to the MTC rules about how long to hold things. A hunk of a diamond ring has been in the safe since August. A teddy bear has resided in the lost-and-found office since summer. The mother of the teddy bear's owner called James the day her little girl left it on a bus, but James hadn't gotten it yet. She keeps hoping the bear's owner will call again.

> *. . . Thank you for holding. . . . What bus was he on, Ma'am? . . . St. Paul or Minneapolis? . . . What time did he get on? . . . If you can give me a more definite answer, I can try to find the bus right away. . . . What color was the wallet? . . . Just a minute, please. I'm putting you on hold. . . . Hi Smitty, guess who? I've got a woman whose husband left his wallet behind. He's 82 and kind of shook up.*

Wallets. Now that's something Edith James gets steamed up about. Not only do droves of forgetful people leave wallets behind. But other bus riders get their pockets picked and call her later, frantic. She has a big box of wal-lets with no identification that she figures have been ripped off and dumped. James doesn't carry a wallet herself. She takes a few necessities in a purse and carries a minimum of cash in her pocket. A secure pocket.

Nothing infuriates James more than callers who assume MTC employ-ees steal the things they find on buses. Most don't steal; she's convinced of it. When someone calls and says, "I don't know why I'm calling you be-cause I know it wasn't turned in," James loves to be able to respond, "It's here."

Most customers behave well. But one customer's behavior sticks in her craw. A woman who had lost her purse was so upset — "really having fits" — that James asked MTC Clerk Dick Day to search a string of buses in the MTC garage. He found it, and the money was in it. James told the woman of that happy fact and made it clear that Day had gone out of his way to do her a favor. The woman didn't even bother to ask James to thank him. "Can you *believe* some people?" James said.

And another woman, about 70, lost her purse and was frantic because her Medicare card was in it. The purse was routed to James. Not only was the card there, so was $840 in $20 bills. "I have your purse," she told the woman when she came to pick it up. "Good." "Aren't you going to check and see that the money is there?" "Oh. I suppose I should." The last James saw of her, the woman was sitting at a bus stop across the street, her purse tossed casually on the bench.

You lost a Bible? . . . Was it in any kind of package? . . . What kind of plastic bag? . . . Was your name on it? . . . I have it. . . . Today? 6 p.m. Tomorrow we're open until 4:30. . . . You're very welcome.

Rarely does James have more than a few minutes between phone calls. If the phone doesn't ring for 10 or 15 minutes, she thinks it's broken. The MTC operator stops sending through calls an hour before the end of James's workday so she can catch up with paper work and arrange merchandise. The telephone and the line of people at the door to identify items would be enough to make most of us lose our minds and call her to help find them. But James likes her job. "I like it because I don't have a lot of people around me all the time. The bosses, you know. I'm on my own down here." But all these people calling! "It's fun in here sometimes. No, it really is."

James has held the job for several years, except for a brief time when she was bumped by an employee with more seniority. He lasted six weeks. Couldn't stand it.

I understand you left it under the seat, sir. What I don't understand is WHAT you left under the seat.

She handles customers politely and, when possible, with a sense of humor. When someone hangs up on her, she says with exaggerated courtesy, "And thank *you*, too."

"At first, some are really grumpy," she said. "I can talk them out of that, maybe. What I can't handle is where they call me and start crying. Like yesterday, this woman called and said she lost her clothes. She was going to stay over to her cousin's and she had a special dress for a party, some night clothes and clothes for the next day. All in a bag. She was so upset I asked the driver to look for it. We're not supposed to bother the driver for anything but valuables, but she was so upset and I felt bad for her." She got the bag back.

Some regular callers to the lost-and-found department know Edith James by name, and vice versa. One old man loses his bus-identification card so often that James can figure out when he is vacationing in Florida. That's when he hasn't called for his card in more than a few weeks.

James is paid $12.25 an hour, the same as MTC bus drivers. She used to be a driver, in fact. She does some pinch-hit driving in the summer, but prefers lost-and-found in bad weather.

When she gets home in the evening, she's glad her husband, Bill, is the quiet type. She said, "He doesn't talk. He gives yes and no answers and doesn't go anywhere." At home, she refuses to answer the phone. "The first 30 minutes, I shut the door and turn on the TV. Like tonight, 'Magnum' is on and I can't afford to miss no parts of 'Magnum.' If *he'd* call, I'd answer. Nobody else."

— P.M.

Edith James got bumped again from her lost-and-found job. An MTC employee with more seniority wanted the post. She's dispatching buses on the city's south side.

Weekend in Jail

Just Like Living in History

Taylors Falls, Minnesota
1981

STAYING IN Taylors Falls for three days is like living in history, rather than being bombarded by it. That's because its denizens don't push the history angle as if their livelihoods depended on it.

History is just there, wherever you turn, and bespeaks a gentler time in our region. A hand-lettered sign, blurred with age but still exhorting horse-owners to "Use Long's Excelsior Liniment," peers down from one of the old beams that holds up the roof of the glossy new Livery shopping mall. There's also the tiny Victorian library memorialized and then blown to smithereens by Thomas Gifford in "The Wind Chill Factor." The library collection has grown to 10,000-plus volumes since 1887, when it moved into the little building built in 1854 as a tailor shop.

Oh, they've finally got around to changing to the Dewey Decimal System from the old 1, 2, 3 classification system, but librarian Marilyn Rimestad still has the first book purchased, the Holy Bible, classified until recently as "1." Marilyn is very concerned about circulation figures, which have dropped from 6,500 book check-outs in 1976 to 2,482 last year. But she figures the library will always be there, even though folks don't spend as much time as they used to reading every era's best-sellers and sipping oyster stew at library board meetings of a frosty 19th-century night.

Heading south on the main drag, where wood smoke curls up from many chimneys, it's difficult to resist coffee at the Chisago House, a newish restaurant that stands on the site where some say the famous orator Stephen A. Douglas held forth back in 1857. Some say not. If Douglas didn't, at least Ken Rivard, 67, does, on Dec. 1, 1981.

"When the circus would come to St. Croix Falls years back, they used to have a parade. They'd come across the bridge to try to get us to come to the circus. I remember the elephants used to line up at the well — they had a big water tank there then — and they'd stick their trunks in the tank and *whoosh*, they'd fill up with water. I don't think we'll see that sight again."

Probably not, but the artesian well half-way up the hill still runs ceaselessly, and a man is putting his 10th five-gallon container of its water into his car trunk. One wonders if he sequesters an elephant in one of the old horse barns up on Angel's Hill.

Night is falling and a reporter must spend the night in the jail across the street from the well. No, he isn't out on a work pass after stealing a horse from the livery, nor has he tried to *really* blow up the library in hopes of making a story. The jail on Government Rd. was built more than 100 years ago and held its share of hoodlums over the years. But now it serves as temporary housing for a very few of the million people who make their way through Taylors Falls each year to see the sights in town and nearby.

Jail owner Helen White, who lives next door at the restored Schott-muller Building, calls the jail a "bed and breakfast," but it bears little resemblance to its British Isles counterparts. The outside is simple, stolid, its 16-by-24-foot walls built of 2-by-4s stacked flat upon each other. To get through the front door, one must first get through an ancient iron grate that squeaks open. Grim.

Once inside, however, the picture changes. The old cells are gone. In their place are a modern kitchen stocked with breakfast makings, cooking pans, china pottery made by local artisans, a vaulted-ceiling living room, a loft bedroom and a spic-and-span bathroom. Art by locals hangs on the new, wainscoted walls. And homemade hooked rugs grace the wood-and-brick floor. This is a lockup worthy of a former Watergate criminal.

But a chill has set in, and the guest must make a decision. Should he turn up the electric heat or stoke up the living room's chrome-trimmed potbelly, which has a generous pile of oak logs stacked behind it. The absence of a television and the presence of a bottle of sherry in his briefcase tells him that potbelly is the only answer.

With a fire roaring and the sherry breathing, it's time for a perusal of the bookshelf, generously stocked with essay collections and mystery novels and magazines about building restoration. Perhaps the public library could boost circulation if the jail's own bookshelf weren't so delicious. Ah, here's a book called "The Guest-Room Book, 1948," full of poems and essays by the likes of Hilaire Belloc, G.K. Chesterton and C.S. Lewis, authors the guest has forgotten since the appearance of "Three's Company" and other contemporary classics. Why not give it a try?

> Those who are shocked at the barbarity of other nations may discover a salutary reminder of our own blindness if they will look for an hour or two at "Morris's British Birds" . . . .

No, that won't do. Ah, here's something, a parody of Housman about how certain men actually murdered their lovers:

> There's Tom who shot his Ludlow lass
> For walking out with Jim:
> (He often gave her powdered glass
> To make her figure slim.)

There's Jake whose buxom dairymaid
Had cracked his heart in two.
He took his oldest razor-blade
And sawed her weazand through.
But Juries blind with city smoke
Can never understand
The simple ways of country folk
Which lives upon the land.

On to Alfred Noyes' graceful appreciation of Thomas Bailey Aldrich and some snippets from Leonard Feeney, S.J., ending with a vignette:

Host (showing guest to room): And now, my dear fellow, if there's anything else you want, just want it.

By this time all the guest wants is another glass of cream sherry and all the potbelly wants is another log on the fire. That done, it's back to the easy chair and some contemplation about earlier tenants who had spent the night in less-pleasant circumstances. For instance the fellow who spent Thanksgiving Day 1882 within its walls: "While making an arrest last week Wednesday Marshal Booth had quite a tussle with a plasterer from Saint Croix Falls, who bit the thumb nail off Booth's right hand."

Ah, the simple ways of country folk which lives upon the land.

And then it's on to Cyril Hare's mystery about an English murder entitled "An English Murder," a suave little book with characters named Lady Camilla Prendergast, Mrs. Carstairs, Sir Julius Warbeck, Robert Warbeck — a young gentleman of fascist leanings — and Wenceslaus Bottwick, Ph.D., a Jewish scholar who is studying in the private library of Warbeck Hall.

The sherry warms the guest's innards, the fire crackles and snaps and hisses as midnight approaches. The English mystery completed (Mrs. Carstairs did it), the guest performs his ablutions and climbs the stairs to the loft, where he curls up under a prizewinning patchwork quilt and thinks about how he didn't even miss the evening's "Saturday Night Live" rerun. And to ponder the history of the little building and tenants like the house painter Beck who got drunk on a Tuesday night in 1881 and "went to sleep on the front porch of Mrs. Guard's residence and woke up yesterday morning in jail."

Morning dawns after a dreamless night that has covered the little building with a blanket of snow. After making an excellent breakfast of eggs, rolls, coffee and cheese, the guest tidies up — one isn't expected to, but one simply wants to, as Lady Camilla Prendergast might have put it — and makes his way out into the snow-covered town where you can live in history.

—D.W.

Lloyd McMichael
War and Remembrance

Minnetonka, Minnesota
1984

September 1944/

LOYD McMICHAEL, a 19-year-old navigator with the U.S. Eighth Air Force, was on his seventh bombing raid. The target was Dusseldorf, Germany. One engine conked out, then another. The B17 kept lurching along on its other two. Recently lectured that no mission was to be aborted, the crew tried to stay with its flight group. It lagged five miles behind the other hundreds of planes, "like a sitting duck," and had to turn around over Germany and head back to England.

Things got so bad that the pilot advised everyone to bail out. McMichael, the navigator, knew the plane was over Holland, but he wasn't sure just where. He and the other crew members had always promised each other to go down with the plane, partly because their parachute training had been a quick speech amounting to "jump, count to 10 and pull the cord." Nonetheless, when the plane was going "bump, bump, bump" and falling fast, the nine crew members jumped.

The pilot didn't survive; he was left-handed, and speculation was he couldn't find the rip cord over his left breast. The gunner was captured by the Germans. The bombardier had heard somewhere that it was wise to delay opening the chute so the enemy wouldn't have an easy target; his chute opened at about the level of a church steeple, and he lived to tell about it.

McMichael and two others landed in a grain field. "Oh God, I prayed," he remembers. "I said about 10 'Our Fathers' before we hit ground."

Some Dutch farmers saw the falling parachutes and came running. McMichael landed hard, wrecked his knee and passed out. When he came to, he feared his crew would be mistaken for Germans, so he yelled, "We're Americans!"

The rescuing Dutchmen turned out to be with the resistance movement. The Germans had launched a massive assault on The Netherlands more than four years before, in May 1940. The Nazis assumed that the Dutch, as fellow Aryans, would cooperate with their plans. They were wrong. The Dutch felt intense resentment about the occupation. There sprang up an active underground press, mass strikes, acts of sabotage, hiding of Jews (such as Anne Frank) and public protests by Catholic and Protestant churches. The Germans, in retaliation, hindered the shipment of farm produce. In parts of Holland during the winter of 1944-45, there was nothing to eat but sugar beets and tulip bulbs.

McMichael and his crewmates were taken into a barn. They were led through a trap door and into a hidden room, about 6 by 8 feet. The hiding place was filled with agricultural products — mostly seed and feed — concealed from the Germans. The room was well-built; there was no clue inside or outside the barn that gave it away. The Americans spent the day there. Not wanting to soil the feed, McMichael used his fleece-lined boot as a toilet.

That night, more members of the underground showed up. They dressed the three Americans in civilian clothes and took them by bicycle to another farmhouse, maybe 15 miles away. Another of his crewmates was brought there. The place was isolated enough that any approach by the Germans would have been detected soon enough to hide the Americans, so the fliers were relatively free to move around the house, but not the yard. The Dutch family insisted that the Americans take the master bedroom, living room and dining room. The family moved upstairs.

Three weeks after the crew had bailed out, the British Army came through and rescued the Americans.

"We never had much of a chance to say farewell," McMichael said. "They got us out as quick as they could. We couldn't even grab our stuff."

For security reasons, servicemen and the underground were not supposed to exchange names or military information. But McMichael had given the family his name and stateside address.

He was sent home to Austin, Minn., where his parents and his fiancee, Dorothy Beckel, lived. He didn't go back to combat but was in the Air Transport Command, getting airplanes to and from Europe and India until the end of the war. He tried to put the parachute jump and the Holland stay out of his mind. He lost track of his crewmates.

He got a post card in Austin in 1945 from someone in the family that had plucked him out of the field. He was never sure exactly who had sent it. He didn't try to correspond. "I was young, still in service. I wasn't concerned. Then the guilt took over for not having written, and I never did write."

April 1984/

Lloyd McMichael, now a 59-year-old accountant, and his wife, Dorothy, were in Europe to visit their son, Steven, a Franciscan brother who was studying theology in Rome. Lloyd wanted to get to The Netherlands. "I had to search for the spot and thank those people." The more time that had passed, the more he realized how brave were the families that had taken him in.

All he could remember about the location was that it was somewhere near the town of Hulst, in southern Holland near the Belgian border.

Armed with only one clue — the 1945 post card — the three McMichaels started the search on Good Friday. Lloyd McMichael went unsuccessfully from person to person, showing the post card. He was about to give up, when someone recognized the name of the sender, "P. Dieleman." That person motioned for the McMichaels to follow him and took them to a farmhouse.

It was the farm where McMichael had fallen from the sky. The woman who answered the door didn't speak English. McMichael handed her the post card, and she got across the idea that it was written by her sister, now dead. McMichael went into charades: He flapped his arms to show he was a flier, he made parachuting motions. The message got across. He was pulled into the house. The woman, it turns out, remembered him; her name is De and she was 11 years old when her family put the Americans in the hiding place.

She took the McMichaels to the barn — the same barn; "they never change anything over there," he said — and found her brother, Jac, who during the war was in his early 20s and with the resistance movement.

"We hugged and kissed many times," McMichael said. "I haven't hugged a lot of guys in my time, but I hugged and kissed him."

The presents started flowing. The first were the best. De Dieleman brought out a pair of leather gloves with McMichael's initials on them and a pair of silk gloves. McMichael knew they were his silk gloves. Only navigators, who needed to write during flights in the unheated planes, wore them. And there were his Air Force boots, which he had painted with his nickname, "Mike."

"With that, I broke down," he said.

Dorothy McMichael, through an interpreter, asked, "Why did these people keep his things all these years?"

"Because they always thought that he'd return someday."

Jac Dieleman went out to the barn and got one last souvenir: McMichael's parachute ring. Ordinarily someone bailing out of a plane would pull the rip cord and toss aside the ring. McMichael said he was so petrified he held onto it for dear life all the way down. Even after he passed out and revived, he clutched and carried it to the hiding place. Forty years later, it's rusted, but a McMichael family heirloom.

After coffee and cake and conversation in the Dutch farmhouse, McMichael had his wife take photographs of him with his boots, his gloves, his parachute ring. Seeing that the Dutch family had sentimental attachment to them, he didn't even consider asking for them. "They had already given me a hell of a lot."

But the family insisted. They were his to take home.

There were other presents: De gave Dorothy a delft plate, given to De by her mother and inscribed with the date of the war's end. Jac gave Lloyd a pair of wooden shoes.

The Dielemans took the McMichaels to the farmhouse where the second family had put him up for three weeks. It was the home of H.J.E. VanWesemael. Again there was someone who remembered him. Again there were tears and stories. They showed him his old navigation maps but put them right away. Clearly, they were *not* his to take.

But he was treated royally, showered with gifts and thanked profusely.

"I was there to thank them for what they had done for me, and they were thanking me for what the Americans had done, and we were all crying and everything."

He walked into the Dutch family's living room where he had stayed for three weeks and noticed a crucifix on the wall. He doesn't remember this, but the Dutch family told him that 40 years earlier he had seen that crucifix and had said, "He saved me."

"I've never been an openly religious person, but evidently I was religious then. I must have been pretty scared."

May 1984/

The delft plate is prominently displayed on a buffet at the McMichaels' home, 16508 Devon Dr., Minnetonka. The wooden shoes are on the mantel. The gloves and boots haven't yet been given an official place of honor and are on the coffee table. The McMichaels are packing a box to send to Holland.

McMichael hasn't started to tell his 8-month-old twin grandsons his war stories, but he's practicing. For years, he has told the story about how he used his boots as a toilet. He told it so often in a Dale Carnegie course that his friends called it the "Boots over Holland" story.

His navigational skills are pretty well gone. He had to get help from his wife to direct visitors to their home.

Of his trip to Holland, he said, "I can't imagine anyone having a more emotional time. Now I've got the duty to find the rest of my crew. I'm also trying to promote a lot of the Eighth Air Force to go back." One other thing — he's trying to find out if the Dutch government ever did enough to reward the brave members of the underground. He knows the U.S. government did — the families got certificates from Gen. Eisenhower's office — but did the Dutch?

He plays down his role in the war — "At the time, I thought I was a pretty romantic John Wayne-type of guy, but it sure wasn't a John Wayne-type of landing, with guns blazing." His primary memory is of being scared. Just how scared he had been came back to him when he was standing in the field where he had landed.

"I was just a kid," he said. "I'd put in one year at [the College of] St. Thomas and went into the Air Force at 18. That was June 1943. I graduated from navigation school in April of '44. Can you imagine? We were supposedly experienced navigators in less than a year."

He said he didn't do any crying about his war adventures when he was 19. "I was a strong soldier and we weren't supposed to cry." He's making up for it now.

—P.M.

The friendship has grown. The people in The Netherlands have sent McMichael a corner of his parachute, a watercolor painting of the barn and a copy of his pilot's death certificate.

Harold Emery Geiger
Bard of Nokomis

Minneapolis, Minnesota
1981

Not for him the flaccid free verse,
Not for him the unrhymed line.
He likes accents, he likes meters,
Calls Black Angus "lowing kine."

WHAT YOU'VE just read is called trochaic tetrameter. Not many poets use such metric forms these days, unless you count Henry Wadsworth Longfellow (1807-1882) of Cambridge, Mass. Longfellow adapted this pattern from the Finnish sagas when he wrote "Song of Hiawatha."

Or Harold Emery Geiger (1899-) of Minneapolis. Geiger has been casting his poetry in complicated metrics for almost three-quarters of a century, ever since he was a student at Minnehaha Grade School, back when memorizing Longfellow was popular.

Not that Harold Emery Geiger retired to a garret upon graduation, dashing off poem after poem, paying no attention to hearth or home, waiting to contract TB, the poet's disease. After graduation from South High in 1916, he served in World War I, graduated from law school, married, sired two children, worked as a bookkeeper, manufacturer's representative, hardware-store owner, Hennepin County deputy sheriff and courthouse bailiff in the T. Eugene Thompson murder trial (about which he wrote a poem). Lines always seemed to be running through his head, like these from 1961:

On the shores of Lake Nokomis
High above its sparkling water
Here we built and here our home is;
Here we raised our son and daughter.

Here I did a lot of hiking
With the playmates of my childhood;
Found the scenery to my liking
While we roamed though virgin wildwood. . . .

Geiger's wife, Alice, died in 1974; now Harold Emery Geiger, 82, lives with his dog, Champ, high above the sparkling waters of Nokomis, and tries to figure out how to sell his recently published first book, "From the Mountains to the Prairies: Selected Poems for Everyone's Enjoyment."

"I was hoping to sell them at senior-citizen centers and at gift shops in hospitals," says the white-haired Alternate Senior King of the 1980 Aquatennial. "My book has a little of everything in it that people might enjoy or be inspired by."

Or just plain chuckle over, as in Geiger's "Eighty Years Young":

Winters are colder; children are bolder
Than they were when we went to school.
I'm apt to grumble at the way people mumble;
My hearing is good as a rule.

My memory's failing; I must use the railing
When making my way up the stairs;
Clothes out of fashion; less of the passion
I had in my early affairs. . . .

Aches are increasing, the pain never ceasing
That settles in knee joint and hip.
Plagued with arthritis and diverticulitis
With its constant insidious grip. . . .

My bowling is shot; my golf not too hot;
I still dance but don't often run;
But I'll keep on trying; why think of dying
When living's so darned much more fun!

The book, which sells for $2.50 ($3 if you want it mailed from his home at 5000 Woodlawn Blvd.), also has nature poems, poems about faith in God and country, affectionate poems to a son, a daughter, a sister, a wife — recalling experiences that ring true outside his immediate family. Geiger rambles agilely around an eight-room home crammed with poetry manuscripts, memorabilia and family photos, Champ at his heels. "My wife would have a fit if she could see that I don't dust every day."

Geiger's too busy for dusting. Champ awakens him every morning at 5 and he busies himself with senior-citizen activities, bowling, golf. And giving poetry readings at places like St. Paul's Landmark Center. Last April senior citizens gave a concert in the Twin City Federal atrium, and Geiger opened it with a poem that shows his powers of allusion and wordplay:

> *... We laugh at the antics of Bench Warmer Bob*
> *As he tells us why we should invest*
> *The money we save from that earned on the job*
> *In the place that he claims is the best.*

> *... We request that you lend us your ears*
> *And your interest, one hundred percent.*
> *We hope you will find as our closing time nears,*
> *The investment in time was well spent.*

> *We are banking on keeping you all entertained*
> *With our songs and the numbers we play.*
> *But the goal we have set cannot be attained*
> *If you're not "Thinkin' Happy Today."*

And he continues to write. On a recent trip to California, he chided his niece for clipping her pet mallard's wings:

> *If I had the wings I was born with,*
> *Over these garden walls I would fly.*
> *Just to see what I'm missing out yonder,*
> *In the air 'tween the sea and the sky. ...*

"The lines just keep popping into my head," says Geiger. Memories keep popping in, too, memories of when he and Alice built their house in 1941, how the maple tree and the kids grew up, what fun he and his wife had in courtship and marriage. On his bedroom dresser, opposite Champ's mattress, is a 1930s nightclub portrait of Alice, her slender arm draped around a smiling Harold Geiger, probably snapped by one of those leggy photographers you always see in William Powell movies. Back then, Geiger affected a pencil-thin mustache, his wife the face of wholesome beauty.

These memories of his wife are obviously difficult, but Geiger works out his feelings in poems like "In Memoriam:"

> *The sun will shine; the wind will blow,*
> *The passing years will come and go*
> *And very few will ever know*
> *That she is gone.*

> *Where e'er I look, I see her face;*
> *I miss the warmth of her embrace*
> *No one can ever take her place*
> *And she is gone.*

I hear her footsteps on the stair
And rush to see if she is there,
But all I find is empty air
For she is gone.

For me, the birds no longer sing;
For me, no summer, fall or spring;
She was my all, my everything,
And she is gone.

A few weeks back, Harold Emery Geiger went on a senior-citizens' trip and there met Sister Anne Eugene Auer, a teacher at Holy Angels Academy. He subsequently gave her a copy of his new book. After reading the book, Sister wrote back: "Dear Mr. Geiger: I have just finished . . . your beautiful poems and want you to know how much they have inspired me! . . . They truly portray the depth of your Faith, Hope and Charity. . . . Do not grieve that you are alone — your dear wife is always with you in spirit and in time will come to take you to the celestial sphere where you will be reunited forever more."

Harold Emery Geiger hasn't belonged to a church for almost half a century, but says he loves this letter from Sister Anne Eugene Auer. "It makes writing the book worthwhile."

This is the Bard of Nokomis,
The silver-maned gentleman bailiff.

What you've just read, Harold Emery Geiger can tell you, is written in dactylic hexameter, well, actually dactylic *pent*ameter with a trochaic measure tacked on the end.

—D.W.

Irvine and Lillian Dubow
Scholarships for Nice People

Little Falls, Minnesota
1984

WE GOT AN interesting press release a while back about the Dubow Family Scholarship. The scholarship, we read, is not for an outstanding athlete or scholar, nor for achievement in a particular field of study. It is not designed for a member of a fraternity, club, organization or religious group.

The scholarship is for a *nice* person.

Irvine L. Dubow, a Little Falls optometrist, was quoted as saying, "You may have an excellent student, but such an individual may not necessarily be a nice person. It is nice people who add to the quality of our lives and who make a community a good place to live."

Eager for a nice story, we telephoned Dubow. He sounded pleasant. He would be happy, he said, to send us more material on his scholarship.

The statement of purpose said "the heritage of Judaism" prompted the scholarship.

"Education and knowledge is something that has to be earned and unlike material things can never be taken away," it said. "For too many years our ancestors were never allowed to farm or own property and were restricted in what they could or could not do. At night in many countries they were confined to the ghetto. The only thing that made life bearable and gave it meaning was the love of books and the love of learning. This allowed the escape of the mind and the eventual opportunities to escape the oppressive confinement of the ghetto. In small part to this memory, the Dubows dedicate this scholarship."

Hmmmmmm. This is a little heavier than *nice*.

~

"Doc" Dubow, as he's known in Little Falls, was seeing a patient when we got to his office at 313 1st St. SE., so we had time to poke around the waiting room. Under a sign reading "We are Proud of our Patients" were newspaper clippings announcing such things as Joel Wilczek's engagement to

Tammi Kahre and an open house to celebrate the 40th anniversary of Joe and Frieda Kedrowski. There was a snapshot of Rebecca and Kip Dubow, identified as grandchildren of Dr. Dubow, and a newspaper story that calls Dr. Dubow "one of the country's foremost experts on gas-permeable contact lenses and a frequent speaker at professional conferences and meetings" and a plaque that says "Dig a big hole in your garden of thoughts. Into it put all your disillusions, regrets, worries, troubles, doubts and fears, and forget."

Dubow appeared. He had nice manners and a nice handshake. He's on the small side and 59 years old. He said his wife, Lillian, was on her way from the Lillian Dubow Travel Agency. Soon she appeared, and she also was quite nice.

It was his idea to establish a scholarship, she said. He said it was her idea to make it unusual. "She's against scholarships strictly for athletics," he said. "We talked about scholastic scholarships and tried to decide where to direct it. Should we gear it to the person who is underprivileged or should we gear it to the good scholar?

"Then we asked, 'What is it we're really looking for? What is it that the world needs?' It needs more *nice* people. More *kind* people. People who will *listen*. People who are *concerned*."

About the scholarship recipients, she said, "We don't do the choosing. The high school has a team [principal, counselors, teachers] that selects them. We don't know who gets it until the day we present the scholarship at the awards ceremony."

The Dubows are establishing a trust to ensure that the scholarships are awarded to Little Falls students "forever." The first-place winner gets $350, and the second-place winner gets a Webster's Unabridged Dictionary. Why a dictionary? Lillian Dubow said, "I guess we're dictionary people. We believe in dictionaries. Each one of our boys received one at some point in their lives, and they hang onto them for dear life. We believe it's an essential part of everyone's life."

This spring the scholarship winner was Jodi Aldrich, who comes from "very nice people, kind people." Mary Jo Wielinski, almost as nice, got the dictionary.

Irv Dubow said he and his wife are not rich ("not by any stretch of the imagination — we're middle-middle-class"), but they feel strongly about education. They said books are wonderful friends. They've traveled the "whole wide world over" with books. They've learned so much from books.

The Dubows outlined why they feel strongly about Little Falls. Irv and Lillian and their eldest son, Burt, then a baby, were living in Winnipeg, Manitoba, in 1950. Irv wanted to move to Minnesota, but he didn't know just where. Driving to St. Paul to take his state board exams, he passed through Little Falls. He liked its looks. He stopped by, and people told him, "We've got enough eye doctors. Don't come." He came anyway. He called Lillian and said, "I've found a place. I've found an apartment, and I've found office space. We're moving to Little Falls, Minn." In those days, said Lillian, wives did what they were told. "I said, 'Fine. Where's Little Falls?'"

They were young and impoverished, he said, but had faith in the future and faith in Little Falls. "It's been a great community and a wonderful place to raise children. Good schools. The boys went through scouting. We hope to pay something back to the Little Falls that was so good to us."

Their four sons are grown now. Burt is an optometrist in St. Cloud; Jim and Rob run a video-game business in St. Cloud, and Rick is a physician finishing a gastroenterology fellowship in Portland, Ore. Irv and Lillian have six grandchildren, all nice.

Irv joked that he and his wife are the leading Jewish residents of Little Falls. Actually, they're the *only* Jewish residents. A few other Jews lived here when the Dubows arrived 34 years ago, but they're long gone. The Dubows belong to the nearest synagogue, Temple of Aaron in St. Paul, and their sons had their bar mitzvahs there. Have they encountered prejudice along the way? "Not one ounce of trouble, ever," Lillian said. "We feel this community has accepted us for what we are."

And what are they? Nice people?

"It sounds crazy," she said, "but that's it."

The reaction to their scholarship idea has been overwhelmingly positive, they said. No one told them they're dippy or Pollyannas. People have said they wish the idea were theirs. (The Dubows wouldn't mind the idea being copied.)

Neither of them had scholarships, Lillian said. She worked to put Irv through college. He always told her she could go to college some day. In 1977 she graduated from St. Cloud State with a bachelor of arts degree in elective studies, mostly in business. He was proud.

"Here's the bottom line," Irv said. "We have so much. We live in a great country and a great community. Most probably of all the countries in the world, this one offers more opportunity to everybody, including minorities, and we'd just like to provide a little bit more incentive so the young people here do have a chance. The little bit we have to contribute we'd like to offer in a positive fashion. God bless."

His wife, beaming in admiration, said, "Nicely put."

❧

One small mystery remained. After Lillian told us, "I think it's very nice of you to come here to do this," Irv said he didn't understand how word of the scholarship had reached the press. From the press release, we said. What press release? he asked. This one, from A La Carte Communications in St. Paul. Never heard of it, he said.

Never heard of Alice Jones, whose name is at the top of the release? No.

We called Alice Jones. It turns out she does public relations for the Upper Midwest Council for Better Vision. She had met Dubow briefly, liked his scholarship idea and was happy to fulfill a council request to publicize it. "I thought he was just marvelous," she said. "Very nice guy."

—P.M.

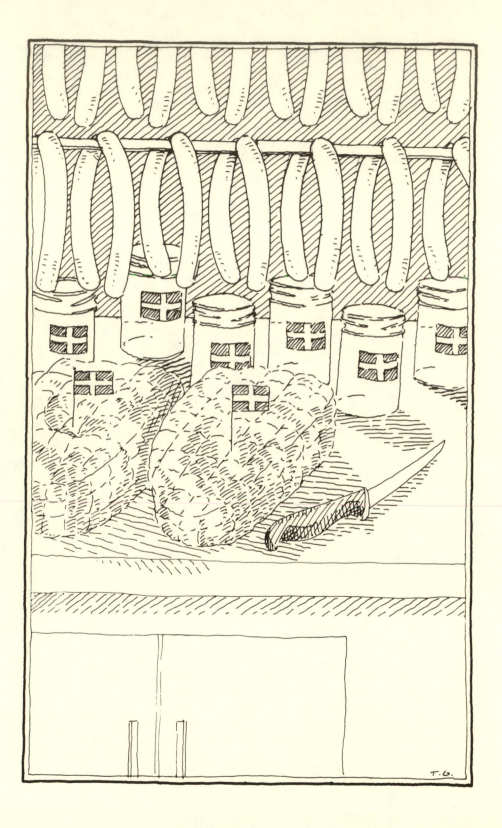

Ingebretsen's
The House that Swedish Sausage Built

Minneapolis, Minnesota
1982

NOT TOO MANY Christmas seasons ago, the folks in front of the meat counter were crowded anchovy-style and a woman who fainted wasn't able to fall down. That hasn't happened since 79-year-old George Anderson was installed at the door as Traffic Control Engineer. Now George hands out numbers to customers as they arrive and won't let more than a manageable group beyond a tape he's stuck on the entrance floor.

We're talking about Ingebretsen's Scandinavian Center, a fixture at 1601 E. Lake St. for more than 60 years, a monument to Swedish sausage, a place where sons and daughters and grandchildren of immigrants still crowd in to stock up on Norwegian medister polse, Danish medister polse, rulle polse, pressed sylte, pan sylte, spekekjott, pinnekjott, dried mutton sausage, home-smoked hams and Jul skinke.

And that's just some of the stuff they make in the basement. If you're the sort to which no Christmas dinner would be complete without reindeer meatballs, salt herring and perhaps a soupcon of gammelost or primost or gjetost or pultost or nokkelost or Jarlsbergost to smear on a slab of denture-shattering knackebrod, well, Ingebretsen's has that, too. Along with fish balls, fish cakes, cod roe, kippered herring, pearl sugar, almond paste, primost, lingonberries and Scandinavian cough drops. And 15 varieties of tinned sardines.

Early one Thursday morning in the basement, butchers are laboring mightily, stockpiling goodies for the Christmas rush that comes every year, while Mamie Gilbertson and Claudia Olson peel russet potatoes that will be mashed, mixed with flour, margarine, salt, sugar and a dash of vinegar and baked into lefses by day's end. Bud Ingebretsen sips coffee in his tiny basement office and tells of his father Charles Ingebretsen (1882-1954), who came as a teen-ager from Sarpsborg, Norway, worked as a dockhand in New York City, made his way to Fargo, where he apprenticed as a meatcutter, then came to Minneapolis to set up his own shop.

"His place was Ingebretsen & Alm on Riverside Av. [present location of Durable Goods]. Then he was on 27th and Lake with Val Ness. Then he was on 4th and Lake and it was just Ingebretsen then. Al Olson was manager and he was driving by this place and he saw it was for sale. It was an Armour & Co. store. Dad bought it in 1921, the year I was born. Al stayed at the place on 4th and Dad came here. Eventually Dad sold the 4th Av. store to Mel Bringgold."

Al Olson and Charles Ingebretsen were partners for many years, and they called their store Ingebretsen's Model Market. In the same building was C. Thomas, a grocery store, "one of the big grocery outfits in town," according to Bud.

"C. Thomas wanted to move right across the street into a new building. But Dad wouldn't move across the street. You see, all the foot traffic was on this side. I can remember the foot traffic was terrific on this side, the south side. Lake St. was on the edge of the shopping district of south Minneapolis then and the street cars let people off on this side. C. Thomas didn't like it very well when Dad didn't move with them."

How did it all work out?

"Well, let's just say that we're still here. And C. Thomas isn't across the street."

Bud's father put him to work cleaning up the store when he was in ninth grade. "I earned a dollar every Saturday. Back then, we bought most of our Scandinavian items from specialty stores. Actually, we only had a small case for those items. And in those days there were sausage places all over. We bought our lamb roll [rulle polse] from Nelson's on Franklin and 10th. Our blood sausage from another place and our sylte from another. As those places dried up, we gradually started making all the specialty meats right in the store."

Today, Ingebretsen's advertising flyer lists 20 Scandinavian specialty items made on the premises and that isn't even counting the jellied veal tongue. Bud and Al Olson, now 90, bought out Charlie in 1953. After Al retired, Warren Dahl bought in, and he and Bud have been partners since 1960.

Bud says that when he was a kid, "We didn't even think of ourselves as being particularly Norwegian, and we didn't think of the store as being Norwegian." But then came the ethnic revival of the '60s, and "People started coming and saying, 'What do you have that's Danish?' or 'What do you have that's Swedish?' "

Bud's son-in-law Craig Bloomstrand, 33, overhears the conversation and throws in his two cents' worth: "I guess years back some people didn't want to be recognized as ethnics. Now we have a fierce pride about it." And the store capitalized on that. In 1973, when the gift shop was opened in the area where C. Thomas sold groceries, the "Model Market" became "Ingebretsen's Scandinavian Center." Bloomstrand and his wife, Julie, run the gift shop as a separate corporation and take great pride in the Scandinavian handicrafts, books and specialty fabrics they carry. "Hardanger needlework is taking off just now," says Craig. "A while ago a woman came in with a 60-year-old piece of unfinished Hardanger needlework. We were able to match the thread perfectly."

How many stores in the country specialize in meat and crafts?

"Probably about one," say the butcher and the craftsman simultaneously.

"Actually, it's a good combination," says Craig. "There's one lady who comes in because her husband likes pickled herring. She buys some of that, and then she comes over here and buys Hardanger fabric." And there's another woman who has cut a deal with her husband. He can watch the Vikings on Sunday as long as he does some cross-stitching between plays. "She made that deal before the [players'] strike, so I don't know how it's working out."

A few steps away Paul Landvik and Gary Coleman are mixing ground beef, potatoes, onions, mace and a special combination seasoning in preparation for stuffing Swedish sausage. Ingebretsen's sells 20,000 pounds of the stuff in the month of December. They fill a water-pressure stuffer with the mixture, and Landvik places a length of beef intestine on the spout. "They ship beef intestines to Denmark, where they clean them, then they ship them back here and we stuff them." Landvik hits a lever and the soft, raw sausage squirts into the intestine, which writhes across the stainless steel table like the original snake back in the Garden of Stockholm, ready to tempt Eve Somethingson on Saturday morning.

~

The store opens at 9 a.m on Saturdays. At 9:05, customers are lined up at the long, like-new, L-shaped refrigerator case that Charles Ingebretsen and Al Olson installed back in the '30s. Before that they had made do with cracked ice and before that, when Bud was a kid, they'd made do with a marble slab. At 9:07, counterman Tib Berg calls out number "24!" He shakes hands with a middle-aged couple, says good to see you again and starts packaging their order.

On this Dec. 4, there are only six butchers behind the counter. But two weeks hence, there'll be 21 of them to take care of the Christmas rush. Handmade krumkake and rosettes are stacked on the porcelain counter, beside imported Vasa bread. Bud Ingebretsen slaps down a package of lamb roll and says "yes-sir, takk skal du ha!" For those not into cod roe and middag polse, that means "Thanks shall you have." Partner Warren Dahl waits on a woman with six packages of Mamie's and Claudia's hand-rolled lefse. She wants enough fresh lutefisk for two. Warren picks up a carcass of the slippery stuff and runs his index finger halfway down. "This should be enough."

"Oh," says the woman, "I'll take the whole thing."

"Yah," says Warren the Charmer. "If you have anything left over, you can make lutefisk sandwiches for Sunday lunch."

Warren puts the fish and the lefse in a bag and the woman worries that the lutefisk smell will penetrate the lefse. "At our house," says Warren, "we put a piece of lefse down, put mashed potatoes all over it, then lutefisk, then we pour melted butter on it, roll it up and eat it. So it wouldn't make any difference." But he obliges and puts the fish in a separate bag.

Down the street at Curly's cafe, Allan Luthi, 35, and Cheryl Hiltibran, 31, come in for breakfast, after buying spekekjott, a dried, smoked leg of mutton at Ingebretsen's. She's German-Dutch, he's Swiss and they've recently moved to Minneapolis from Illinois. Tonight they're having a wine and cheese party and they wanted "something different."

Luthi says, "We don't go to Ingebretsen's real often, but if we want something in particular, we know we can get it there." Hiltibran says, "There are interesting things to look at, too. We also bought some Christmas tree decorations in the gift shop." They found out about the store from Luthi's business associates, Norwegians who sell cross-country skis.

Back at the store, all sorts crowd around the counter and ogle the bulk goat cheese, homemade liver pate and dried beef, smoked ham shanks, salted pig's feet, meatball mix, fresh veal, rolled rib roasts, fish that's fresh and fish that's salted. Sort of like peeping Thomas Wolfes lusting after the contents of their refrigerators. Others examine the long import food case. Vern Westin who comes in from Chaska frequently because "it's the only good Swedish grocery store around," looks at a two-pound tin of anchovies that sells for $14.98.

Uff da.

Syd Erickson of Columbia Heights stands near a seven-foot redwood statue of a Viking carved by Warren Dahl's friend Donald A. Nelson. Warren says that it's one of the few Swedish Vikings. You know he's Swedish because he has a wooden head. The Swedish Viking holds a Hagar the Horrible cartoon strip in his left paw. Hagar's friend says, "There will be no peace until all men learn to understand each other." "True, true," says Hagar. "How are we going to get everybody to speak Norwegian?" Tit for tat.

"54!" cries Loren Johnson, a salesman by weekday and counterman by Saturdays, "because I like it here."

"Already?" says customer Syd Erickson. "I usually have to wait a half hour." Shirley Erickson is English-Scotch-Irish-Dutch and says she's put up with Syd's lutefisk for 42 years. It's 10 a.m. now and the big lutefisk tray has been refilled. Dorothy Schoemaker of St. Louis Park needs a hunk. "Yah, I'll take that one." It quivers on the scale. "It looks so horrible," she says, "but it tastes so good."

Outside, you see blue-haired ladies parking in the bank lot across the street. And you know they're coming this way before they close the car doors. In come Ole Rolvaag's son Karl with his wife, Marian. They were high school classmates in Northfield 50 years ago and tied the knot after meeting at a class reunion and now live on Bowstring Lake, near Grand Rapids. Marian never heard of Ingebretsen's before marrying the former governor.

"Her father was on the Carleton faculty and she lived on the Yankee side of Northfield," explains Rolvaag, who picks up a wooden box of salt cod, a Jule kage, a giant toothpaste tube of cod roe, then heads for the cheese counter for a chunk of goat cheese that resembles petrified peanut butter.

Marian says she's getting to like some of the stuff, but that lutefisk requires "lots and lots of butter." Already she has bought a bumper sticker in the gift shop. It says "When lutefisk is outlawed, only outlaws will have lutefisk."

There's a lot of funny stuff in the gift shop. And a lot of elegant stuff. And lots of expensive stuff. Lisa Rusinko Rykken, 26, grew up in northeast Minneapolis, is of Russian descent and is enthusiastic about Hardanger embroidery. Customers swarm around her as she picks through fabrics, listening to a tape recording of Mike and Else Sevig singing "Jeg er Saa Glad Hver Julekveld," known to folks not cognizant of Peer Gynt yarn swatches as "I Am So Glad It's Christmas Eve."

What's a nice Russian girl doing in a place like this?

"Oh, I was introduced to Hardanger embroidery by Emilie Kennedy."

Emilie *Kennedy?*

"Emilie *Nystuen* Kennedy."

Oh.

"I've been at it for less than a year and I just taught a course in it at the Norwegian-American Cultural Institute. They paid me $11 an hour. And I'm here spending my pay."

Back in the butcher shop, Warren Dahl shows a customer a chunk of Swedish Jul skinke, a pickled fresh ham that's sold only during the Christmas season. Counterman Red Knickerbocker retires to the backroom for a smoke. A Depression-era advertisement propped on the import counter announces fresh milk-fed veal for 12 cents a pound, dressed walleyed pike for 11 cents.

A woman says to her husband, "Did you forget the primost?" Tib Berg hollers "1!" and the six butchers start on their second 100 customers, waiting for Christmas week, when they'll be joined by 15 fresh colleagues and 79-year-old George Anderson, Traffic Control Engineer at the House that Swedish Sausage Built.

—D.W.

Scott Weisinger
Unemployed on the Range

Winton, Minnesota
1983

SCOTT WEISINGER sold the pool table for $150 and the pickup truck for $500. He got cash for the gun collection he had started as a kid. He sold everything he could from the bait shop that went belly-up last summer, and he still owes the bank $1,400 on it. He did everything he could to keep his family off welfare. His unemployment benefits from his days as a miner ended in June, and his attempts to find work on the Iron Range have fallen through time after time. This summer, the Weisingers went on welfare.

His mother, Rena Weisinger, said when Scott wasn't around, "What hurts me the most is he's losing his confidence. He used to think the world was his oyster, and he doesn't think so anymore."

Scott, 25, said later his mother was right. "Pride left a long time ago. It's simply a matter of survival now."

In the past four years, he has worked in the mines only six months. He has come to realize, finally, that he has no future in Winton, no future in the north woods. He has begun to search for work around Minnesota. He says he would move to Siberia if he could find a job that pays well enough for him to support his wife and three children. Minimum wage won't do it.

When something comes along — and Scott still says *when*, not *if* — he'll likely have to leave behind the house he built. Up here in the north, when a man says he built a house, he doesn't mean he hired a contractor and an electrician and a plumber to build him a house. It means *he* built it. Scott did everything but put up the ceilings, and that was only because he couldn't lay his hands on the equipment he needed. Three years ago, he might have been able to get $70,000 for his house, with its three bedrooms and family room. Now he'd be lucky to get $40,000. That's if he could sell it, which he doubts. Houses aren't moving in Ely and Winton. He's in no hurry to landscape a house he can't sell.

Scott and his wife, Cindy, who's 23, had thought their family was complete with their two boys, Christopher, now 7, and Bryan, 2. Five-month-old Monique was a surprise. They delight in having a little girl, but a third child may compound the problems of starting over somewhere else. A fourth is unthinkable. Scott had a vasectomy, paid for by the government.

Somehow it seems incongruous for a big, strong Iron Ranger to talk unblushingly of love, but Scott said of his family, "We're all real close and we love each other a lot. That's what really helps — love. We're working it out together."

His future once looked great. Already at age 8, he was tearing apart engines and putting them back together. The summer he was 12, someone paid off a $2 debt by giving him an old boat motor that didn't run. He fixed it and traded it for a motorcycle that didn't run. He fixed the cycle and sold it for $400. All this took a summer, but he had fun.

In high school, he had a locker next to Cindy Tuomala. She couldn't stand him because he was so sure of himself. One day when he had finished studying welding at the vocational-technical school, he saw her in Ely. Cindy recalls, "He picked me up and put me on his car and wouldn't let me go until I promised I'd go out with him on a date. It was close to kidnapping. I promised, reluctantly, and I asked my mother, 'How do I get out of this?' I did go out with him and found out he was a gentle man. We got along pretty good after that."

He got a job with Erie Mining as a welder and was laid off in October 1979. He became a driller's helper in June 1981 at Reserve and earned $10.83 an hour. Plus overtime, and there was a lot of it. The money went for the house he put up on the lot next to his mother's. He worked the midnight shift, got home at 8 a.m. and worked four to five hours on the house. "Had no choice," he said. "Had to get a roof over our heads."

On Jan. 3, 1982, he was laid off. He thought unemployment would last until that spring. He has never gotten back.

Last summer, he tried the bait business. He said he trapped his own minnows, worked 20 hours a day and couldn't make the minimum wage. "We're losing all our tourists," he said, "and everything is going downhill since they passed the Boundary Water Canoe Area. The big-money guys are gone, the doctors and the lawyers. They were the ones with the big boats and motors, who'd spring for fancy meals and resorts. Now you see kids with canoes and food they bring up from the Cities. The only thing we get them for is gasoline and occasionally a meal."

He answers every help-wanted ad he sees, said his wife and mother — his two biggest supporters. The closest he got was a job as a janitor with the Ely school system. It pays $1,300 a month. He drooled at the chance. "That was the ship I should have been on," he said. Five hundred people applied, three were interviewed, and Scott came in second. He was one of 300 people taking a Civil Service exam for two jobs in highway maintenance. No go. He was one of 5,000 men seeking 100 jobs with Potlatch Corp., a timber-products firm in Cook, Minn. No go.

"Your hopes go up, and then they're shot back down," he said. "Now you go there three-quarters expecting no job. The really rotten part is there aren't many jobs I can't do, and I can't find one. I wired this house, I did my own plumbing. Really, I can do just about everything. I'm a good worker."

People in Winton say Scott is an excellent welder, but welders are a dime a dozen. They say Scott really can do anything, but there's little to be done. He takes an odd job where he can, but that doesn't feed a family.

In June, the unemployment ran out. The Weisingers get $623 a month in Aid to Families with Dependent Children for the kids and $130 a month in food stamps. Cindy makes $150 a month as Winton city clerk. They have kept up with $276 mortgage payments.

Scott putters around the house, fixing things here and there. He fixes things that people bring around. He smooches up his kids. He makes hamburger casseroles for the family. He fishes. He worries. He pulls out gray hairs.

"This place is dying. When I was a little kid, you couldn't cross the street in Ely, there were so many cars. Now Ely is dying, and Winton is near dead."

Of course, the Weisingers would like to stay in Winton. Said Cindy, "I don't have to worry about my kids at all. Everybody is so friendly, everybody helps you out, everybody knows each other. There's lots to do here. We don't have the cultural things the Cities do, but in winter we have snowmobiling, skiing, skating. In the summer there's fishing and swimming, three-wheeling and barbecuing. We don't have to drive a long way to find our fun."

But there's no way to stay. Scott doesn't know how to find work away from Winton. Every stab he makes leaves him frustrated.

"How do you get out of the rut you're in? It's like I see the world going by, and I can't do anything to get on it."

—P.M.

When we couldn't reach Scott, we telephoned his mother. She said that Scott and Cindy are separated and that he has not found steady work. Eventually we got him on the telephone and he said, "My life has gone to hell. I don't want to talk about it."

Cedric Adams
The Traveling Troupe Remembers

Minnetonka, Minnesota
1983

THE PARTY thrown by Diane Frandrup Sparrow on June 1 for the folks who performed with Cedric Adams was wonderful. Lots of "look who just walked in," lots of toasts and hugs and kisses, lots of remembering the innocence of 30 years ago. And also a few tears for the fallen. I felt good just being there, close to people who had been close to Adams, once the brightest multimedia star in the Upper Midwest firmament.

I grew up with Cedric Adams. His jowly visage grinned out at me from the Sunday paper I delivered. I heard his infectious chuckle over the airwaves, his mellifluous voice, telling me all sorts of stuff I didn't need to know. "Your heart," Cedric Adams intoned, "pumps enough to fill a railroad tank car every two days."

My parents and their friends called him Cedric and always turned off the lights after he signed off at 10:13 p.m., so that pilots flying over western Wisconsin would know it was 10:13. Later, at Charlie's, I ate a sandwich named after him. But I never got to see the man up close. But just think! The folks who were coming to Diane's party had snuggled up next to him on the long drives into America's heartland.

A kid from my hometown once saw Cedric close up, and the rest of us envied him. Bobby got all the way to Minneapolis and appeared on Cedric's Saturday night amateur show, "Stairway to Stardom." Bobby did his impression of Yogi Yorgesson singing a dialect song called "Yohn Yohnson's Vedding." When it was all over Bobby placed first on the applause meter. Cedric said, "My, for such a young man, you certainly have mastered a fine Norwegian dialect." And Bobby replied, "Vhut dew yew mean by dat?"

❧

Diane Frandrup Sparrow left final party preparations to her 86-year-old mother, Bertha, and sat down in her townhouse to tell me the reason for the party and what to expect.

Diane is bright, gregarious and not a bit bashful. She grew up on a farm near Cannon Falls, went on to perform with Cedric and such folks as Arthur Godfrey, Ken Murray, Rosemary Clooney, Milton Berle, Garry Moore and Harry James before semi-retiring to raise a family. Today she sings part-time and also teaches skin care with Mary Kay Cosmetics.

"I started singing with Slim Jim [Iverson] when I was 3. Later I went on Cedric's 'Stairway to Stardom' as a yodeler. I won several times and finally, in 1947, when I was 8, Cedric told me I was getting to be part of 'CCO and that I could start traveling with him if I wanted."

She wanted. For eight years, Diane made 40 trips a year traveling with "Cedric Adams' Open House" to little towns all over the five-state area, yodeling her heart out and singing Betty Hutton-type tunes.

"It was a 2½-hour show, sponsored by various companies — NSP, Pillsbury, Coca-Cola. We'd set up in a school auditorium or an armory. Cedric would warm up the local audience, then introduce the acts. There were usually about five acts of young talent that traveled out of Minneapolis in station wagons."

Between the yodeling and the pantomime and the baton twirling and the adagio dancing and the magic acts and the door prizes and the modeling demonstration by Aquatennial queens, there was free Coke for everyone, the women from Pillsbury would bake a cake right up on stage, NSP people would give lighting demonstrations "and Melvin Greer of the 620 Club on Hennepin Av. would show the folks out there how to carve a turkey."

Sounds almost like a '50s version of "The Prairie Home Companion" without the satire.

"That's right. And at 10 p.m., Cedric would go on the air and do his news show. When it was all over he'd talk to people and there'd be supper at a local restaurant and the drive home. People loved the show, there was never an empty seat. All the people coming tonight were part of that show."

Diane said the idea for a party was hatched when Neighbors asked if she'd like to reminisce with a few fellow troupers about the old days with Cedric.

"But I lost track of some of the people, so I called 'CCO. On Memorial Day, I was interviewed by Ray Christensen and told him listeners could help me get in touch with people. As soon as the show was over, the phone started ringing. Some people have died. Others have other engagements tonight. Jim Rosen, one of our adagio dancers, can't come because he's a fireman in Richfield and has to work tonight. The other dancer was his sister Rosann, who has to attend a graduation tonight.

"But there'll be about 25 people here, including spouses. Pat Dunn Jones, our baton twirler, flew in all the way from Texas. She should be here soon. I'm so excited!"

⁓

When all company members and wives were finally assembled, the stories about Cedric and his program came thick and fast, gave a measure of the man they grew to know and love as kids:

Diane Frandrup Sparrow: "Cedric took me to New York when I was about 10. On the plane, he told me he wanted *me* to write *his* column about our trip. I said OK, but then in the excitement I forgot. Weeks later he called me aside and told me he was very disappointed in me. That really hurt, because he was like a father. I said I'll write the column now. He looked at me and said 'Too late.'

"Cedric wanted us to learn, to be responsible."

Bill Sowden: "Our pay was commensurate with pay for any young kid who wanted to work with a great guy and get lots of exposure. Cedric was paid $500 for a show and out of that he paid his staff. I made $20 a night the first year, $30 the second. He didn't have to, but he always took us to the best restaurant in town. We always went first class. And if we were 50 miles from Gaylord, we'd always make a detour for pie."

Marilyn Peterson: "I was majoring in music education at MacPhail. Cedric took me aside and asked if I really wanted to teach. I thought about it and decided not. Later, when I started my company, Cedric wrote about it."

Curt Balcom: "We had these Pillsbury people along and the producer told us to run out to a store and get the biggest bottle of Bromo-Seltzer there was and sneak it into the dry cake mix. We did that and Cedric was in on the joke. Well, they mixed it up and Cedric, you know how he was. He started laughing and then he stopped laughing.

"Nothing happened. The cake batter didn't foam up or anything. They put it in the oven on stage and then we were sure something would happen when it heated up. Cedric kept glancing at the stove, just on the verge of bursting out. When the cake was baked the Pillsbury women took it out and it looked like any other cake. Even tasted the same. And then, you know, Cedric had to tell the whole crowd about the joke that didn't work."

Diane Frandrup Sparrow: "My mother always sent along a box of homemade walnut fudge for the group. I'd hand it to Cedric and he'd say he'd have to sample it. Well, you know his sweet tooth. By the time he'd finished, there wasn't much left for anyone else.

"You know, I had my first ice cream soda when I was traveling with the show. Pat Dunn and I walked downtown in some town and she took me to the restaurant and we shared a soda. They had sodas in Cannon Falls, but with 11 kids, our family couldn't afford them. I've never had one since. And remember when Cedric came out with that pamphlet about his 25 years as a journalist? He'd make us go out between acts and sell them to the audience for 50 cents. I've been a saleswoman ever since."

Bertha Frandrup, Diane's mother: "Did Diane always talk this much on the road?"

Bill Sowden: "Diane was always a little sweetie. She was the youngest so she just remembers more. Right, Diane?"

Marilyn Peterson: "After the show, we'd usually get to a restaurant at about 11 p.m. Cedric's steak would come 15 minutes later. At about that time, some old farmer would come up and want to talk. Cedric, he'd slide the steak over and say, 'How many cows are you milking?' "

Pat Dunn Jones, just in from Dallas, Texas: "No, I never set any country auditoriums aflame with my baton, but when we had the accident, they used my electric baton to flag down help."

Bill Sowden: "I remember after the accident, Cedric called us all and said no questions, just all be at Sno-Fo Manufacturing at such and such a time. We came down there and Cedric told us he knew we'd torn or soiled our clothes in the accident. He said go in and everyone pick out a coat. No cheap stuff. No gabardine. Take Harris tweed, something good."

More talk of the accident that occurred in 1951, when the car driven by Curt Balcom slid off an icy road coming back from a show at Annandale. Talk of how Cedric wept, about how he sat with his broken ankle on a hard chair in the waiting room until he was certain the kids were all treated. Talk of how the nurse refused to treat Tubal, a black man, and of Cedric's anger when he found out. Talk of how Cedric wrote a column right after, talking about the bravery of the kids.

Jack Nordin: "After my time on the show, I never quit entertaining. I work in a bank, but I'm still available as a magician or a clown or a juggler. Here's my card."

Bill Sowden: "Sure, we go out and work to make a living. But we still remember the days of hyacinths and nectar and try to stick with it."

All good things must end. Cedric Adams got busy with network broadcasts, and the 15,000 miles a year consumed too much of his time. The troupe broke up in the mid-'50s after eight years and all went their separate ways, some for flirtations with the big time, others to families, school and less glamorous employment. Cedric Adams died in 1961, at age 59, and the Upper Midwest mourned. When in 1961?

"February 18," answered Tubal Wilson, quick as a fox.

⁓

Then it was time for lunch. And more talk, talk, talk. Talk of the party on Cedric's Chris-Craft on Lake Minnetonka. Talk of this town and that. Talk of future luncheons with the troupers who couldn't attend. Talk of troupers who would never make it to a luncheon again. Talk of how Cedric was probably Up There, looking down on them and chuckling his chuckle.

Toward the end, they all raised their glasses as Bill Sowden, now a company president, proposed a toast: "Cedric, we loved you, we thank you, we are your family. And for the others who are gone, God bless you."

—D.W.

Ma Thao
'What Is Doing This Killing?'

St. Paul, Minnesota
1983

MA THAO is afraid to sleep. He forces himself to stay awake as late as he can, and he usually wakes up in a cold sweat after only three or four hours of rest. "I think so much I can't sleep," he said.

What he thinks about is dying. Thao is a 30-year-old Hmong, and in the past five years more than 70 young Hmong men in the United States have died in their sleep of a mysterious syndrome. Their hearts apparently stopped. The men had seemed healthy; their autopsies give no good reason for their deaths. Doctors are stumped.

Minnesota has about 10,000 Hmong immigrants; California is the only state with more. At least 11 local Hmong men have died of the sudden-death syndrome. As the deaths increase, so does the fear. Some Hmong men set alarm clocks to ring every half hour so they wake up and assure themselves they are still alive. Ma Thao said his wife gives him a jab in the ribs when his night breathing becomes irregular.

Fear is ruining his life, he said. "This morning I got up at 4. I feel normal — a little bit tired. Some nights I wake up with bad dreams. Sometimes I see the old country, Laos, and I see the war. I see people dead. When I dream, I see people die."

He said he saw much fighting when he was a truck driver for the U.S. Army in Laos. But then he could cope. "I used to sleep the whole night. Eight, nine hours." Now he goes to bed at midnight or 1 a.m. and wakes up at 4 or 5, unable to fall asleep again. "I worry, and I cannot make my body to sleep," he said.

He is becoming more and more nervous and has blacked out several times. A doctor told him last week that he should not drive a car. Consequently, he lost his job. He was an employment counselor with the Lao Family Community, Inc., an agency that helps Laotian refugees, and much of his work involved driving immigrants to job interviews and to work. Now he's an unemployed employment specialist with nowhere to look for work.

He worries about money. Thao, his wife and three children (ages 6, 5 and 3) live in a modest flat at 664 Hall Av., St. Paul. The living room is decorated with a few folding chairs and a kitchen table. "I need to work," he said. "I don't know what I can do if I cannot drive a car. I am a little bit mechanical. I can fix the car."

He speaks English slowly, quietly and with dignity. His face showed pain when he said, "My body and my mind were different before. I cannot tell you exactly what's wrong, but I can give you an example. Pretend you move to another country. You don't know the language, the law, you know nothing about that country. No money, and everything changes in your life. If you do that, what happens to you here?" He tapped his forehead.

"If only I could sleep."

∾

What is causing the sleep deaths of the Hmong men?

"There are quite a few theories, none of them good," said Dr. Neal Holtan of St. Paul-Ramsey Medical Center's International Clinic. "It could be the heart, electrolytes in the blood, stress, body rhythms. We have no good answer at this point. With so few clues, it's hard to even come up with a research project."

The startling thing about the Hmong sudden deaths is the absence of findings during autopsies. Most other young people who die unexpectedly in the United States do so when they are awake — often when exercising strenuously — and their autopsies show heart damage or some other cause of death. Not so with the Hmong.

"It's the unpredictability and seeming unpreventability of the syndrome that is sending shock waves through the community," said Jane Kretzmann, state coordinator of the refugee program office.

Almost all, or perhaps all, of the affected Hmong are men. Most of the deaths occur during sleep. The vulnerable ages seem to be 30 to 44. Early speculation was that warfare gases or chemicals used in Southeast Asia were causing deaths later in America, but interviews with the victims' families show that only a small number who died were exposed to chemical warfare. The first deaths here were reported among Hmong refugees from the mountains of Laos, but more recently there have been unexplained deaths in the United States of other Southeast Asians, such as other Laotians and Kampucheans (Cambodians).

It's unclear whether the Hmong died in this mysterious way when they were in their homeland. Most Hmong here say they did not. Speculation by some medical authorities is that the Hmong in America have succumbed to severe culture shock.

The federal Centers for Disease Control in Atlanta is looking into the mysterious deaths. It has not ruled out "emotional triggers" as the cause of death.

Dr. Garry Peterson of the Hennepin County Medical Examiner's Office performed the autopsy on the latest victim of the syndrome, Chou Xiong of

Minneapolis, who died Feb. 22. Authorities said Xiong seemed to be in good health when he went to bed, but by 4 a.m. he was breathing with such difficulty that his wife rushed him to the emergency room. He died there half an hour later.

Peterson said, "There is a lot of anxiety in the Hmong community, and there well might be. The risk to Southeast Asians is high."

In some of the victims, medical professionals are finding subtle differences in the heart's conduction system, Peterson said. Their hearts are wired differently but not necessarily abnormally. He explained there are all sorts of small anatomical differences in people. For example, the blood supply to the gall bladder has several major variations in human beings — none of them "wrong," just different.

Whether it's because of the heart's wiring or something else, the Hmong seem to be vulnerable to an arrhythmia (an uneven heartbeat) that develops for some reason. "Emotional or respiratory, I don't know. It could be triggered by a frightening dream," Peterson said.

He said that if a Hmong man should die of another cause, say a car accident, it would help the sudden-death research to perform an autopsy. However, the Hmong community is reluctant to permit autopsies. "In a routine case, probably permission would not be granted," he said.

Dang Her, director of the Lao Family Community, explained the reason for that. Many Hmong believe in reincarnation, he said. They fear that parts of their bodies will be missing in their next lives. Autopsies were not performed in their old country, and they thought that in autopsies all body parts, down to the finger joints, were taken apart. Medical examiners got better cooperation when they explained that only the heart and brain would be examined.

Her, for one, does not fear for his own life. He doesn't have the time or inclination to fret, he said. Yet he is deeply concerned for the Hmong community here. "We must find out what causes these sudden deaths," he said. "This is so frustrating."

Every theory has holes knocked in it, Her said. When Hmong people noticed that most of the deaths occurred in small apartments, the next death was in a big house. When poison gases were suspected, the next death was of a man who had been nowhere near the battles.

Meanwhile, Her's office, located in the YMCA building in downtown St. Paul, continues to help Hmong with English classes, employment searches, legal questions and naturalization problems. In every gathering of the Hmong, he said, conversation turns to the mysterious deaths.

～

Leng Vang is deeply bothered. Vang, who is on the staff of the state refugee project, has bad dreams and wakes up and stares out the window, trying to calm himself. "Sometimes I cannot sleep all night long. Some of us have to set our watch to go off every 30 minutes or every hour." For the last year and a half, he has set his alarm many times each night, usually every half hour. If he doesn't wake up quickly when the alarm sounds, his wife frantically wakes him.

"What is doing this killing?" he said. "Is it the broken heart? Is it the loss or the guilt? Is it some kind of rare disease we don't see?

"You see, Hmong men took their responsibility as a man very different. Here they feel responsible for the family's survival, but there is little they can do. They worry. In the old country, we were used to the land and had an understanding of what we could do to survive. Coming to a new society, they do not know what to do to survive. That's what's creating the stress.

"This is a free country but there is so much you have to understand. We are not used to private lands. We lived up in the highlands with not much government. It is entirely different here. This is like being a bird in a golden cage — it's nice, but it's restrictive. The bird can stop eating and die."

—P.M.

Ma Thao is alive but not well. Shortly after this story ran in the newspaper, he and his family moved to La Crosse, Wis., with the hope his health might be better in a smaller city. His nervous spells have continued, and he has not found work. The latest medical research indicates that the mysterious nighttime deaths of the Hmong may be stress-related.

Main Street, U.S.A.
Home of Minnesota's Nobel Laureate

Sauk Centre, Minnesota
1981

HARRY SINCLAIR LEWIS (1855-1951) began taking notes for his fifth novel above Rowe's Hardware on Sauk Centre's Main Street in 1916. An obscure novelist, he hoped his satire of small-town life might sell 20,000 copies. Publisher Alfred Harcourt thought 40,000 copies would be more like it. When the furor died down after its publication in 1920, "Main Street" had sold millions and the Sauk Centre kid no one thought would amount to much became the bumptious bull in our literary china closet, the first American to win a Nobel Prize for literature. Books about small-town life haven't been the same since.

Sauk Centre hasn't been the same either, once readers watched Carol Kennicott take her fictional walk down Main Street. Thousands of literary pilgrims have made the trip to this prototype for Gopher Prairie, even though Lewis called his fictional town "a continuation of Main Streets everywhere."

Journalists also make it to Sauk Centre. Some are quick to pick up on Lewis's unflattering portrait of a town where people contract a "village virus" that debilitates them spiritually and culturally, turning men into boors, women into gossips.

• In 1975, when Sauk Centre dedicated its Sinclair Lewis Interpretive Center, The Mankato Free Press chided the town for renaming its institutions after Lewis or his book: "You seldom hear a dog boasting of its fleas."

• In 1980, a Minneapolis Star reporter described Sauk Centrites as "beady-eyed" and "making all kinds of money off the man who would have quite happily razed the whole damn place."

• A reporter from the Boston Globe arrived a few months ago, sat down in a local coffee shop and asked people if there was much bigotry around town.

All this and more despite frequent disclaimers by Lewis. On Aug. 4, 1921, the Sauk Centre Herald ran a letter Lewis, its former employee, sent from Cornwall, England: "It has come to my attention that a certain number of people in Sauk Centre believe that . . . 'Main Street' portrays real people and real scenes in Sauk Centre . . . this is totally erroneous. . . . Practically all of the characters and scenes in 'Main Street' are either composites, combinations of the things and persons I have noted in the scores of American towns I have seen in all parts of the country, or else they are totally imaginary.''

Spoils a good story, doesn't it?

Spoiling it even more is a hard look at heroine Carol Kennicott, who battles ''the village virus'' in the book. Mark Schorer, Lewis's biographer, states that Carol is incredibly naive, has nothing to offer Gopher Prairie, proving that there are always foolish people in the world.

Donald W. Griswold, editor of the Sauk Centre Herald, makes two other points that visitors sometimes forget. First, the book is fiction. Second, even if it were based on fact, Sauk Centre has changed since Lewis spent his miserable childhood here. Griswold thinks it was miserable because Lewis was a mean kid. But biographer Schorer blames the child's misery on his lack of friends and his clashes with a practical, uncommunicative father, who didn't understand his gangly youngest son's penchant for reading Tennyson and daydreaming of Guinevere, Sir Lancelot and all that.

Dave Jacobson, Sauk Centre High School teacher, enjoyed his childhood in Sauk Centre. He's president of the Sinclair Lewis Foundation, which supports the Sinclair Lewis home and the Interpretive Center. The home attracted 26,000 tourists from 1970 to 1980 and the center drew 45,700 since 1975.

Jacobson was responsible for introducing ''Main Street'' into the high school's curriculum after being razzed by his army buddies because he hadn't read the book. ''Now I think Lewis is important. We don't have to apologize for attracting tourists because he grew up here. We're certainly not exploiting him the way Hannibal, Mo., exploits Mark Twain. We've tried to keep the interpretive center as objective as possible.'' (The center stresses that Lewis led an unhappy childhood in Sauk Centre and admits that Lewis's artistry has been in question for decades.)

Jacobson grants that some tourists stop at the center just to use the restrooms, but says that some stay on to look. ''We overheard one father say to his son, 'Don't you know him? He's from Minnesota, the first guy to fly across the Atlantic,' '' Jacobson said.

''Some students get very involved with 'Main Street' and others are indifferent. Some get one thing out of the book — they want to get out of town, go to Minneapolis. That's natural. No doubt Lewis had a difficult childhood. It's difficult for all kids, so they identify. But when they return for class reunions, they're looking for work here. They want to bring up their kids here.''

Lewis himself returned again and again, seeking acceptance, a sense of belonging and romanticizing his own childhood. Don Hanson, 86, owned the drugstore that stands at The Original Main Street and Sinclair Lewis Avenue. ''When he came home he and his older brother Claude [a doctor in

St. Cloud] always got together at our fountain for ice-cream sodas."

Hanson remembers that some people around town were pretty riled up after "Main Street" was published. "But I thought it was a descriptive book of small towns. I thought it fit."

It also brought recognition. Hanson's drugstore is on the dust cover of his 1946 Living Library edition of "Main Street." When Schorer's biography made a big splash in 1961, Don was featured in Life magazine. "But the best one was when I got a post card from Virgil Sieben. Virgil was in the merchant marines and he sent me a card saying he'd heard me being interviewed on the 'Voice of America' when he was at sea."

Why did Lewis wander most of his life, from New York to Europe to New England, back to Minnesota and finally to a lonely death at the Clinica Electra in Rome? "I can't really say," said Hanson. "His folks weren't like that at all. Doc Lewis practiced medicine above my father's store. Used to come in and show our customers letters from 'Red' and how much money he stood to make."

Nor was there much wanderlust in Dr. Will Kennicott, the stolid Gopher Prairie physician who found Carol working at the St. Paul Public Library, wooed and won her, then dragged her back to the town where he practiced medicine and wondered why Carol lacked enthusiasm after her first jaunt down Main Street.

Let's take a random sampling of the famous street to see what's happened since Carol arrived just before World War I:

> She was within ten minutes beholding not only the heart of a place called Gopher Prairie, but ten thousand towns from Albany to San Diego.
> Dyer's Drug Store, a corner building ... Inside ... pawed-over heaps of toothbrushes and combs and packages of shaving-soap. Shelves of ... nostrums for consumption, for "women's diseases" — notorious mixtures of opium and alcohol.

Dave Medhaug's nostrums in his Main Street Drug Store are neatly displayed these days, although the "Doctor" and "Dentist" signs on the second floor of his 1904 building are fading. Medhaug remembers reading "Main Street" when he was a kid growing up in Rushford, Minn.

"Small towns are much the same everywhere. When I go back to Rushford to visit my mother, she always talks about so-and-so running around with so-and-so. I think it was the forest — not this particular tree — that Lewis was dealing with when he wrote the book."

> A small wooden motion-picture theater called "The Rosebud Movie Palace" ... a film called "Fatty in Love."

Today's "Main Street" theater is showing "The Devil and Max Devlin," starring Elliot Gould. No one on Main Street was willing to speculate on whether this represented an improvement over Fatty Arbuckle.

Dahl and Olson's Meat Market — a reek of blood ... Howland and Gould's Grocery. In the display window, black, overripe bananas and lettuce on which a cat was sleeping.

Pamida Discount Center has replaced the downtown meat market and Ken-Mart grocery features yellow bananas, meat wrapped in clear plastic, with nary a cat to be seen.

The Bon Ton Store ... the largest shop in town ... clean!

The Boston Store provided Lewis's model for the Bon Ton. It burned down in 1925. J.C. Penney stands in its place. Clean! Close by is another large shopping complex, Bushey's Rexall Drug and Ben Franklin Store. Helen Lewis clerks there. Her late husband, Carl, was Lewis's nephew. She remembers the novelist as "very friendly, a good talker and very nervous. He just couldn't sit still." Helen read "Main Street" and "Babbitt" (1922) after she married Carl in 1941. "It just wasn't taught here when I went to high school. I thought 'Babbitt' was real good. It was more interesting than 'Main Street.'"

Helen has a grandson in Minneapolis named Jeffrey Sinclair Lewis, inspired by her son's reading "Main Street" at Sauk Centre High School.

The Farmers' National Bank. An Ionic temple of marble. Pure, exquisite, solitary.

The old State Bank building, 1900 A.D., provided Lewis the prototype for Carol's favorite building on Main Street. The Ionic columns are still there, but today it's a beauty salon called "The Hairoscope."

A raw red-brick Catholic Church with a varnished yellow door.

That would be St. Paul's Church, built in 1904. The raw brick has taken on a patina of age, as have the wooden doors. The church's beautiful altar looks Old World. Not so, says Father Elmer Torberg. "When I came here, I thought it was something special, maybe imported. But no, a church artist came out here and told us that it was a supply-house item at the turn of the century."

A fly-buzzing saloon ... thick voices bellowing pidgin German or trolling out dirty songs — vice gone feeble and unenterprising and dull — the delicacy of a mining-camp minus its vigor.

According to Fred Schultz, 76, there's alway been a saloon in the building where the Short Stop Bar dispenses potables. "That place was never short on antifreeze when Ben Schoenhoff owned it," says Schultz. Nor is it today, with its working-class clientele. A sign above the bar says, "Our credit manager is Helen Waite. If you want credit go to Helen Waite."

Things can get rowdy at the Short Stop, says John Middendorf, 19. "Sometimes we call it 'the Zoo.'" Middendorf says, "When we read 'Main Street' in school, we thought it was a bunch of B.S., but not now."

John recently helped move a friend from the first floor to a second-floor apartment. "You should have seen all the old ladies looking out the window. Then we moved the furniture out of the house altogether to another place. They were looking again. It reminded me of when we read 'Main Street' in school." But he admitted that if old women in neighboring Melrose had been nosy under similar circumstances, he wouldn't have thought about "Main Street."

> *The Minniemashie House. It was a tall lean shabby structure . . . .*
> *In the hotel office she could see a stretch of bare unclean floor. The*
> *dining room beyond was a jungle of stained tablecloths and catsup*
> *bottles.*

The renovated Palmer House has not one, but three dining rooms. Formica replaces tablecloths and on Mondays, Opportunities, Inc., gathers in the tiny Kennicott Room for lunch and discussion of attracting industry. On Tuesdays, Rotary meets in the Minniemashie Room to partake of the salad bar and manly fellowship, barbecued sausage and talk of tax-indexing, contrasts that the satiric Lewis would have cherished.

Some people speculate that Lewis's ghost clunks around the hotel where he once clerked. Co-owner Al Tingley says no. "If Lewis comes to town, he comes in a whirlwind. A friend from Texas — a Lewis buff — came to visit us in 1974. We took him out to Lewis's grave. When he knelt to kiss the marker, a whirlwind came out of a blue sky, picked flowers right out of an urn, dashed them to the ground and was gone."

And that's not the only evidence. "Last year the foundation was having a fund-raiser scheduled for 1 o'clock on the lawn by the Lewis home. It was a beautiful day, the sky was clear and we were all set up. At 12:55, it got darker, and another whirlwind swooped down and scattered paper cups and napkins all over the place."

At that point, Tingley looked up at the sky and said, "Thank you, Sinclair." And Dave Jacobson said, presuming that Lewis could, why would he do a dumb thing like that?

Tingley said, "I told Dave, 'That's just what he would have done. That was just his style.' I think Lewis is getting the biggest kick out of our project."

Harry Sinclair Lewis, the bumptious bull in our literary china closet.

No whirlwinds descend when visitors take an after-dinner stroll along Sauk Lake, where kids played childhood pranks on the lonely redhead, the gangly outsider. The same lake that inspired Lewis to create a summer home for Will and Carol. Now it's dotted with busy resorts like Johnnie's Big Sauk, owned by transplanted Iowans John and Gwen Bierman, and the homes of folks like Glenn Domine, who moved in from a Detroit suburb and extols the virtues of the good life in Sauk Centre.

Standing on the bridge above the old dam on Main Street, visitors watch young and old sit in their little boats, pulling in panfish. The sun, a red disk, drops slowly into the horizon, casting a warm glow on the glassy surface of the lake that Lewis referred to again and again after leaving home. So perhaps he wasn't just smoothing over old animosities when, in 1931, he wrote a reminiscence for "O-Sa-Ge," his high school's yearbook:

> If I seem to have criticized prairie villages, I have certainly criti-cized them no more than I have New York or Paris, or the great univer-sities. I am quite certain that I could have been born in no place in the world where I would have had more friendliness . . . [nor] half the fun which I had as a kid, swimming and fishing in Sauk Lake, or cruising its perilous depths on a raft. . . . It was a good time, a good place, and a good preparation for life.

That was 20 years before he came back home for good on a frosty day in January. A women's trio sang "I Heard a Forest Praying," and young Frederick Manfred delivered the eulogy. At the cemetery, a gust of wind came up and scattered some of his ashes on the artificial grass, blew some into the air. One wag said, "Red Lewis scattered over 80 acres of Stearns County."

—D.W.

Don Hanson died soon after our visit to Sauk Centre, and we counted ourselves lucky and proud to be granted the last interview with the last man in town who personally knew its famous son. The last we heard, Main Street was still there and gearing up to celebrate the 100th anniversary of the birth of Sinclair Lewis, with guided tours of his haunts; a play about him, "Exile from Main Street" by Lance Belville of the Great North American History Theatre, and a new book by Palmer House owner Al Tingley, called "Corner on Main Street."

Vern Bienfang
Hiring the Handicapped

Minneapolis, Minnesota
1983

LET'S MAKE it clear right away: Vern Bienfang is no softie. He doesn't hire handicapped people because he feels sorry for them. He hires them because most are hard-working and dependable and appreciative. He's tough and expects a lot and kicks their cans out of the door if they screw up.

So there.

Bienfang can't stand the idea that people might think he has a soft heart. "Ask my wife," he said. "I'm a nasty person." He started hiring people he calls "limited" in 1960, when the economy was flush and it was hard to find people who would stick with low-paying drudge jobs. He hired some people with limited mental abilities. "I found out — they work and they stay," he said.

Bienfang, 45, is the executive steward for the Dunfey Corp. in Minneapolis. He has 120 employees who do behind-the-scenes work at the Northstar Hotel, Marquette Inn and the 50th floor of the IDS Center. They do the cleaning, upkeep and repairs — from scrubbing kitchen pots to polishing brass rails — in 14 restaurants, eight bars and five kitchens.

Of those 120 people, he said, all but about five are limited in some way. He has a totally blind man who loads dirty dishes at night. He has a man whose epileptic seizures don't keep him from doing a good job with a vacuum cleaner. He has a young woman who started as a night dishwasher and now is a supervisor.

He has employees who are retarded, slow, paralyzed, brain-damaged and hearing-impaired. He has dwarfs and amputees. He has people who can't read and write, people who have emotional problems, people with severe speech impediments, people who have birth defects because their mothers were alcoholics.

He said, "Damn it, I do it only because it makes good sense, good business sense. If a person finds a job they're happy with, they do good work and they stick with you. It's as simple as that." So there.

Now listen to what other people say about Bienfang. They say he's a softie. Strict, but caring.

Jeff Geltz is Bienfang's assistant. He's 23, from New Hampshire, holder of a bachelor's degree in hotel administration. Never before had he worked with handicapped people. He had heard of Bienfang. "I knew he worked with all these retarded and handicapped people, and I got scared," he recalled. But he also knew Bienfang has a reputation for running a tight ship. "He knows what he wants and he gets it. He's there when you need him."

Geltz said Bienfang helps the new employees find apartments. Bienfang lends them money to get them on their feet. He senses when something is wrong, and he sits the person down and finds out what needs to be done. He says to an employee, "You've really been screwing up, but I know why." He brings around a woman on payday who helps them with budgeting.

"Some of these people are still here because Vern has so much compassion," Geltz said. "Others are out because they can't live up to his expectations. He doesn't fire people for being slow, but he does fire people who aren't willing to make it, who won't try. And he puts great emphasis on trust. If they lie to him, just once, they're gone."

Heinz Pollinger is one of Bienfang's bosses. He is the food and beverage director of the posh restaurants on the IDS's 50th floor. Pollinger was born in Switzerland and has worked in restaurants and hotels in Europe and the United States, including the huge John Hancock Building in Chicago. He said Bienfang's stewarding operation is the best he's seen.

"He has excellent people," Pollinger said. "Turnover is low. They know the business — from how to handle the equipment to how to lower the accident rate. We have fewer problems with the health department than in other places because his kitchens are so clean. It means fewer headaches for me because his people show up and do what they're supposed to do. They don't talk back as much as the average individual does."

Pollinger said people are sent from all over the Dunfey chain to tour Bienfang's operation and meet his employees. "It's nice to see these kids working, to have a chance," Pollinger said. "If more hotels and restaurants would know of their benefits, they would hire them, too. I'm sure of that."

❧

One more testimonial: Florence Comeau is 49 and a night supervisor at the Marquette Inn. She is deeply indebted to Bienfang. She's one of the few employees he doesn't consider limited; her only handicap is being a widow with limited education. Comeau's husband died of heart problems two years ago, and she had to find a job. She went through career counseling, gathered her courage and sent out more than 50 applications. She got only four interviews and flopped in them all.

Someone suggested she see Bienfang. As it happened, he was looking for an older woman to work for him. He wants a spread in employee ages so his team is like a family. He liked Comeau and figured that because she successfully raised a family she could supervise his people. He offered her the job. She said to him, "Oh, my God, I can't do that! I'm still having problems with my own grief." He said, "Come in tomorrow morning and take a crack at it." She did, and she did well.

Comeau hadn't been around mentally handicapped people before and didn't particularly want to be. She had enough trouble at home. An adult son had been in a swimming accident in 1975 and was a quadriplegic. She said, "I had to lift him into the bathtub and give him as much dignity and modesty as I could." She found out that dealing with Bienfang's employees had some parallels with dealing with her own son. She found she needed to dispense a mixture of love and help.

"This job has put some purpose back in my life," she said. "I feel they're all my children. I do a lot of listening. If they're happy and giddy and crazy, I get a little crazy too. If they're quiet, I can be too. I found out it's not hard to like any of these people.

"They take a real sense of pride in what they accomplish. Housekeeping is always at the bottom of the heap, but I like to find ways to let them know they're appreciated. Everybody needs a little pat on the back, especially in jobs that are repetitious."

Of Bienfang, she says, "He has a monumental temper when he gets going. He can instill a little fear. I see him chew out someone for doing something colossally stupid, and tease and joke with them later."

Is there more to his motivation than good business sense?

"Oh, hell yes, but he'd never admit it. Something in his life touched him deeply, but he doesn't want anybody to know that. He just wants people to know he expects a good day's work out of them. He knows people. He showed some kind of insight when he hired me. Vern was the only one who saw a possibility in this over-the-hill lady who was definitely the grandma type. This job fills such a void in my life, and I owe it to Vern."

∽

What *did* touch his life?

Nothing in particular, he said. Oh, yes, there were his two aunts and an uncle with muscular dystrophy. He watched them deteriorate until they died. "I grew up with it so it doesn't bother me," he said. "A lot of people don't understand disabilities. That's why I like mainstreaming; everybody gets exposed." And, oh, yes, two of his six children (three adopted, three biological) have emotional disorders.

But that's not his motivation, he said. And it's not religious; he doesn't have time for church. If anything, it's the role that chance plays in life. He said to the reporter, "Hell, tomorrow it could be you. You can have a car accident on the way home. You might like to have one of these jobs yourself someday."

He doesn't pretend to put every person in the right job immediately. "They've got a lot more on the ball than people give them credit for, but you've got to get them doing the right thing." He moves employees around, gives them more responsibility than they think they can handle, switches them from days to nights and vice versa. "Vacuum running and pot scrubbing are burn-out jobs. You've got to move them around. You've got to keep people challenged," he said.

Ann Hanke is his favorite success story. "Annie, my God, you couldn't ask for a nicer girl," he said. He found her at the Career Orientation Center in Emmetsburg, Iowa, a school that specializes in training people who need extra help to find work. He hired her as a dishwasher three years ago. She did so well he promoted her to silver polisher. Now she's 24 and supervises eight people.

She has her own apartment near Loring Park in a building where about eight other of Bienfang's people live. She said, "We have lots of fun. I was scared about moving to Minneapolis, but I got used to it."

He hires a steady stream of employees from the Iowa school and from other programs for the handicapped. He was dubious the first time a totally blind man was referred to him, but the man worked out fine. "A lot of people there can't handle books — the figures and the reading. But they turn out to be hard-working people," he said. "What's nice is, after a while, they don't need me. They can go on and find a job anywhere. I hate to lose the good ones, but I love to see them get ahead."

He does have his prejudices. "I can't handle Lino Lakes [rehabilitation center] people — kids who have emotional problems and are sneaky and fast. I'm limited myself; I can't work with them. I've tried. Lord, I've tried, but I get mad. They're smart like foxes. They outthink, outmaneuver my kids and it doesn't work." Also, he won't take drunks or mental patients who are in and out of institutions. He wants dependable, long-term employees.

Long-term is right. The average length of employment for his people is six years. This in a trade where the average turnover rate for stewards is 200 percent a year; Bienfang's is 15 percent, at most. Most who leave are those who are promoted out of his department to become busboys or maids.

He first hired people with limited abilities when he was working in Oklahoma in 1960. He continued the policy when he came to the Sheraton-Ritz in Minneapolis six years later. He switched to the Northstar in 1968. Dunfey took it over in 1979 and his territory has expanded. Dunfey has supported Bienfang's idea of hiring people with limited abilities, only partly for the federal tax breaks they bring. The firm also has hired 15 Laotians as housekeepers.

Dunfey people say Bienfang hovers over his employees. He told one last week, "Damn it, you stink. Go take a bath." He made a young man promise to call him immediately after his doctor's appointment to say if his seizure medications were changed.

He tries to scoot away employees when they show up for work two or three hours early, eager for overtime pay. He gives his best tour of his operations to parents scared about their handicapped child working in the big city. He sends employees to a dentist who gives them a break on the bill.

He refers them to a hairdresser who doesn't charge them full price. He knows many of their landlords and he trains them to call him if an employee is sick or in trouble or behind in rent or didn't come home at night. (The cause for the latter has ranged from seizures to romance.)

His employees say Bienfang often works from 7 a.m to midnight. He said he gets two or three hours of sleep a night. "So what?" he said. "My family comes here to see me. I go home to see them. My wife works and the kids go to school, play basketball, have friends, play in the band. They have a life of their own. I love my job and they know it."

His choice of vacation proves it. He traveled alone on USAir's "all-you-can-travel" plan for 21 days and visited 33 hotels, checking their kitchens and stewarding operations and mentioning here and there that his employees have worked out well.

"Yeh, you're only as good as what's behind you," he summed up. "I tell the kids, 'If you were a bunch of duds, I'd go nowhere.'"

—P.M.

A Wisit From St. Nicholas
Plagiarism, Norwegian-style

Minneapolis, Minnesota
1983

BEFORE I BEGAN working full time for the Minneapolis Tribune in 1981, I contributed occasional pieces to the editorial-opinion pages, many of which I wrote in Scandinavian dialect. I have little chance to do that these days, but this Christmas I tried my hand at some derivative verse. Try reading it aloud, exactly the way it's spelled, and you could make a hit at your next Sons of Norway banquet:

> Vuss da nate before Chrissmuss, an' all trew da house,
> Not ing-a-ting vuss stirring, not ee-wenn a mouse.
> Da jung vunss vuss packed lake sardeence in vun bed
> Vile wish-unss uff rommegrot danced in dare head.
>
> Ma, she cooked lew-ta-fisk in a nightgown of puce.
> And me? Ay yusst sucked on a big cud uff snoose.
> Den over da hoghouse aroce such a cladder,
> Ay yumped from da tee-vee tew see vhut vuss da madder.
>
> Avay tew da front porch ay tromped in may bewtss
> Lake Ingvald, da hired man, on one uff his tewtss.
> Den vhut tew may vundering ice should appear?
> A Yohn Deere corn binder, pulled by eight vite-tail deer.
>
> Vid a little old drifer so nimble an' kvik,
> Dat I sviftly de-dewced dat he musst be St. Nick.
> Fasster den Pug Lund, da vite-tailss day came,
> An' he visseled and shouted and called dem by name:

"Now Astrid! Now Birgit! Now Rundvig an' Ragne!
On Torbjorn! On Torsten! On Ole an' Magne!
Pass da manure pile, get on da ball,
Speed tew da farmhouse and climb op da vall!"

An' den in a tah-vinkling ay heard on our rewf
Da prancing an' pawing uff each little hewf.
Ay vent tew da fireplace tew trow on a stick,
An' down trew da shimney slid yolly St. Nick.

Hiss eyes day vuss blue, hiss smile it ver sveet,
Hiss nose vuss bright red from tew much aquavit.
Hiss cap vuss from Monkey Vord, his bewts verr Sears' Best
An' hiss bundle uff gifts put hiss back tew da test:

A krumkake baker, for Inger, my vife.
For me, a Rapala fish-cleaning knife.
Ski poles for Sven (pluss a novel by Undset).
For Lena? Membership in Nordmann's Forbundet.

Nick didn't make small talk, tewk giftss from hiss sack,
Lake Hadacol for Grandma an' her miss-rub-bel hack.
A truss for poor Leroy, for Ingvald some schnapps,
And for Ole a "buster fuzz" tew vord off da copss.

He hitched op hiss trouserss, viped his noce on hiss sleeve,
Consulted hiss sked-yewl, said "Yee I gotta leeve."
Den, laying hiss finger inside uff his lip,
Nick dug out vet snoose, den gave it a flip.

He sprang tew da binder, tew da deer gafe a vissel
An' away day all flew, lake a Pershing crewce missile.
Ay heard him giff holler, ass he drofe out uff sight,
"Ya, Glad Jul tew all, and tew all a gewd night."

—D.W.

Al and Ag Gilgosch
70 Years Married

St. Paul, Minnesota
1982

SEVENTY years ago today, the girl with the smallest waist in White Bear Lake married the nattiest dresser in Ramsey County.

"When she first saw me on a blind date," Albert Gilgosch recalled, "all resistance was gone."

"No, no," his wife, Agnes, corrected. "I didn't want him. I just couldn't get rid of him."

Pretending to toss her a dirty look, he continued, "I can honestly say we never had a serious argument in 70 years together."

"Thanks to me. I don't argue," she insisted.

"Maybe we'll make it to 75 years," he said. "If we do, it's because I'm amiable and congenial and I never argue with a woman. I always get the last word, but usually it's, 'Yes, dear.' "

They *do* say nice things to and about each other, but they try to keep the level of humor high and schlock low. You can bet that Grandma and Grandpa Gilgosch of St. Paul will get most of the good lines at the party in their honor this afternoon. It's going to be a small, intimate affair — immediate family only — at their daughter Alvina Thornberg's house in New Hope. Fifty people or so. That includes their four surviving children and most of the 15 grandchildren and 16 great-grandchildren, from as far away as Florida and Washington.

Al and Ag, as they're called, have slowed down some, but not much. She dropped into a conversation something about, "When I was raking leaves the other day . . ."

She also mentioned that when Al was putting up the storm windows a few weeks ago, a bee stung him on the chest. Daughter Muriel Kane suggested Ag put meat tenderizer on the wound, and she responded, "The only meat tenderizer I have is a wooden mallet, and I don't think I should use that on your dad."

Agnes LaFond was born 89 years ago to a French family living in what is now Shoreview. Al was born 91 years ago in Germany, and he was brought to America when he was six months old. It was lucky for him he was still a "suckling" (his word; "sounds like I was a piglet, don't it?") because nursing babies traveled free. If they hadn't, his parents would have left him in Germany.

His father, a brewmaster in the old country, was assured there were lots of good brewery positions in Minnesota. There weren't. He took a less grand job in a Winona sawmill. Al, one of the older of 13 children, had to quit school after fourth grade. He left home at age 13 and supported himself in various creative ways, such as managing an "educated horse" at fairs.

Going west to become a cowboy, he got as far as Montana when his money ran out. He asked for work at a ranch and was assigned to bake bread, which he had never done. Al tossed in a package of yeast, and when the dough started oozing out of the oven door, he realized he had used too much yeast (in fact, the whole winter's supply). He looked over his shoulder, expecting bullets, and hopped a freight back to St. Paul.

He went to work as a salesman for Haynes Bakery in St. Paul because he liked its horses. He met Ag and fell in love with her and her beautiful black hair and her slender body. He still calls her legs "crochet hooks" because they were so slim. She had been asked to do some modeling, but she refused because "they didn't talk good about models in those days." Ag was earning about $5 a week as a pieceworker, sewing fringe on rugs at the Crex factory in St. Paul. Al made about $7 a week, and they rented a duplex for $15 a month.

Did they have a family right away? "Oh, no, no," he said. "We waited 10 months."

"Nine months and three weeks," she corrected.

That first baby arrived with difficulty. Ag gave birth at home, and the doctor ran short of chloroform. Al didn't think Ag would live through the birth, and he was petrified, partly because his own mother had died in childbirth when he was 4. He was dispatched to the drugstore to get more chloroform, and he swears his feet never touched the sidewalk, he ran so fast. They named the baby girl Viola, and they had four more children in the next 15 years — Earl, Allan, Muriel and Alvina. (They lost Earl to a heart attack in 1962, two weeks after their 50th anniversary. The timing makes them nervous about celebrating their 70th.)

Muriel was named for Al's favorite cigar. He started smoking cigarettes at 15 and was told by doctors to quit smoking before he was married. He has had asthma and bronchial infections all his life, but, what the heck, there's nothing like a good smoke. What he usually puffs on now is a pipe with a cigar standing upright in the bowl. People used to tell him he wouldn't live to be 30. "They're all gone now, the ones who said that," he said.

He didn't have to fight in World War I because he was classified as an enemy alien, meaning German-born. Even Ag had to be fingerprinted because she married a German. "I never left Minnesota and they did that to me!" she harrumphed, still upset about it. "He's imported, but I'm domestic."

About the time of World War I, he gathered up $800 and started his own business. He spent $250 on a 1913 Ford, stocked it with cheese and sausage and began the wholesale food distributorship called Gilgosch and Co. He takes credit for introducing to St. Paul grocery stores such products as Nestle's cocoa, Borden's cheese, Mrs. Grass's soups, colored margarine and canned dog food.

He worked 14 or more hours a day, six days a week. Al and Ag were married seven years before they went to a dime movie. Their first vacation was when they went to Spokane, Wash., for their silver (25th) wedding anniversary. "See, every time we got a few dollars ahead, the business needed a new truck or something," he said.

Al made a few extra bucks along the way in the stock market. "I did very, very good," he said. Forced by his family to tell all, he admitted he *did* make a mistake by not buying Minnesota Mining for about 25 cents a share. His judgment then was, "Oh, who wants to buy stock in a little sandpaper company? It'll never amount to anything." His decision to buy Nelco Chemical was a lot better.

Neither Al nor Ag were much interested in amassing a fortune. All he ever wanted was a house and $10,000 to buy a tree farm. He was getting close in 1929 with blue-chip stocks, but he lost most of it in the crash. After he retired, he picked up on the market again, and he still offers pointers to grandchildren who ask.

The Gilgosches lived simply and frugally. "We never had a grocery bill or a butcher bill," Ag said. "We lived on what he made."

"I said, 'We ain't going to get it unless we pay for it,' " he said. "That's why you see so many poor people these days. Both the husband and wife work, and they both need a car and a houseboat and everything, and they use that credit, credit, credit. We didn't believe in that. We believed in hard work."

They still do. They had a cleaning lady for a while but Al felt "just like we were losing our happy home, having someone else clean it. It's our dirt." Ag may not air the mattresses and wash all the windows every spring and fall as she used to, but they keep up their house at 667 N. Lexington Pkwy. very well indeed.

One of the best things about their house is that it usually smells of cookies and home-made soup.

She grows flowers and hands them out to friends, relatives and hospitals by the armful. He's in charge of vegetables — a bushel and a half of carrots this year and enough beets for her to can some 20 quarts. Spare tomatoes went into three big batches of spaghetti sauce last month.

Do they feel well?

"I feel all right," she said. "But the other night I had a cheese sandwich and woke up at 2 o'clock with heartburn."

They have had their share of medical problems. She has arthritis and high blood pressure and has had operations for "female problems." She buried her gallstones in the garden for a strange sort of compost. He has had two operations for colon cancer and is trying to wear out a second pacemaker.

"But we're pretty good," he said. "People don't get old from work. They get old from sitting around. Rot to death. When I die I want to die with my boots on." That must mean he isn't ready to go because he was wearing bedroom slippers. (His heel spur gives him his only pain.)

He calls himself the Metallic Man — silver in his hair, gold in his teeth and lead in his fanny.

Until several years ago, Ag refused to accept a gift of an automatic washing machine from her children. She gave in only because she had caught her finger in the wringer of the old washer. Her dear husband commented that it was lucky it was her finger, not her chest.

Al has always been a worrywart — a bleeding ulcer sent him to the hospital several weeks ago — and what he usually worries about is whether he has enough projects to keep him busy the next day.

"I often get up at 3 o'clock and get breakfast and think," he said.

"Get breakfast? You just make coffee! You call that breakfast?"

"That's all you ever make for me, coffee."

"That's all you want!"

"As old as she is," he said, addressing his guests, "you'd think she'd get over being so ornery to me."

He can no longer drive because his eyesight has failed, and they rarely leave the neighborhood now. Instead of going to church on Sunday morning, they sit in their living-room chairs and say their prayers and read the Gospel. They don't watch much TV — Ag said it's mostly "crap," a word that her shocked grandchildren didn't know she knew — but she does know the intricacies of the "Dallas" story line.

They say they never expected to have their marriage last 70 years. "I thought we'd be gone by now," she said. "People ask how we made it so long and I say, 'The good die young.' I told him we won't have anyone coming to our funerals, all our friends are gone."

He added, "We say to each other in the evening, 'Well, we made it through another day.'"

Wouldn't they like to say something sweet about each other? "Like what?" she asked.

Like, aren't you glad you married him?

"Too late to change my mind."

Tough talk, but she patted his hand as she passed by.

—P.M.

Ag and Al have moved to Lake Ridge Health Care Center in Roseville, Minn., and are doing well. She's 92, he's 94.

Lou Snider
No Melancholy Baby She

Minneapolis, Minnesota
1982

*I never had big, wild ideas. All I wanted to do was live quietly, peace-
fully. And I've done that.*

— Lou Snider, pianist

She's a true professional. She's all style, a total pro.
— Jeff Strate, former co-producer of KSTP-TV's Sunday Extra
    and creator of the Pink Flamingo award

Lou Snider is a pianist who's been in good company ever since she sat
down at the piano bar in Al Nye's restaurant on E. Hennepin Av.
many years ago.

Night in, night out, six nights a week for years, five nights a week these
days, the diminutive blonde musician has had Frederic Chopin as her constant companion. The composer-pianist's portrait hangs above her as she
pounds out the tunes requested by a faithful following who come to eat and
drink and sing at the Polish-flavored eatery.

❧

Wednesday night, Jan. 6 — The mercury has reached 11 below and
Nye's Polonaise Room is quieter than usual. Fifteen couples have slogged
through the snow to dig into mammoth cuts of prime rib or lobster tail or
Boczek Duszony z Kapusta Kizona — heaps of snowy-white sauerkraut and
slabs of tender spareribs. Bartender John Battner says that some nightspots
would "give their right arm for a crowd this big on a night like this." But he
wishes it would be busier, "because that's when time flies." He's also tired
of the piped-in music. "Makes the place sound like a funeral parlor."

He won't have long to put up with that because it's almost 8:50, time
for the arrival of Lou Snider, who comes in all bundled up. She limps to the
bar — she's been handicapped since she was a baby — grabs a Tab with a
slice of lime, smiles at Doris the waitress, who says, "Lou, go and entertain

us, dammit," then proceeds to her spot in the northeast corner. Chopin looks down on her, a stern Polish taskmaster. Awaiting Lou at the piano bar is a well-dressed man with a beard, sipping brandy from a snifter, talking quietly to his female partner.

Lou sits down at Nye's new Yamaha ("Someday, I'll just drive this away"), surveys the seven empty stools, flips on the electronic drums and plays "Blessed Are the Believers." When that's over, she smiles at the bearded man, says "You gonna sing or just sit around?" then breaks into "Could I Have This Dance?" and then "Stardust."

Hoagy Carmichael's tune prompts a response from the beard: "I guess they put him [Carmichael] away this week."

"Yeah," says Lou. "I guess he even wrote a song for his own funeral, something with Gabriel in it."

Karen the waitress comes by and Lou says, "Make his a double, so he'll sing," then starts on "Old Buttermilk Sky." The guy begins to sing softly. The ice has been broken and Lou, who always tries to maintain close contact with her customers, sees her advantage. "You harmonize on this one, 'I Fall to Pieces.' It's a Patsy Kline song." The beard obliges, after which Lou asks, "The last time you were in, didn't you sing 'Older Women Make Good Lovers'?" He nods, then sings. He doesn't rattle the rafters like some piano-bar tenors, but sells the song very nicely.

Then Lou solos on "It Had to Be You," ends with a flourish and says, "Faithfulness will get you anything. We know that, don't we? It's almost as good as flattery." Lou has a habit of making cynical remarks about the songs she sings, but her melodic laughter after each remark suggests that beneath her black velveteen jacket beats a heart the consistency of Golabki, Nye's tender cabbage rolls.

"Let's do 'Suddenly, There's a Valley,' a very pretty song. Jaye P. Morgan did it in the '50s, when I was 12. Oh, I forgot I told this guy [the reporter] that I used to play for Slim Jim Iverson. Ha ha."

The beard and his lady get up to leave. He stuffs a dollar bill into the brandy snifter in front of Lou. He says he's been coming to sing with Lou for about a year. Do most piano-bar musicians mix it up with customers the way Lou does? "The good piano-bar player does. But lots of others, they just sit there and play and the customer can take it or leave it." And out into the night they go as Lou sings "There's a fire softly burning, supper's on the stove."

"At my home," comments Lou, "you can turn that around — supper's softly burning . . . ha ha."

Roxanne Haines drops in for a song or two. "Are you ready for your song?" asks Lou, and they begin to sing a medley, concluding with Roxanne's favorite, "As Long As He Needs Me." The duet sounds pretty good, but Roxanne isn't satisfied. "Everytime we do it I mess it up. I have sung with Lou since I went to my first piano bar, the Sconce next to the Orpheum. I was 19. Lou is really talented. One thing about her, she makes everyone sound good. Some piano-bar players don't want you to sound good.

They'd rather sound good themselves."

"Gee," says Lou to Roxanne, "I like your new hairdo. Makes you look like Liza Minnelli." Then some talk of old movies and who played in what musical and how Lou likes old tunes, old movies. "Old things are nice," says Lou. "Except for you, Frank."

Time has flown pleasantly to 11:30 and Frank Williams, a husky gray-bearded fellow, has ambled in. It's time for his song. Everyone seems to have a song. Frank's is "Old Man River" — "Get a little drunk and you land in J-A-I-L-L-L."

Frank tugs at his Greek fisherman's cap, wants to buy Lou a drink. She nods at Karen and the waitress brings Lou her night's martini. "I'm on a diet. And I think it's time for our Revenge Songs." So she and Roxanne proceed through the litany: "I'll Get By," "Just Because You Think You're So Pretty," "Some Day You'll Want Me to Want You," "I Want to Be Around to Pick Up the Pieces." Then Lou launches into a series of pop tunes based on Chopin's works. She's also capable of rapping out a polonaise or two, but says classical music "isn't my thing."

Soon it's 1 a.m. and time for Lou to bundle up for the trip back to her husband and family, to stay there by the fireside bright. In her four-hour stint, she's played and sung and talked with no break to a total of eight customers. The cold weather has kept customers away many times, but that doesn't bother Lou. "I've played at Nye's for 16 years. Sixteen years straight. Well, as straight as I can get."

～

Friday noon, Jan. 8. Lou's version of straight turns out to be very straight indeed. She picks at a luncheon steak, wishes she weren't on a diet and talks about her life, how lucky she figures she is to have such a good job and such a fine family.

Lou's life, however, did not begin on a happy note. In 1936, when she was 1 year old, her father suffered severe depression because his wife was dying. So the Elk River farmer shot all four of his children (they all survived), leaving Lou lame for life. Then he hanged himself.

Lou was able to pick up the pieces. "I was lucky. I got to live with my Aunt Laura and Uncle George [Crandall] on Buchanan St. in northeast Minneapolis." Lou attended Michael Dowling School and Marshall High, away from her own area school "because all the kids there knew about my background." As a child she "diggled around on my aunt's piano. And so my aunt got the idea I should take lessons. I took them from a neighbor lady, a Mrs. Hines."

After high-school graduation, she became an office worker, but didn't like it. "In 1954, I auditioned for Slim Jim Iverson's talent show. As it happened, Slim Jim's pianist had just quit and he hired me on the spot." She met lots of musicians, and a few of them got together and formed a touring rock 'n' roll band. "It was called Lanny Charles and his Harem, and we ended up playing at the Trocadero in La Crosse [Wis.] for three years." After the group broke up, she tried a piano-bar engagement in Austin, Minn. "I was fired the first night because the club owner said I didn't have enough rapport with the crowd. I swore I'd never try *that* again."

In 1960 she went to visit friends in La Crosse and met a truckdriver named David Snider. David apparently told her, "If you'll be m-i-n-e mine, I'll be t-h-i-n-e thine, and I'll l-o-v-e love you all the t-i-m-e time," because they were married that year and they still are. Their union was blessed with twin boys, Ken and Klint, 21, and daughter Luanne, a sophomore at Coon Rapids Senior High School, all of whom like to sing, "off-key sometimes, but don't put that in the story."

Lou is proud that her sons like to listen to Elvis Presley, rather than punk rock. "I can't figure out how they can be *paid* to do that stuff. It's not music. It's screaming and hollering. It's just *noise*."

How does David Snider, who now operates a small trucking company, feel about her being away from the fireside every night? "He's learned to live with it. He even visits other piano bars occasionally to see what's going on. And my policy is that I never eat dinner with a customer. Once a wait-ress asked me it I'd have dinner with her and two customers. I didn't tell her she shouldn't, but I asked her to think about her loyalty. Was it to her husband sitting at home with the kids or to some guy sitting at the bar? I think she got the point.

"Actually David and I have a neat little deal going. We have time off when other people don't. I don't think my job is a grind. And I make much better money than I could if I were working 9 to 5. I can grocery shop when other women are working. I have time to cook and sew and read, nothing constructive, ha ha, and answer the phone for him. And we have a lot of time together. Some piano-bar players don't like what they do. That's sad. But even if I didn't like it, I'd do it anyway because the hours are so good. And Al Nye has been just fine to me."

Not that there aren't hazards when you sit behind a saloon keyboard. "Drinking is a big problem if you don't use your head all the time. Everyone wants to buy you a drink. And some musicians accept them. My waitress has orders to always ask me before she brings a drink. I don't blame the customers. It's not their fault. It's your responsibility to say no. I'm lucky that way. I have a very temperate crowd. And I try to be sensitive to their problems. If an AA comes in and he's trying hard, I cut out all my alky jokes as long as he's there.

"Y'know? It's a funny thing. My job gets easier all the time. Know why? People are drinking less than they used to and you get fewer calls for 'Mel-ancholy Baby.' I'd say that about 40 percent of my customers drink pop or orange juice."

Lou says the customers she likes even less than drunks are people who won't tolerate the kind of sing-along music most of her customers like. "They just sit there and stare at you, like why can't you play something I like. But I try to educate them. There was one customer who tried to hog the show. He resented it when someone tried to sing along when he was singing. So I chided him, I cajoled him and finally he came around. Sometimes I feel like a schoolteacher. Y'know the university sent questionnaires to people in various occupations. I filled it out and they wrote back and said I had the aptitude to be a high-school English teacher. Imagine that! Sometimes I think in my business kindergarten teacher would be more like it."

Soon it's time for Lou to go home, cook supper and prepare for Friday night, and big moments in her career haven't even been touched upon. "Oh, yeah, I've had them. There was the time Hubert Humphrey came in. He didn't come to sing along, of course. He was there for a political meeting of some sort. But he came by and talked to me." And last summer when Lou Snider was awarded the Pink Flamingo by KSTP-TV's "Sunday Extra." "I don't quite know what to make of that, or what it means. I guess I'm in good company if Governor Quie got one."

"Sunday Extra" co-producer Jeff Strate explained later that Lou's award, unlike Quie's, was meant to be positive. "We gave Lou the award because she's such a great trouper and has such a big heart. She'll play "Tie a Yellow Ribbon" for her customers 10,000 times and still come up smiling." Strate says when Lou was given the long-legged bird, she broke into a rendition of "Yellow Bird." She could have played "Flamingo," but Strate thinks her fans probably like "Yellow Bird" better.

~

Friday evening, Jan. 8. It's colder even than Wednesday night, but Nye's Polonaise Room is hopping and the strains of "Yellow Bird" collide off huge portions of Nozki Wieprozowe z Kapusta Kizona (hocks and kraut to you). There's no getting a seat in front of Lou, so people sip their drinks at tables set up around the piano bar. The northeast corner of the room is a world unto itself, as young fellows in trenchcoats come in out of the cold for a drink at the main bar, ignoring the music, the jokes, the verbal thrusts.

Lou plays constantly and talks to the big mixed crowd as if she were in her own living room. A guy with a black mustache sings "Some of These Days." Three young girls stand there, wait for stools, do a dance that indicates they're not part of the 40 percent orange-juicers. An ample older woman named Betsey catches on and does a chaste little hula. Someone tells a slightly risque joke and Lou says "Ahem! Now we're going on to finer things." "Mockingbird Hill." When she finishes, Betsey looks at her husband and says, "Don't you have two hands, for God's sake?" He looks back at her quizzically, "CLAP! For God's sake. CLAP!"

Lou has a "cheat book" of words and music open at the Yamaha, but she seldom glances down, except to write requests on a notepad so as not to forget the people who make requests but can't get up to the bar. Lou plays "I Wonder Why," and then people argue about who introduced it, Rosemary Clooney or Liltin' Martha Tilton. Lou asks someone else if he's sold his house yet.

Burly Frank comes in for "Old Man River" and when he finishes people holler "ALL RIGHT!" Lou asks him if he ever studied to be a Swiss yodeler, then breaks into "Red, Red Robin." A photographer comes to take Lou's picture and she looks out into her audience and solemnly scolds: "I have just one thing to say. I hope all you guys are with the right ladies tonight. Ha ha."

Ed Byron, a regular, sings "Mack the Knife" and rips through the complicated lyrics with confidence borne of much repetition.

With a confidence borne of much repetition, Lou's stubby fingers fly across the keys as she plays the lilting "Music Box Dancer." Lou complains she has a stiff thumb from removing wax off her kitchen floor this morning. Harriet Levandowski gets up for her regular Friday-night rendition of "Flaming Mamie, Hottest Baby in Town." She tells a reporter that when she married her husband, Frank, she thought Levandowski was a rare disease, "but now I know different."

After that, Lou plays "Don't Sigh and Gaze at Me," and pants into the microphone. Then she takes her only break of the night, sitting at a table with some middle-aged couples. Then it's on to "Oh, What a Beautiful Morning" and "San Francisco." ("That's the request favorite of all time. 'Misty?' No, that's worn out.") A guy says he's from Arkansas and Lou asks "Don't you wonder what the hell you're doing up here at this time of the year?" Then it's time for "The Whiffenpoof Song." When the crowd gets to the "gentlemen songster" part, she pounds it out for all she's worth and a multitude of voices soar through the dining room as one.

Then it's "Follow Me" and photographer John Croft finally has it figured out. "That's it! Helen Reddy. That's who you sound like. Helen Reddy."

"Nah, I don't listen to Helen Reddy. I don't listen to many records at all. I'm too busy up here mouthing off. Ha ha." It's late and the dining area is emptied out, but Lou's audience is bigger than ever. Time for a medley from "The Sound of Music." Everyone joins in on "Edelweiss" and when they get to the part about "bless my homeland forever," Lou says, "Homeland? Homeland? That's Nordeast, isn't it?"

That it is, Lou Snider. That it is.

—D.W.

When this book went to press, Lou Snider was still tickling the ivories at Al Nye's on Hennepin, coaxing songs out of folks who want to sing, but don't know if they can. She was too busy to tell us if she still loved her work, but judging from that smile on her face, it's a good bet she won't be quitting soon.

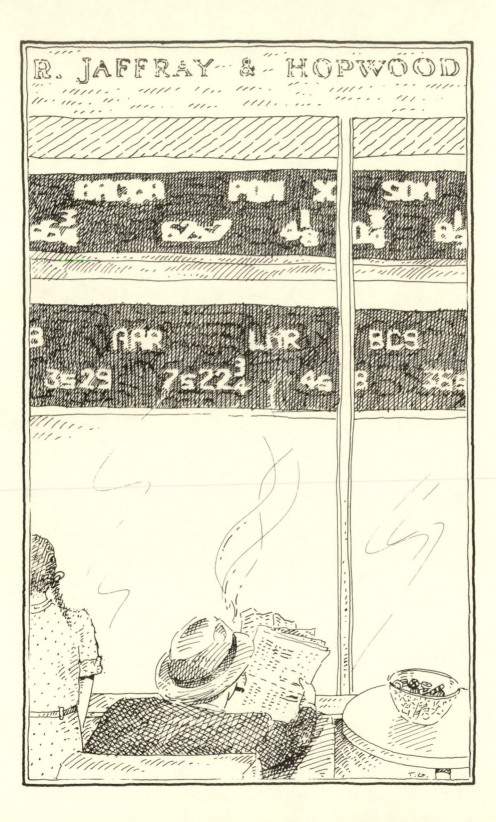

Tape-worms
At the Brokerage House

Minneapolis, Minnesota
1983

Wʜᴇɴ ɪ ᴡᴀs a kid in Sheboygan, Wis., in the 1950s, my dad sometimes would take me downtown on a Friday afternoon for what
he called a business trip. He went about his business, and I'd tag
along.

One of my favorite stops was the Security National Bank. At seven
stories, it was the city's tallest building; the restaurant on top was grandly
named the "Sky Garden." The bank's basement vault was lined with safe
deposit boxes. My father explained that adults rented metal boxes to keep
important things safe and secure and private. I was a little disappointed that
my dad kept only boring *papers* in it.

Next door, there in the bank basement, was a brokerage house, Wayne
Hummer by name. My dad would stand around with the other guys, watching the ticker tape. There'd be lots of businessmen and as many old-timers
killing an hour. It was definitely a male environment — full of big-man
chairs and cigar smoke. Conversation was about home repairs, bargain
stocks and the Milwaukee Braves. (My brain developed a permanent glitch;
the sight of stock quotations makes me think of third-baseman Eddie Math-
ews.)

It was a male club, but the men didn't seem to resent the presence of a
little girl. As I remember it, a bowl of candy was available to juvenile visitors. I know school tours were welcome. I learned to count in eighths, and I
had lots of attention from talkative grandpas. I got to eavesdrop; I knew
who was having wife troubles. I also heard the story a hundred times that if
my dad hadn't let a broker talk him out of Burroughs stock, we'd all be rich
today.

I didn't learn enough about the market to be of use to me now, and my
father isn't around anymore to teach me. I occasionally wander into a brokerage house and find the atmosphere intimidating. The more prestigious
the place and the higher it is in a skyscraper, the snootier the receptionist.
Brokers sit in little cubicles, ear to the phone and fingers on the computer

keyboard. Few places have ticker tapes to please the public. With no patient old-timers around to answer dumb questions, new customers have to attend courses about the market. No kids hang out, much less hang out with free candy. What happened to the old guys and the kids?

∾

To find out, I walked over to Piper, Jaffray & Hopwood, Inc., in downtown Minneapolis. It's one of the few local brokerage houses with a place for the public to sit and watch the electronic ticker tape. This bullpen, as it's called, is a vanishing American institution, I learned. At Piper-Jaffray, the bullpen is smaller than it used to be. It's down to four plastic-covered chairs, a coffee table (but no free coffee), an ashtray, a wastebasket, a computer terminal and a window overlooking the ticker tapes. Sometimes people are bunched up four and five deep, but there's little encouragement to spend time. Why?

"These are colorful people and we like having them, but rent's up and heat's up and we can't afford to give them much space," said Steve Berghs, senior vice president and resident manager. "Before, we needed to have a bullpen to attract customers and now we don't. It's not economical to have them here. The greater percentage are just watching, not trading. They may have a portfolio, but they may not have done anything with it for years."

Then why doesn't Piper, Jaffray get rid of its bullpen?

"For the same reason we're probably not moving into the Piper, Jaffray tower when it opens up," Berghs said. "For the sense of history."

No longer do employees rip off a hunk of printed tape and scurry to the blackboard to print stock quotes, but a bit of tradition is carried on by the hangers-on in the bullpen.

Bullpen regulars — called tape-watchers or tape-worms — fall into several categories. The first is the businessmen and businesswomen. Most dash in to punch up a quote on the computer screen and leave immediately. Some spend part of their lunch hours with the ticker tapes, especially when they're dieting and want to avoid the sight and smell of food. A few are full-time investors, who spend hours every day at the library and various brokerage houses.

The other major group is the retired people. Here, too, there are subdivisions. Some are active and knowledgeable in the market. Regulars tell about one old guy who looked dirt poor and used rubber binders to hold his shoes together, but every once in a while he would execute a bond deal that would make eyes roll.

Other old people are looking for a warm place with a comfortable chair. Some admit they haven't traded in a decade. As Berghs put it, "Their wives kick them out in the morning, and they go from Piper to Schwab [a discount brokerage with a bullpen] and back to Piper."

The day I was there, two elderly men greeted each other like long-lost brothers.

"I'll be 86 in April, and I'm not senile yet," one said.

"Yeah," said the other, "but are you making any money?"

Piper, Jaffray keeps its tape-worms in a little room separated from the brokers. They used to be able to wander about at will and sit at brokers' desks when the brokers were off at lunch. "Pretty soon you got a customer giving advice to another customer," Berghs said. "Sometimes they got pretty good advice, sometimes more sound than they got from the brokers. But the Securities Commission didn't like it."

Because the ticker tape can run as much as several hours behind the market, brokers don't use it. Piper, Jaffray has 70 brokers in this office and only 20 can see it from their desks. Computers do it all, better.

Who are the bullpen regulars?

Catherine O'Leary is one. She's an 80-year-old widow who doesn't trust the Social Security system or brokers, "so I take care of myself." She takes the bus downtown several times a week, has coffee for a quarter at Joe's in the skyway and then watches the stock quotes at Piper. She is selling some of her stocks to make her bookkeeping simpler.

As a girl, she wanted to be an architect but couldn't because the field was closed to women. She taught math, physics and chemistry: "men's subjects, which made it hard to find a job." She married a young doctor fresh out of school, who once sold a pint of blood to buy medical books. He practiced in several Iowa towns, and they raised six children. He got into the stock market, she said, but didn't do well because he didn't take the time to study the market. "He'd buy good stocks but didn't sell them," she said.

She took over the portfolio. "In those days it was about the only thing a woman could do at home. I learned from a very wonderful broker with Merrill Lynch. Very knowledgeable. Brokers now are more or less clerks. Some don't even follow your direct instruction. In those days, they educated you."

When she was in her 60s, she raised two grandchildren. Her husband died eight years ago. "Doctors don't always die rich," she said. She's carefully watching her investments and switching from stocks, mostly utilities, to Treasuries. "I just want to cover my tracks and be able to buy my coffee tomorrow."

Another regular is a man in his early 30s who earns his living by investing. He didn't want to be called by name here because he perceives public resentment against what they call the idle rich.

"Most people think those who trade in the market are flaky," he said. "A lot of my peers' parents have been wiped out in the market. Rather than admit they made errors in judgment, they say trading in the market is gambling. 'Stay away,' they say. They prefer to think they lost money on the equivalent of a roll of the dice, not that they were stupid."

He works hard at his craft. "We're doing the same thing Irwin Jacobs is doing, but he's in a suit and a fancy office," said the young man in blue jeans. "He's an entrepreneur, and we're tape-worms."

He carries a briefcase stuffed with corporate reports, Xeroxed charts and Wall Street Journals. As he talks, his eyes are on the ticker tapes, which to the novice move at a dizzying speed. He follows literally hundreds of stocks.

"Everyone talks about the great information age we have. That's crap. Interest in finance by the average person is increasing and the number of financial services is increasing, but information available to the public is decreasing. Good information is available only to those who pay for it." He would like to have a Dow Jones news retrieval wire at home, but it costs $1.20 a minute. He stands around the bullpen instead.

∿

I didn't get any tips during my day at Piper, Jaffray, except from the tape-watchers who said don't trust your broker. Get smart. Do it yourself.

But I wish I had trusted my broker. Before the rush was on, he wanted me to buy CPT.

—P.M.

The Piper, Jaffray brokerage office did move into the new corporate headquarters in 1985. The bullpen was abolished. "Economics, you know," said Steve Berghs.

The Sausage Makers
Pigs' Heads and Garlic

New Prague, Minnesota
1984

THE PHONE call came in the middle of the night. As it rang for the third time, I still hesitated. I knew down in the pit of my stomach that *they* had found me again and that I had to get involved whether I wanted to or not. I picked up the receiver, absently watched the TV flicker through a pretaped program of "Julia Child and Friends." How ironic, I thought. But I guessed that's how things come down when you live your life in the fast lane.

The voice on the other end came slow and deliberate, in cryptic English with undertones of Middle Europe: "You missed it last time. But we're doing it again. Tomorrow. Be at Stanley Simon's warehouse on Central Av. by 9 a.m. Come in the door at the back." I told the voice that I had a conflict, but that I'd try to work it out with my editor, try to make it to the warehouse on Central.

"See that you do," said the voice of Theophile Mares, followed by a *click* and a *buzz*.

So I called my editor, told her I wouldn't be in on Monday. I laid out inconspicuous clothing, sensible boots. I brushed up on correct pronunciation of proper names I'd use the next day. Afterwards, I sipped a kirsch aperitif while riffling through a dictionary studded with whorls and curlicues you'd never find in Webster's. For I knew that a false verbal step on the morrow could prove to be a disaster. I turned in earlier than usual, not so much for sleep, but to escape the questions that inevitably would come from a wife who wishes I'd find a safer occupation, like fighting offshore oil-well fires.

Early next morning, I headed south on snowswept 35-W, trying not to worry about the wind-chill factor. And wondering just how far they'd go and how many risks they'd take to preserve the past, this willful group of men I'd meet at the end of my journey. An hour later, I was parked next to St. Wenceslaus Church in downtown New Prague. I walked into a darkened tavern on the main drag, trying to look as if I did that sort of thing every morning. "They're over at the warehouse," said the woman behind the bar. "Leave your car where it is and walk over. Use the door at the back. Don't bother to knock."

I crunched my way through the brown-sugar snow of alleys and back streets and arrived at the back door of Simon's warehouse, wondering how I ever got involved with *them*, who murmured inside. I walked through the old door at the back into the dimly lit warehouse, a reporter who came in from the cold. A makeshift stove sputtered, crackled, gave enough warmth to turn my taut cerebral capabilities into mush.

Armond Meyer stood at the stove, toasting bread. For all the tension, I was glad I'd made it to the meeting. I knew that I'd finally have the answer to a question that had haunted my waking and sleeping hours for the past two years. Before the day was over, I'd know how to make Jitrnice, a Czech sausage so tasty and so fragrant that Julia Child and friends would weep at first bite.

∾

The faces in the warehouse are familiar. I'd met them two years ago in the Sportsmen's Bar, when Neighbors visited New Prague. The meeting had started innocently enough. As old men played exotic card games in the back room, J.B. Hartmann and Theophile Mares began to talk about Jitrnice. Hartmann said it was just plain liver sausage; Mares said it wasn't. Men around the bar took sides, speaking English and Czech, and the argument lasted deep into the day and was continued on the next, with no solution whatever. It was not a pretty picture. The conundrum was duly reported in the Minneapolis Tribune, after which the discussants wrote to tell me that I would have my answer the next time they got together to whomp up a batch. That time came and went several times as conflicts kept me from the event.

But now *they* have me where they want me.

"You can peel onions, Wood," says Theophile Mares, handing me a razor-sharp toad sticker. "After that, peel the garlic." And so I hunch over, tears streaming, and the cabal sets to work in Stanley Simon's warehouse, while chief spicer Stanley, who doesn't smoke or chew tobacco, peers into one kettle of simmering pig cheeks, then another where two pig livers bubble away.

Don Vanasek, a retired plumber, explains that the group begs and borrows pigs' heads whenever a farmer butchers a hog. They freeze the heads until they have a suitable number, then they gather at the warehouse, sort of a clubhouse filled with fishing tackle and Stanley Simon's ice-making machines and the soda pop Stanley sells in warmer seasons. And they put together the sausage that their fathers and grandfathers made before them.

The night before, they'd boiled the meat and skin and snouts off 10 pig heads and now they're getting the rest of the ingredients ready. Theophile Mares boils pearl barley and farina on a hot plate. John (Spunky) Simon comes in and wonders if they need more natural casings. "Yah, and more marjoram," says cousin Stanley Simon, who sniffs at a pint jar half-full of marjoram, or marianca, as the Czechs call it. "And I wonder if we should put some nutmeg in the Jitrnice this time."

"*Nutmeg!?*" says Spunky. "What in hell you making, Tom and Jerrys? Forget the nutmeg."

It's already 10:30 a.m. and Theophile Mares says it's time for beer. Ed Bartyzal, 78, huffs and puffs in with a song on his lips: "Jitrnice jelita, des so dobra dobricka . . . ." ("Blood sausage is very good for your stomach.") Mayor-elect Ray Schoenecker drops in from his feed mill next door to see what his brother-in-law Theophile Mares did with Schoenecker's gloves the day before. Bob Ziegler, who donated some pork hocks, comes by to see that no one is abusing them and so does Frankie Sticha, a retired farmer, who donated three pig heads.

There's talk of how fathers and sons got together at hog-butchering time and made a country party of Jitrnice-making, how Stanley Simon learned the secret of spice from his mother, how Theophile Mares' late mother, Mary, helped tie the sausages just a few years ago, how she died last year at 93, how the group's ornate Enterprise sausage-stuffer is on loan from Spunky Simon's mother-in-law, Agnes Rezac. Theophile Mares runs over and stirs the simmering barley, then brandishes the old wooden spoon: "This is a spoon after my mother yet."

A couple more beers into the day, the ingredients are ready for grinding, and the men take turns at the crank. Spunky's son Chuck drops in, on leave from the Marine Corps. He joins in, straining the chunks of meat and fat and cartilage from the heady broth. He brought his California girlfriend home on his last leave, and she wouldn't eat some of the stuff that goes down pretty good in New Prague. Has he thought about finding a new girl?

"Yeah, I've thought about it," he says with a grin.

The whole procedure brings back memories for Frankie Sticha. He and his wife used to make Jitrnice in their farmhouse basement. Now his wife has Parkinson's disease and can't manage, so Frankie feeds the grinder with the sweet meat from close to the bone. It comes out in fragile worms at the grinder's other end. "Ooh," says Frankie, "I used to get so sick on those days. Too much sampling."

"Put some more dry bread in," says Stanley Simon. "Put another onion in. More garlic now."

Don Vanasek smiles. "We do it different every time, but it never seems to make much difference." Theophile Mares says, "Yah, but do we have any eyeballs in there this time? We should have some eyeballs." Soon, the meat and bread and farina and barley and onions and garlic are ground, and it's time for the grand master, Stanley Simon, to step up. He sniffs the spices, he tastes the meat, he pours on the pepper, and then he plunges his arms into the big kettle of meat. Knead, sample, add, add, sample, knead. He throws in a jar of nutmeg and his cousin Spunky shakes his head.

"Stanley! You wash your feet this morning? Wait till Stanley gets in there to mix with his feet, just like we stomped sauerkraut in our bare feet when we were kids.''

City Administrator Jerry Bohnsack, a German, drops by to see what's going on. So does Spunky Simon's wife, Evelyn, who brings some grub to sustain the Jitrnice team.

Finally, Stanley pronounces it good enough to stuff. Chuck Simon says not enough garlic, but his uncle Stanley says that will take care of itself once it's cooked again. There should be enough, I think, having peeled at least 10 buds of home-grown garlic donated by Jessie Machs, only to have Spunky take the bag away from me and peel God knows how many more. And so the stuffing proceeds in Agnes Rezac's ornately painted old machine, which looks like a cross between Gutenberg's printing press and something bordering on the obscene. Stanley takes moist, clean intestines, slips them over the spout, then spins the overhead wheel. Meat squirts out into the intestine casing. Once it's a foot long, it's cut and handed to Theophile Mares and Armond Meyer. Mares ties with strings; Meyer, 74, insists on doing it the old way, tying the intestine together in an intricate knot. But Meyer has to go for a physical at the clinic, so Mares goes it alone as the snake-like sausages pile up on the card table he sits at.

Spunky Simon cooks the tied rings of sausage in their own broth, then lays them to cool on a floor scattered with butcher paper. Toward the end, with 150 "white" rings cooling on the warehouse floor, it's time to make "black." Stanley Simon does this by pouring a quart of deep maroon pig blood into the mixture, after which sausages squirt out of the stuffer as if they'd been colored with cherry Kool-Aid.

And lunch sizzles and simmers on Simon's double-barreled woodstove. White and black Jitrnice from parties past. Venison bologna. Out of the cooker comes the plumpest ring bologna ever seen. "That's Leonard Pexa bologna," says Spunky Simon.

"Leonard Pexa *bologna!?*" exclaims Frankie Sticha. Did they grind up Leonard just to make bologna? No, no, no, says Spunky. But it's special bologna because when Leonard Pexa makes bologna, he grinds up the whole cow. T-bones, sirloins, the works. Mayor-elect Schoenecker is back for lunch, too. He slices into the Leonard Pexa bologna with a hunting knife and comes out with a morsel that's a far cry from the products out of Austin, Minn. Everyone chews and oohs and ahs.

Soon 180 rings of white and black Jitrnice are lined up on the floor. It's time for a trip to Spunky Simon's Sportsman's Bar for a brandy, then supper at home. As we all sit there, Armond Meyer comes in from his physical. He's happy, he says, because the doctor said that he's going to live until he dies. And then we talk some more about Jitrnice. Gee, 180 rings and all from a few begged and borrowed pigs' heads, dry bread, 50 cents worth of cereal and a few seasonings. A pretty cheap mess of vittles.

"Well, no," says Spunky Simon. "There's really only one constant ingredient in Jitrnice. For every pig's head, you need a 12-pack of Schmidt's. And that costs money.''

Night must fall and so I make my way back to Minneapolis. Now I know that Jitrnice is made up of some pig, some vegetables, some cereal, some spice and a closely knit organization. So far, so good. But two things nag in the pit of my stomach. First, on the seat next to me, I've got a sack of fresh sausage. What if I'm stopped at the border? Bloomington has one of the stiffest garlic ordinances in the seven-county metropolitan area. And what about that piece of metal Stanley Simon found in the grinder? He said it was a .22-caliber slug that killed one of the pigs. But could it have been J.B. Hartmann's Knights of Columbus ring? Remember Hartmann? He was the fellow who told Theophile Mares two years ago that Jitrnice was nothing more than liver sausage. Where had Hartmann been all day? He wasn't at the warehouse and he wasn't at the bar with his presumed friends. I wonder about that. I guess that's how things come down when you live your life in the fast lane. . . .

—D.W.

The last time I saw The Over-the-Hill Jitrnice Gang was in October 1984. After a morning of wild-mushroom picking with one of their number, Theophile Mares, my wife and I stopped at Simon's Bar for a beer. Most of the gang was sitting around, drinking beer, eating smoked carp, planning the next sausage-making tournament. Oh, and one more thing. They were yucking it up about the state meat inspector who read the above story in the Star and Tribune, then came to New Prague to nose around and find out whether or not the gang was selling the sausage. No such luck. In New Prague, Jitrnice doesn't last long enough to sell.

George Hanson
Funeral Director

Kenyon, Minnesota
1982

Gᴇᴏʀɢᴇ ʜᴀɴsᴏɴ has planned some 2,000 funerals, but he hasn't gotten around to planning his own.

"Those who are left will have to worry about that," said Hanson, who's 82. "I have enough to do while I'm living."

He amended his statement to say he has one request: "I sure hope they tuck a cigar in one of my pockets." He buys his Lord Clintons by the case, and people say if you see a cigar coming around the corner, you'll see George Hanson a second later. He said he can't remember when he started smoking — "ever since I took my thumb out, I guess."

The comedy quits when Hanson talks about his career as a small-town funeral director. These people he buried, he knew them. He knew their hopes in life and their wishes in death, he knew their survivors, he knew many of their ancestors. Some morticians ease out of the business when they reach the age when their own mortality troubles them. Not Hanson. He stayed active as long as he was able, because, he said, he believed he was helping people.

"I'd often have a widow or widower asking to see me some days after the funeral. I'd think they wanted more thank-you notes or some such thing. I would ask if there was something I could do for them and they'd say, 'Can I just come in and talk?' You know, that was one of the biggest paychecks, having them have that confidence in me.

"In the big city, you don't have the contact with people you have here. I always thought there was probably a little more milk of human kindness stirred because we knew the people we were dealing with."

Did it bother him to work on the bodies of his friends?

"No, I knew their troubles were over. Some of them went through a lot, suffering, before they got to our preparation room. A few times, when someone close to me, or the son or daughter of a friend, had died, it was hard. But even that was better then working on someone I didn't know."

His funeral work now is limited to answering the phone for his son,

Don, who runs the business. George is not in the best of health and doesn't get out of the house much. Conveniently, he lives in an apartment on the second floor of the funeral home. Even if Don Hanson is working across the street on his other business, taxes, there is a Hanson minding the mortuary. People don't like to get a phone-answering machine when they call a funeral home.

George Hanson was born in Red Wing and moved to Kenyon when he was 11. He took the then-standard six months of mortuary training at the University of Minnesota. He trained under his brother, R.B. Hanson. As did most morticians in those days, the Hansons also sold furniture.

He found he liked the mortuary business. He had toyed with the thought of other occupations. His first idea was the Lutheran ministry, following in the footsteps of his father and his grandfather. Both were pastors of the Hauge Lutheran Synod, a conservative Norwegian group.

"I knew I wouldn't preach on what the mother church wanted, and I would have been quietly defrocked. I'd *have* to preach on what was on my mind. That wouldn't have gone over well with those old-timers. Besides, I couldn't say 'Amen' or 'Hallelujah!' after every third sentence. I got along pretty well with my Lord all these years without that.

"So I started to consider medicine, like my brother, Adolph, who was 11 years older. I'm glad I didn't go into medicine because I would have been responsible for life and death both." He paused to let that sink in, and he took a few pulls on the cigar.

"I haven't told you the major factor yet. The major factor is that I didn't want to spend seven years in medical school because I had met the one and only girl, and I couldn't wait." She was Edna Lee, daughter of a farmer east of town. George heard her sing "When Irish Eyes Are Smiling" in the girls' glee club, and he fell in love. She was a freshman and he a high-school senior. When he saw her walk across main street near the old theater, George said to his brother, the doctor, "There goes the girl I'm going to marry." He hadn't even dated her yet.

What did Edna look like when he first saw her?

"I can't remember everything," he said, changing from his refined voice to his grumpy-old-man voice. "There on the wall, there's a picture of her as a bride and also a picture of her on our golden wedding, and from the two you can imagine what she looked like then. I also have a photo of her at 5 years old, if that'll help, but why you'd want to know what she looked like that day is beyond me.

"You know, she didn't have much of a choice but to marry me. I was pretty persistent, yah."

So on the 15th of June in 1922 they were married. Not only was she a wonderful wife, he said, she also "fitted in perfectly" as a funeral director's wife. "She was a perfect hostess, I can tell you that." For years, she did all the hairdressing on the female corpses, a job now performed by George's daughter, Eileen Strandemo, who lives next to the funeral home.

The funeral business had its disadvantages. "My wife and I couldn't go to a movie together or attend the same church service, because one or the other would have to be on the fool telephone all the time." Don remembers that when he was on high-school athletic teams, his dad could never get to an out-of-town game.

Then there was the problem of all the caskets stored in the parlor at home. The Hansons used to live in a small house, the parlor of which was used for visitations and for casket storage. When there was a funeral, the Hansons had to move out eight or 10 caskets to the back porch for a few days.

The services were almost always at a local church. He guessed four out of five were Lutheran services. Many were in the Norwegian language, and some of the old-timers still want hymns at their funerals to be sung in Norwegian. He can understand that. Some hymns are more beautiful in Norwegian. It's difficult, though, to find a soloist who can handle the pronunciation.

But back to his wife — George said that in addition to being the perfect wife for a mortician, Edna was the perfect mother. She produced children in just the right order — boy, girl, boy, girl — and she raised them right. She did everything right, but she got cancer. She suffered for 10 years, and she died on the 23rd of June in 1977. He wouldn't talk about that funeral, except that the Hanson Funeral Home was in charge of arrangements.

Don had come back to Kenyon in 1955, when he and his dad set up a partnership. With their having too little work for two men, Don started a sideline of income tax and accounting. Don and his wife have three sons, but none is interested in the funeral business. The 22-year-old is in the Air Force; the 24-year-old is a senior at Arizona State studying criminal justice and special education, and the 27-year-old was last heard from two years ago, when he was drifting in California.

George Hanson has been thinking over his life, partly because his granddaughter, Ann Vold, a nurse in Rochester, gave him a Christmas present of an empty journal. It's a present he had to promise to give back to her, "someday when I'm gone." He is jotting down some thoughts for her — some his own, some he "borrows" from the Bible, some from other writers. He is finding he has no regrets. "Yes, I think I have served a ministry in my life. I really think so. I've touched a lot of lives in my own way. There's no experience like death, you know."

He was with some people when they died, including his father and a good friend, Dr. Edmund Bakke, who died in his arms at home. "It was better in the days when people died at home, in their own surroundings and usually with someone who loved them. They didn't have to say anything, just hold a hand, be there. I don't want to make it romantic. It may be horrible to see someone die. Death is not always pleasant. The greatest mystery in life is death, but yet it's the only absolute certainty."

He's not the kind of person who believes in a heaven with streets paved with gold and beings sitting around playing the harp all day, he said. "We'll have something to do. No man, and no woman, is happy sitting around idle."

He pointed out that the Bible doesn't record the words of people who rose from the dead. "You'd think they would have recorded something Lazarus said. They must not have wanted us to know. You don't need to know, you just have to believe.

"And believe me, you'd better believe it."

—P.M.

George Hanson died in August 1983 at the age of 84. His son, Don, said the funeral was "the traditional service at the church, nothing different or unusual." The church was full. Memorials went to the First Lutheran Church and the Kenyon Cemetery.

Kirkland Anderson Sr.
A Neighborhood Institution

Minneapolis, Minnesota
1983

KIRKLAND ANDERSON lingered over a late breakfast at Curran's restaurant in south Minneapolis, dragging deeply on a cigarette. He spoke of growing up on a farm near Bolton, Miss., of migrating to Minneapolis and of ending up operating Kirk's Mobil, his 22-year-old service station at 400 E. 46th St.

Anderson is a courtly man who speaks quietly, deliberately and with a keen sense of life's ironies.

"I was the youngest of 11 children. We farmed 120 acres, raised corn and cotton. My father always said if you *do* something, you'll *have* something.

"So when the other farm families went to town on Saturdays, we worked on our truck garden, shelling beans and peas, picking melons. Then my folks would load up the truck and drive to Jackson to sell our produce.

"Education was hard to deal with in Bolton because they had nothing beyond sixth grade for blacks. But my parents believed in education and so all of us were sent to Jackson to live with relatives. My mother paid them in milk and eggs and other produce, and all of us graduated from high school. Two out of 11 graduated from college. All of us, I believe, had some college."

Anderson graduated from high school in 1946 and a year later headed north to study at the University of Minnesota, where his older sister, Percia, already was enrolled. "As the youngest child, I was spoiled. If my mother hadn't died in 1944, I probably never would have come up here. She wouldn't have let me leave. But she was gone, and I took the train to Chicago and then to Minneapolis. For a young man from Mississippi, that was a frightening ride. Between Chicago and Minneapolis, I never saw a black person. I kept saying to myself: 'There has to be a black somewhere.' I'd look out the window at section gangs, and even they were all white."

He studied at the university, then went into the service during the Korean War. He returned to Minneapolis in 1953 and married Alice Gaskins, a registered nurse, in 1954. Five children blessed their marriage; with mouths to feed, further study at the university was out. Anderson got a job as a postal clerk, bought a house in south Minneapolis. "I did fine at the post office, because I believe I'm a hard worker, but I guess I'm not a person who likes to be told what to do. Maybe it was growing up on a farm, I don't know."

That's where the service station came in.

"About two blocks from our house, Mobil was building a new station. I kept watching the building going up. You know, you always have your own business in the back of your mind. When the building was finished, they put up a sign that said 'For lease' and a number to call. I called. About 25 people applied, and I got it.

"I'm not mechanically inclined, you know. I'd never even changed a tire in my life."

That was the least of Anderson's problems. The year was 1960; times weren't great. "I think about 75 percent of new filling stations were going under, so banks wouldn't touch me. My wife wasn't working because the kids weren't all in school yet." Finally, Anderson managed a $5,000 loan from A.C. St. Paul, a credit union for black railroad employees. "I'm proud to say I never missed a payment."

Still, he had second thoughts about his new life, as he raced around his brand-new station from 7 a.m. to midnight. "In the beginning, I'd have gotten out if I could have afforded it. But I owed so much money I'd have put our house in jeopardy if I'd have paid off my debts and looked around for something else.

"I still don't like the business very much; I'm still not mechanically inclined. Recently I thought of selling out. I guess you could say I had burnout. But now I've got a second wind." That's because sons Duane and Kirkland Jr. both work at the station these days. That gives their father the luxury of late breakfasts at Curran's and more time to be the front man, to manage, to look after the business, and also to hope that Duane might be interested in taking over when he retires.

"I guess I've always wanted to be a clinical psychologist, or at least finish a degree. Now that I have some time, I've been thinking about going back to school, maybe to something like the University Without Walls, where they give you credit for work experience — not to make more money, but just for the satisfaction."

～

Several hours before my interview with Kirkland Anderson, I'm nudging my old Detroit beast toward the 46th St. entrance to Interstate Hwy. 35-W. The beast is hitting on what sounds like about 3½ of its eight cylinders. It's 7 a.m., so I wheel into Kirk's Mobil, which Kirkland Anderson Jr. has just opened for business. He's 24 and attended the University of North Dakota, where he majored in office management and started as a running back on the football team. He hasn't found a job yet, so he's working for his father. As he sets up the windshield-washing equipment on the service islands, mechanic Hank Roundtree rolls tires out of his service bays onto the front driveway, waiting for customers with mechanical problems.

In essence, Kirk's is an old-fashioned neighborhood station. No fresh sweet rolls for sale here — or Hula-Hoops, or luncheon meat, or a teller in a bulletproof glass booth. The immaculate restrooms have shiny old Nibroc towel dispensers. Above the cash register in the office are shelves stacked high with Pyroil brake fluid, Supreme antifreeze. Also air filters, oil filters, headlamps. There's a Soo Line calendar and several maps of Minneapolis tacked up to help motorists who finally break down and stop in to see where the heck they are and where the heck they should be. A sign on the door leading to the shop says, "Insurance Regulations Prohibit Customers from Entering Shop Area. Thank You." On the wall a clock advertising Brown Velvet Ice Cream says that it's 7:30.

Customers already are lined up at the self-service pumps, and folks from the neighborhood drop by the office counter to shoot the breeze. A fellow carrying a briefcase drops his car off, saying, "Don't do anything before I call to find out what it costs." A middle-aged guy parks his Chevy station wagon on the driveway, comes in and asks Hank Roundtree when he starts the mechanical stuff.

"Nine o'clock. That's when my eyes open."

The guy with the Chevy says he just sits home nowadays, doesn't run around at night the way he used to.

"Yeah," says Hank Roundtree. "You can't go to the bars and pick fights with your own kids."

Kids from Field School across the street start filtering in to buy RC Colas and Reese's Peanut Butter Cups from two very busy machines. Young Kirk Anderson seems to know the kids and their families. He also remembers when he attended Field. "One day we had a field trip. We came over here and took a tour of my dad's station." Across 4th Av. an old man comes out of the Angelus Convalescent Home, looks at the activity, then hobbles back through the morning mist.

Other folks drop by, start conversations — "How ya doin'?" "How ya doin'?" Walt Palmer, an insurance salesman, drives his Buick Riviera onto the rack, and Hank Roundtree gets to work on its exhaust system. The shop smells of V-belts and oil and acid. A balding man points his finger out of an advertisement on the west wall at a customer who isn't supposed to be standing in the shop. The man says, "If your car is four years old, replace the belts. No matter how they look." The customer shudders.

A roly-poly follow comes in. "Hi, Hank. Whaddya gonna do free for me today?"

"You're getting it right now."

"What's that?"

"Conversation," says Roundtree, banging away on Palmer's exhaust system.

An elderly man walks into the shop and slaps Roundtree across the chops with a glove: "Choose your weapons, as they say." Roundtree shrugs and goes back under the car.

Walt Palmer hangs around, makes himself a cup of coffee from the dispenser. Probably the only 10-cent cup of coffee in south Minneapolis. "It's not great," says Kirkland Jr., "but it's hot." "I like to deal with these guys," says Palmer. "They're very accommodating." By 8:30, Roundtree has my Detroit beast at bay with a probe stuck in its poor old tailpipe. The probe is hooked up to his pride and joy, a $12,000 Sun Performance Analyzer, the dials of which flop up and down perilously. The oscilloscope measures cylinder performance in an electronic dance with engine death. So it has come to this: my Detroit beast in intensive care.

"You've got problems," says Roundtree, "See here. See this line jump? No. 3 cylinder isn't operating. And see here. Your hydrocarbons are running 1,600 and they should be at about 400. Your carburetor mix is too rich. Now if I do this [he moves a dial] this arrow should go down. Understand?"

(Ah . . . yeah, Hank. Really simple.)

Roundtree, a native of Mississippi, got into the business working at Merle Ness's Standard station at Grant St. and LaSalle Av. "Back then we had pliers and screwdrivers. They didn't have all this stuff under the hood, like your car. They call that progress. But Merle sent me to school. He was the greatest boss I ever worked for; died a couple years ago."

Since then Roundtree has attended various schools, including North Hennepin Community College, the Vo-Tech at White Bear Lake and Minnesota Business College. He's worked at Kirk's for four years. He's happy to have convinced Anderson's son Duane to enroll in an automotive course at Dunwoody. He smiles. "It took some talking, but now he's going and that's good. He's sharp."

Out at the self-service pumps, a woman in a white trench coat leans gingerly over the rear fender and administers a dose of petrol to her muddy car. Jerry Hamilton, a truck driver recovering from an accident, drops by to kill time. We discuss last night's movie about the woman dying of cancer who finds adoptive parents for her 10 kids. Someone says that Ann-Margaret did a great job as the woman. And I say yes, and how about the husband? A great portrayal of a hillbilly. Kirkland Jr., Roundtree and vending-machine serviceman Carl Tramel howl, then simultaneously point at Jerry Hamilton. Hamilton is white and from Tennessee. It's obviously a standing joke around Kirk's.

Jerry Hamilton answers a phone, because Kirk is calling on another phone to order a part for Walt Palmer's exhaust system. Margaret Koepplin limps in with her pickup. The transmission is making funny noises, she says. "It's got 200,000 miles on it, and I don't know if I want to fix it." Hank backs up the pickup, drives it forward, backs it again, jumps out. "It's the carrier bearing," says Hank. "That'd be about 60 bucks."

"Fix it," says Margaret Koepplin.

Roundtree returns to my beast, finishes installing new plugs, makes some minor adjustments amid the acrid fumes of carburetor cleaner, and the old beast breaks into a contented purr. He shows me how the timing is "not even a hair off. See?" (Ah . . . yeah, Hank. Anyone can see that.) He looks contentedly at the dials of the Sun Analyzer and pronounces the old beast good enough to get back out into the jungle. Overlooking the scene is a silver sign that says:

Award of Merit
Presented to
Kirkland Anderson
in Recognition of
Service to Motorists
Since
1960

Kirkland Anderson Sr. stands behind the counter just before noon and figures he's been fortunate. "You know? We have some of the same customers we had when we started. Some of them move to the suburbs, but they come back and say, 'Remember me?' Now we're serving the children of our first customers.

"Years back they tore up 46th St. to widen it. I called Mobil and told them because they give you a break on rent when that happens. But even during all the mess, we had just as much business, if not more. That was so strange that Mobil people came out to look. That made me feel real good."

Anderson said he's made his share of mistakes. "I guess I was service-conscious rather than price-conscious, and I held out five years too long before putting in self-service. It just seemed too impersonal to me." Even now, 35 percent of his business at the pumps comes from full-service; 40 percent of his gross comes from the shop. Another angle that helps during a mild winter with too-few car starts and tows is his commercial business, such as the 35 to 40 Minneapolis Rogers Cablesystems vehicles that get all their gas at his pumps.

Cartrell Cooper and Obie Kipper drop by to chew the fat. Cooper, a longtime neighbor, says, "Kirk's is the best in the city." Kipper, who moved out of the neighborhood to Bloomington, settles into a chair and says he still comes to Kirk's for all his gas. Anderson tells of being held up three weeks ago by a guy with a revolver at his side. "It never happened to me before in all these years. But it sort of makes you paranoid. Until now, when someone reached in his pocket for change, I never thought about it. Now, when they reach in their pocket, I wonder what's going to come out of that pocket.

"But it has only happened once. This is a good neighborhood, a nice neighborhood. We don't advertise, but we donate to charities and we try to be active in the neighborhood."

(Anderson makes no mention, but in 1972 he and Alice Anderson were in the news, regarding racial conflict at Washburn High School. The Tribune even editorialized: "The . . . Kirkland Andersons of Washburn . . . are the problem-solvers who defy the stereotypes of the times and offer hope for the future." Two years later, Alice Anderson won an American Association of University Women award for helping deal with racial problems at Washburn and for organizing volunteer tutors at the school.)

"And if someone wants to raise money with a car wash, they can come here. We have about eight car washes a year. You know, you can spend a million bucks advertising, but if you don't treat customers right when they come in, that advertising doesn't mean a thing."

Just then, a woman pulls up at a full-service pump, and the man who wanted to be a clinical psychologist, the man who never changed a tire before 1960, strides out, leans down to her window, says, "Good morning. How are you this morning? What can we do for you today?"

—D.W.

Mary Claire Kent
On Her Way to the Opera

Minneapolis, Minn.
1984

To whom it may concern:

Please consider this a letter of recommendation for Mary Kent. I have known and worked closely with Mary Kent for almost two years as her vocal coach, and I believe she possesses the potential to become a major singer. She has not only a beautiful voice but also all the abilities necessary for an operatic career. Please give Mary Kent your serious consideration . . . . She is very deserving of any help you might be able to offer her.

Sincerely,
William Vendice
Conductor, Metropolitan Opera
New York, N.Y.

MARY CLAIRE KENT has the voice for opera, the experts say. She has the powerful body, the stamina, the determination, the diligence, the character. And now, it's certain, she has the strength to do what needs to be done — beg for money.

Last Sunday evening Mary Kent threw a fund-raiser in her own behalf. A $14,000-a-year secretary for Pillsbury, she needs to raise $20,000 to move to New York and study opera for a year. Good teachers there charge at least $75 an hour, and serious singers should be taking three lessons a week. Then there are photographers' fees, apartment rent, groceries now and then, the right clothes, resume writers' fees, even charges to audition with some companies.

It's not easy for Kent to ask for financial support. She told her benefactors at the fund-raiser, "It's humbling to have to ask for help."

But she's getting good at it.

Jim Masterman found himself offering his posh Union Depot in St. Paul for the fund-raiser. He and restaurateur Gordon Schutte contributed several thousands of dollars in hors d'oeuvres and champagne. Mary Kent prevailed upon five friends to help her address 600 party invitations that asked for minimum contributions of $25. Friend Connie Schrandt kept track of responses and donations. Another friend, Mary Jo Rolczynski, said she would do anything to help and was given cloakroom duties, with the dollar bills on the plate going into the Mary Claire Kent fund. William Vendice of the Metropolitan Opera flew to Minneapolis to be her accompanist and to coach at the benefit.

Vendice said Kent did very well Sunday with three arias and "O Holy Night": "This was some of the best singing I've ever heard her do. She warms with an audience."

Especially this audience, packed with 150 relatives and friends, co-workers and church friends, supporters all, people who couldn't wait for the end of an aria to start cheering, people who believe in Mary Kent, mezzo soprano.

"Yes," Vendice said, smiling. "A very loving audience."

He said he has never seen a hometown get behind a young singer the way the Twin Cities is supporting Mary Kent.

It's not only the quality of her voice that makes people want to help her, everyone agrees. It's her personality — her depth, her soul, some would say. She says it's the Lord who is smoothing the path to New York.

She raised about $5,000 Sunday. Now she'll go after grants and hope that Vendice will help her with another Twin Cities fund-raiser when he's here with the Metropolitan Opera in spring. She plans to move to New York in September. Not bad for a Minneapolis kid who didn't see her first opera until she was 26.

~

Mary Kent, you see, never intended a career in opera. One thing led to another. It's been only the last two years that opera beckoned. Her Minneapolis voice teacher, Nancy Grauff, said, "Mary's voice grew and grew. Everything happens in its time."

Grauff and William Vendice won't make promises that Kent will become a famous opera singer. "Nobody can say what the future will bring," Grauff said. "So much chance is involved. But at least she won't be saying at 45, 'I wonder what *could* have happened.' "

Single and 32, Kent is old for an opera student these days. Most go to a conservatory at 18, get a few degrees and have their names known by 30. They're done with studying and are on to the doing by her age. Either that, or finding another career.

Mary Kent and the people who believe in her don't worry about her starting late. They think it will benefit her in the long run. She is training in a manner reminiscent of singers generations ago who studied privately with a teacher or two, rather than in classrooms.

Grauff said that many talented young people sing themselves out at an early age; they attempt too much, too soon, to the detriment of both voice and career. "It's too easy to get conveyor-belt training. It takes time to develop a big voice, and the soul and character to go with it," according to Grauff.

She pulled out a New York Times story headlined "Where are the great singers of tomorrow?" that says, "The real and lasting big star personalities are the ones that stay put and develop in the hinterlands until they are ready to burst on a wider public."

Singing, said Kent and her teacher, is a physical activity and requires the same sort of muscular training that Olympic athletes undertake. She trains not only the mouth, the lungs, the vocal cords, but also the upper body, the stomach muscles, the rib cage, even the legs and feet. Almost every day, she does exercises prescribed by Annette Atwood, a physical therapist who specializes in training singers' bodies. Kent's size-16 body is powerful.

"Lying on the floor and kneeling to sing an aria takes terrific endurance," Atwood said. The exercises she prescribes for singers are modified for their needs. They work on proper head and neck alignment, on putting the hips and pelvis in the right position. Kent, for example, does modified sit-ups; traditional sit-ups put a strain on the neck and vocal cords, the last thing a singer needs.

Kent's character, her teachers say, is even stronger than her body. They told of a recent incident in which she wanted to audition for the Santa Fe Opera's apprentice artist program. The cut-off age was 28. Kent, four years too old, got advice from some quarters to lie about her age. She couldn't. "If I have to found a career on deception, I don't want it," she told Grauff. She applied truthfully and learned they want to hear her sing, regardless of her age. Kent shrugs off the glory: "One reason I couldn't lie is I can't keep track of lies well enough to do it successfully."

"Mary," said Nancy Grauff, "is not the kind who would bite her grandmother in the neck to get a role. She's not just a singing machine. She's not the type who gets up to sing and has nothing to say."

Mary Kent was brought up in south Minneapolis, one of five children. (After her mother died, her father remarried when Mary was 18 years old, making a family of 11 children.) She went to Incarnation Catholic grade school and Regina High. After a year at the University of Minnesota, where she had intended to study nursing, she dropped out to pursue music. She studied at the Children's Theatre and performed there. She also took private voice lessons with Oksana Bryn of the MacPhail Center for the Arts.

Even though she was involved with music, she was feeling empty, insecure and lonely, she remembers. She was searching for God and not finding Him. Raised Catholic, she had lost her faith after high school. One day in 1975, when the 23-year-old Mary Kent was walking along Lake of the Isles on the way to take a swim, she had what she calls the ultimate spiritual experience.

"I heard the gentle voice of God speaking to me. He said basically, 'There really are two kingdoms. You need to decide which to serve.' He said that if I didn't chose His kingdom, He would no longer be able to protect me. I gave my life to God, and it's not been the same since. It's gotten better and better."

She withdrew from the musical scene for a few years as she matured spiritually and emotionally. Then she began singing in churches, joined a Christian fellowship group and worked at a retreat house in Wayzata, lettering prayer cards. She worked for five years as a waitress and two years drawing bike maps for the Minnesota Department of Transportation.

Her main concern was her God. "I lost a lot of friends. Some people thought I was absolutely crazy. My brothers and sisters questioned my decision."

She knew she was right. "Before, I was an emotional wreck. I became a happy person."

In 1979, the time was right to study music again, she said. She began studying with Nancy Grauff in Grauff's south Minneapolis home. Kent said, "After I gave my life to God, I gave Him my career too. I looked to Him for direction, and I believe He gave me the answer. He gave me a wonderful teacher, who did wonderful things for me."

She sang at weddings and with her Christian group. She sang the National Anthem at a Twins game on Father's Day. She became the cantor at Incarnation Catholic Church (the parish in which she grew up) and still sings there. She began working for Pillsbury as a secretary. One of the best things Pillsbury did for her, she said, was to send her to a career development seminar, which concluded she should become a professional singer.

"This becomes one of those stories where you know something is meant to be," Kent said. "Everything works."

Her accompanist, Narissa Strong, introduced her to John Gilmore, a tenor with the Metropolitan Opera, when he was here with the Met in 1983. "I love to read autobiographies of singers — it's my favorite pastime — but I wanted to talk with someone who is in it now. Someone my age. He spent a couple of hours with me." Gilmore suggested she talk with Vendice, the Met conductor. But how could an unknown singer arrange that?

Through Weight Watchers, as it turned out. Kent went to her regular meeting one evening and stood in line with 150 people to be weighed in. She heard the woman next to her say, "I sing with the Metropolitan Opera." The woman was Constance Webber, and Kent glommed on to her.

"In that short conversation, she decided she wanted to help me. She hadn't heard me sing. She didn't know a thing about me. That's what's so crazy. She told me later she saw herself in me before she made her big break." That break was singing in "The Sound of Music" with Mary Martin.

"Connie said, 'You write a note to William Vendice and say you want to work with him.'" So John Gilmore told William Vendice about Mary Kent, and Constance Webber handed him a note about her. Kent got a letter from Vendice saying he would be most happy to work with her.

That was in June of 1983. Two months later Kent went to New York. Petrified. "I was talking to people who were used to polished performers! And I certainly was not." She worked with Vendice for 10 days. "What impressed him most was the condition I was in when I got there and the condition when I left. He told me the progress was phenomenal. I knew I was raw material, but I had high hopes."

There were, of course, disappointments: She competed in a Schubert Club competition — her first competition — and did horribly. "I forgot my words in the middle of the song. Fortunately, there were only three people in the room. Unfortunately, they were all judges." They were kind enough to let her finish, then disqualified her.

In another audition — this time for the Met — her knees were shaking so much that the clanking may have drowned out her voice, she said. She wasn't hired. "What was valuable was that Bill [Vendice, the Met conductor] went back and read the judges' papers. He told me what I need to work on: stage presence. They said I looked like a church singer, which I was. Opera is much more dramatic. I do feel I have natural acting ability, but it takes time to come out." She signed up for drama lessons.

She learned that nose abnormalities were causing problems with her voice. A Minneapolis doctor who has helped many singers, Robert Rosenberg, operated to repair a deviated septum and remove a spur. Just three weeks after surgery, when the swelling still was extensive, Kent could tell she had increased range on both the high and low ends. Grauff told her, "With what I hear today, you have my blessing to pursue a career."

And she agonized over whether as a born-again Christian she could be in opera. It wasn't only the troubling stories that some opera singers sleep their way to the top. Also, she didn't think she could play the part of a seductress, a pagan, a villain who flings herself on the funeral pyre. She turned down Grauff's suggestions for roles to practice: "No, that isn't fit for me."

In recent months, Kent has changed her mind. "What I came to realize was that just because I'm singing something doesn't mean I endorse it."

Many operas, she said, are about good versus evil, and she may play the part of evil. But sometimes the good triumphs. When evil wins out, it's because the central character has a fatal flaw. Maybe the audience will go away with a better understanding of how to make the right decisions, she said. Maybe her personification of evil will help someone. "God has given me an operatic voice. That is my gift. I don't necessarily have to be singing Christian music to serve Him."

So she's learning seductive stances and come-hither looks.

But there's something different, something magical, when she sings a positive piece, something she believes in. Such as, "O Holy Night" at her fund-raiser. When she let loose with "O Night Di-viiiiine," it was chills-down-the-back time for many in the audience.

Larry Salzman, who is married to Mary Kent's twin, Martha, said, "Certain voices break *glasses*, and other voices break *me* up. I cry every time

I hear her. I shouldn't say this, but the only other person who does that to me is Dolly Parton."

"Oh Larry," said his wife with disgust.

"OK," he said, "Dolly Parton almost made me cry once."

⌒

Ann Lamers, a former roommate of Kent's, said she used to get a kick out of watching Kent practice facial gestures and listen to the nonsense syllables she sang. "I'd sit in the bedroom and just giggle."

A Neighbors reporter and photographer went to Kent's voice lesson with Grauff. What her old roommate says is true. The facial contortions and strange sounds were even weirder than usual because it was only five days before the fund-raiser and Kent was having some sinus problems — minor headaches, some congestion at the top of her head that needed dislodging.

We wanted to hear her burst into song, something like the Hallelujah Chorus, but no way. They started with breathing exercises. We found out Kent can hiss from here to Saginaw. A most impressive SSSSSSSSS. Then singing! "Ka-kee-kee-koo-koo," she sang. Lovely. And strong. We wondered if the neighbors' goblets shattered. Kent's "Ming-ming-ming-ming-ming" must have been perfect because Grauff exclaimed, "Good, Mary!" Half an hour later her "Vah-wee-vah-vee-vah" was a lot better than an early "Vah-wee-vah-vee-vah." Or so Grauff said.

We expected to hear a lot of words like "largetto" and "mezzo-forte." Instead we heard "mucus" and "gloppy." There was much discussion of the swollen tissues in her left nostril, and even an examination with lights up the nose. "Lucky you don't have hemorrhoids," we said, and they cracked up.

They did tongue exercises, hardly glamorous. In fact, obscene. The two of them can roll their tongues like rolled roasts. And they can open their mouths, which they call "oral cavities," so wide that they're a joy to nurses taking strep tests. We thought people were born with big mouths or little mouths, but they said singers put a great deal of effort into stretching theirs.

As professional as they are, they know their facial contortions can be viewed as funny.

"Sunday she will look glamorous and sound magnificent," Grauff said. "People will think, 'Why can't I be Beverly Sills or Mary Kent?' "

They worked on head and neck position, jaw alignment, stance. "Strong in the body and strong in the chest," Grauff kept saying. They worked at clearing the glop in her head. They worked at using her forehead, her cheek bones, her lower teeth and her chest as sounding boards for the big voice. They concentrated on her rib action. At times one might have thought she was training as a gymnast.

But please, we kept thinking, sing something with *words*.

She finally did. A mournful, haunting. "Must the winter come so soon . . . . It is a long winter here." Kent said it's from Samuel Barber's "Vanessa" and it's not about a Minnesota December. It's about a lost soul.

~

"I've seen how many good people there are in the world who want to help," Mary Kent said. "It's built my faith in mankind. That's corny, I know, but people have been very kind to me."

If you want to be very kind to Mary Kent, checks of any denomination are welcome at the Incarnation Church Scholarship Fund, 3817 Pleasant Av. S., Minneapolis, Minn. 55409. Contributions are tax-deductible. She promises a hand-written thank-you note. Who knows? The autograph of Mary Claire Kent may be valuable someday.

P.M.

Readers responded like crazy with encouragement and about $4,000 in contributions. Mary Claire Kent is on her way.

Gunnar Petersen
Adventures on the High Seas

Bloomington, Minnesota
1982

RETIRED HONEYWELL engineer Morrie Peterson used to drop off his wife, Winnie, at the Masonic Home and Care Center, 11400 Normandale Rd. Winnie would visit with old folks. Morrie would drive back home, drink a cup of coffee, then drive right back to pick up Winnie. He figured that was sort of ridiculous, so he volunteered to do a bit of visiting with the old folks, too.

That's when he hooked up with Gunnar Petersen, 86, a Norwegian immigrant who had no one to talk to. Morrie wanted to keep his Norwegian in fine fettle. What better way than to talk with a fellow who grew up in Norway? But Gunnar proved to be more than a linguist. Morrie wrote Neighbors recently that his new friend had lots of good stories to tell and asked that we come over to Bloomington to meet him.

Gunnar Petersen sat ramrod straight in a chair in the middle of the Peterson living room. He's a tall man, with a bit of a paunch, and the face of a friendly hawk that always threatens a smile. He has a Norwegian accent as thick as primost, a cheese he favors, and he whistles to himself if not directly addressed. Gunnar is blind, but his mind's eye sees those days in the foggy fjords of his past as clearly as if they were yesterday. In his mind's eye, he sees the rugged island he was born on, the freighters and sailing vessels he shipped out on. He sees his late wife, Natalia, and he sees the ceiling of the Sistine Chapel in Rome.

Gunnar was born on the island of Vesteraalen, north of the Arctic Circle.

"I was apprenticed as a painter and decorator, but there was no work on the island. And I figured I wanted to see the world, so I quit my apprenticeship and asked my bother Ted if he could get me a job. He was working on a freighter and by golly he found me one."

That was in 1913, when Gunnar was 16. "I shipped out on the Roald Jarl as a deck boy, cleaning cabins and serving food. I got 25 kroner a month. No, we never had lutefisk. We had meat and fish, not vegetables.

We're not much at eating vegetables. By golly it was pretty tough back then."

Gunnar's first voyage was from Trondheim to Archangel, Russia, where they picked up lumber and headed for London. "By then the war was going on, and we never even went uptown."

In the next six years, it was on to Antwerp and Baltimore and Bombay and Calcutta and Shanghai and Singapore and Surabaya and Tokyo and Vladivostok, exotic places for the kid from Vesteraalen who made it around the world eight times before he settled down on dry land. His all-time favorite cities? "Oh, Sidney and Brisbane, Australia. They were so *clean* and the people were nice.

"Calcutta, oh God, boy-oh-boy, I was in the railroad station and there were people lying around with no clothes on, nothing but skin and bones. I found two young girls lying there and took them to a restaurant. They wouldn't let them in, so I gave them $20 apiece. Then they were rich."

Gunnar gave away lots of money during his years on the high seas. "When we'd be in Baltimore, there was this priest, Father Adams, who'd come aboard to talk to us. He was a wonderful feller. I'd always give him five or 10 dollars. Because priests don't get paid much, you know." When Gunnar wasn't giving money away, he was getting himself into all kinds of adventures.

∽

"I always tried to get on an American-built ship. The food was better and so were the cabins. Finally I got on the Cato, an American ship. We docked in Italy. I got a couple days off to go to Rome because I wanted to see the Sistine Chapel. I figured if I ever wanted to get back in the painting trade, I'd better see that. I got there and I was stopped by a Swiss Guard. I asked him if there was anyone who could speak English because I'd picked that up here and there. The Swiss Guard said 'Uno Momento.' Then he came back with a priest. And the priest said, 'Gunnar! What are you doing here? There's no water around here.' It was Father Adams from Baltimore. He showed me around the Sistine Chapel — it was beautiful — and I asked him if I could sketch the part with the clouds on the ceiling and he said sure. I sketched it in my notebook. There were all kinds of cardinals and arch-bishops, but Father Adams said, 'Never mind them. I'm going to show you St. Peter's.' By the time it was time to get back to Pompeii, I was broke, so Father Adams paid my way. He was a wonderful feller."

∽

"Once during the war, I was on an old ship hauling iron ore to Germa-ny. The food was so rotten that I just couldn't eat it. We got to Lubeck, and I went downtown to get a decent dinner. I got back to the harbor, and the ship was gone. The German soldiers came and took me to prison. For 15 days, I was a prisoner of war. They'd take us out into the yard and make us walk around in a circle. That was breakfast. Finally the Norwegian consul in

Lubeck got me out and onto a Swedish ship back home."

～

"Another time, there was an English ship short two men. So I signed on and hauled machinery from Liverpool to Vladivostok. When we got to Russia, the English company sold the ship to the Russians and there I was in Vladivostok, out of work. So I had to ride the Trans-Siberian Railway. It took seven weeks and the food was just terrible."

～

"On the 17th of January in 1917, we were three days out of Gibraltar on the Anna, hauling straw from Spain to Scotland. A German submarine came to the surface, it shot a shell in us just under the water and we started going down. The Germans boarded for food and gave us five minutes to get off. I had my jacket on but I didn't have time to get rubber boots on.

"There were nine of us in one of the lifeboats. I thought that was the end of me. Boy-oh-boy. The boat ran full of water and three men had to bail all the time. I froze my feet and that's bothered me ever since. I still have to wear wool socks to bed all year.

"We were out on the North Atlantic four days. No, we didn't talk much because we were too busy bailing. We were rescued by a Dutch ship bound for New York. We asked if they'd take the lifeboat on board. They said sure and when they were hoisting it on, it broke in two. When we got on the boat, they filled us full of genever [Dutch gin] so we could barely walk, but my feet were in such bad shape I could hardly walk anyway.

"You know, the Anna was an old tub. During the war the companies put all those old tubs out on the water and then the Germans sank them and the companies collected the insurance. I ended up in London, broke, with hardly enough to buy clothes."

～

Gunnar doesn't figure that the company bothered to insure him. He finally got back to Norway and shipped out on other vessels, including a Finnish sailing ship.

"You know, you're not an able-bodied seaman if you haven't been on a sailing ship. On a sailing ship when the wind comes down from Antarctica, the rigging gets full of ice. And you have to take in some sail.

"I followed a Scotsman up the rigging. The spar blew down on him and he was killed. They put him in a canvas bag and slid him over the side. Then the captain read a piece from the Bible. He was a nice feller, and I thought to myself why couldn't I have been ahead of him on the rigging. Then we headed for Venezuela to pick up a load of guano. You know what that is. Ha ha."

～

Gunnar stands up, then sits down and Morrie Peterson comes in with a coffee cup. "Here's your medicine, Gunnar." Gunnar sips and licks his thin lips. It's apricot brandy. His innards warmed, he continues his story.

"After the war, times were tough. I was in St. John, Newfoundland. I figured I'd set out to see the world and, by golly, I'd seen it. So I *kvit*."

He emigrated to Boston but didn't like the East Coast, so headed for Minneapolis in the spring of 1919. "I knew there was lots of Scandinavians up here so I came and I guess it went all right."

Gunnar landed a job as a church decorator with the Thomas Gatey Studio. "The pay was real good, $1.25 an hour, you betcha."

He traveled for the company, painting Catholic church interiors in such places as Duluth; Regina, Saskatchewan; St. Louis. He even had a shot at selling New York City's St. Patrick's Cathedral on the services of the Thomas Gatey Studio, but got there too late. But the job that stands out in his mind is when Gatey assigned him to do the dome of the Basilica of St. Mary.

"The dome was blue with gold stars," recalls Gunnar. "But Father Reardon was a real tough guy to get along with. Nothing was good enough. So finally one day, I took my paint coveralls in to Mr. Gatey. He said, 'What the hell are you doing?' I said, 'I can't get along with Father Reardon.' So Gatey got us together and said, 'What's wrong with you two? Here I got a painter who has actually seen the Sistine Chapel, Father, and he's not good enough for you.' After that it went better."

After 10 years, Gunnar got out of church decorating and into painting and wallpapering fancy homes along Lake Minnetonka. In 1931, he was up in Aitkin, Minn., on a fishing trip when he met a schoolteacher, Natalia Rom. They were married and settled in at an apartment on Franklin and Columbus. "The Depression, that was tough. One year I worked only three weeks. You know, if we didn't have money saved up, we'd have had to go on *relief*. But we made it, by golly."

Gunnar and Natalia had no children, and they busied themselves with activities at Central Lutheran, they went north fishing in the summer and Gunnar remembers shopping at Ingebretsen's Model Market on Lake St. for delicacies from his homeland.

Gunnar retired in 1961 and spent the next 20 years with Natalia at their home in north Minneapolis. Then Natalia died, Gunnar lost his eyesight and ended up at the home, where he met his new friend, Morrie Peterson.

"The food is doggone good at the home," says the man who ended up a POW in his search for a decent meal almost 70 years ago.

(Winnie Peterson explains that Gunnar asked if he could keep a jar of gammelost, a smelly concoction, in the refrigerator at the home. "A nurse found it and thought it was something else and threw it away." Now on Gunnar's chart there's a note to eager-beaver nurses: "DON'T THROW THAT STUFF AWAY!")

"Ha ha," says Gunnar, smacking his lips at the Swedish sausage dinner that Winnie's preparing. "Minneapolis has been good to me. I can't complain." He shakes his head. "But, you know, I kept a log of my sailing days.

And when I moved into the home it got misplaced. I sure wish I had that."

Without the log, Gunnar has to rely on the penetrating vision of his mind's eye to recall those adventurous days on the high seas, in Rome at the Sistine Chapel, hanging off the ceiling of St. Mary's Basilica.

"That Finnish sailing ship was so beautiful," he says. "I can still see it. Some nights now I'll wake up and see it and I'll wonder where I am."

—D.W.

Gunnar is still going strong at the Masonic Home, where Morrie and Winnie visit him every week. He occasionally visits the Petersons, according to Morrie, but has given up on the apricot brandy, if not the gammelost.

Jamie Schell

Day in the Life of a Boy

Rollingstone, Minnesota
1984

Blessings on thee, little man,
Barefoot boy, with cheek of tan!
With thy turn-up pantaloons,
And thy merry whistled tunes.
— John Greenleaf Whittier's "The Barefoot Boy"

TEN-YEAR-OLD Jamie Schell doesn't run around Rollingstone barefooted — he's usually Nikefooted — but he does have the spirit of Whittier's boy. He fishes and plays ball and otherwise enjoys what life has to offer in a small Minnesota town.

We met Jamie at Joanie Schmit's bait shop. His friend, Jeff Wood, also 10, had just bought a walleye lure for 50 cents. It was bright purple, the color so fashionable these days, but Jeff had no opinion on whether walleyes go for trendy colors. The boys contemplated this as they stood under a sign at Joanie's that says: "When God created the earth, He made it two-thirds water and only one-third land. It only seems natural that two-thirds of one's time be spent fishing." Jeff and Jamie had an opinion on that: It's true.

They said they were going fishing that afternoon in Winona, seven miles away, but they planned to hang around Rollingstone the next day, "fishing down by the lumberyard." The stream has no name that they know of. When you go fishing there, you say you're going down by the lumberyard and people know what you mean. Anyway, they said, sure, come along the next afternoon, after Little League practice. Jamie said we could meet him at his house at 9 in the morning. He should be up by then.

The place looked like a Norman Rockwell painting: seven pairs of blue jeans in various sizes flapping on the washline; a flagpole surrounded by red and white petunias; a rope-and-board swing hanging from a tree; a 10-year-old boy clipping grass along the sidewalk; a house in A-1 condition (albeit a modern one-story instead of a frame farmhouse); a small black mutt yipping a warning.

Snuffer (a.k.a. Snuff and Snuffers), after formal introductions, became quite docile. Clipping as he talked, Jamie said that his family got the dog from the Winona pound and that people there couldn't tell his breed. He's the family's fourth dog, following "Pepper I" (who jumped up and scratched people and killed chickens) and then "Fearless" (a black lab with a nice personality who liked to fling snakes around) and "Pepper II" (hit by a car after only three or four months).

With the comforting summer sounds of the wind in the trees and the snip-snip-snip of grass clippers, Jamie started in on his autobiography.

"I've lived here all my life — so far anyway." His dad, Jim, "loads barges and empties trucks of whatdayacallum, soybeans." His Grandma Schell owned the cafe downtown and now his uncle and aunt do and his mom works there and his grandma still bakes pies for the cafe and she plays the organ for Sunday mass. He and his sister, Tara, who Jamie said would be 13 in five days, never go to bed at 9 in the summertime. His folks go to bed at 10, but he and Tara stay up until midnight or 1 and they sleep till 9. There are a lot of Schells in the Rollingstone phone book, but not as many as Speltzes, who take up a whole column and a half. There's a Schell Hill, where his dad was raised, but that's no big deal because lots of hills are named after people, like Hoffman Hill. His Great-aunt Jessie Schell just died, but maybe she was his dad's great-aunt. "I can't remember all that stuff."

By this point he realized he had only 10 minutes until baseball practice, and he gave a quick tour of the house — including his mom's bowling trophy and his dad's pool trophy and the funny little statue that says, "I've been reading so much about the bad effects of smoking, drinking, overeating and sex that I have finally decided to give up reading."

He volunteered to show his karate awards (five trophies, three medals) from his class at the Winona YMCA. They were nice. He also pointed out two guns on his bedroom wall. "I can shoot 'em both but this one [the 12-gauge shotgun] would knock me on my butt." We admired the Incredible Hulk bedspread; he said thank you.

～

The baseball field is in an incredible spot — on the edge of town, with a background of hills so green that you'd think you were wearing dark glasses even when you're not.

The kids were tossing around a few balls when coach Terry Henke arrived. He told us he had wanted a team for 10-year-olds and under (largely because he has an 8-year-old) but was told there weren't enough kids who wanted to play. But he persevered and went to the school and asked who wanted to play ball. There were enough sign-ups to form two teams. "Pretty easy."

Henke works nights at a Winona silk-screening and printing company and is an easy-going guy who likes to see kids having fun on the field. This day he had 22 — 11 boys and 11 girls.

As he hauled out equipment (good stuff; even the 10-and-under league will get uniforms), the kids regulated themselves.

"Are you trying to *kill* me, Sarah? You're aiming for my eyebrow!"

"I'm sorry, I didn't mean to throw it that badly."

"Ow!"

"Nathan, go on third."

Some of the kids were puny and uncoordinated and had gloves as big as their chests. Others looked like miniature pros who had the basics down and were working on refinements, such as taking vicious cuts at the ball and pulling up the sweat pants just right.

Terry got his kids working on fielding practice. He tossed up a ball and soundly hit it. Instead of the thunk we expected to hear, there was a disappointing clink. Metal bat. Oh, well, life can't be all Rockwell. There's sunshine and grass to whistle through and mothers with babies in strollers and so what if the bat goes clink?

We chatted for a bit with Pam Wood, a 31-year-old beautician who is the mother of Jamie's friend Jeff Wood and of bat boy Shawn Wood. She said she's lived in Rollingstone all her life. "I appreciate it more all the time. Even the scenery — I'm taking more time to appreciate it. Sometimes the kids whine, 'There's nothing to do here.' But they're learning there's a lot to do." She said that Jeff's main attributes are not athletic and that he didn't want to play ball this summer, but that she told him, "You play. It's here. Take advantage of it."

"Hey, Pam," interrupted Matt Gaffron, who's 11. He wanted to bring her up to date on the play he's writing on his home computer. We asked for a summary. It's called "Vacation Horrors," and, he said, it's about "a hotel in Detroit called Happy Hotel. A woman, Charlotte Hawkins, checks in. She's a murderer. Three cheerleaders — Missy, Sally and Frieda — check in. That night Charlotte sneaks into the room and stabs Frieda in the chest with a knife. They call Sherlock Holmes into the case. That's the first act."

Matt told us what happens, but we'll keep up your suspense, in case you can make it to Rollingstone tomorrow. Matt had planned to produce it Friday until he found out this would be in the Saturday paper. He postponed it two days to take advantage of the free publicity. He said to tell you admission is 50 cents and the play will be produced at his house, a new dark-green house at 203 Edgeview Dr. In town you'll find more information on such details as time of production. "I'll work with my advertising director on that."

He plays the part of a bellhop and is also the director, producer and comic relief. Jeff Wood is part of the stage crew.

Asked where the profits go, Matt said, "Maybe I'll buy the kids something like Popsicles. They'll work for almost nothing." Except for one high school junior who wanted to be paid. Matt dropped him from the cast.

The next chatty visitors at the ballpark were Brian Bartlett, 6, and his sister, Angela, 5.

"Hey, where's that bell coming from?" Brian wanted to know.

We said from the church. Those are church bells for a funeral.

"Who's dying?" Brian asked.

An old lady named Hulda Jacobi, and she's already dead.

"I think she's at the graveyard," Angela said.

"Was she a nice lady?" Brian asked.

We said we didn't know. We'd never had the chance to meet her.

"But was she *nice?*" Angela insisted.

We said she probably was.

"Well," Angela said, jabbing her finger upward, "if she's up there, she's nice."

Jamie Schell brought our attention back to baseball. He was the first-baseman on an 11-person team. (The coach didn't want to cut players so early in the season.) Shortly after Jamie announced, "I'm having a terrible day," it was his turn at bat and he hit a homer. He slapped his teammates' hands as he rounded home. Life in Little League is changeable, and Jamie's next memorable play was to muff a catch, allowing the runner a double. Jamie stood alone on first, practicing spitting on the ground. He's quite good.

In the next inning, Jamie hit what looked to be a double but became a homerun. An outfielder shouted, "We almost had him." The game got ragged and soon any decent hit for Jamie's team became a homer.

A little later. "OK, the bases are loaded," the coach shouted. A girl on third yelled, "I wanna go home!" Little Angela Bartlett, only 5, shouted from the sideline: "Foul ball." This is a town that knows ball. It also knows sportsmanship: Today's Sports Hero and Our Close Personal Friend, Jamie Schell, missed tagging out a runner by a hair and admitted, "I didn't have my foot on the base." A girl on the other team jumped out of the dugout in glee and said, "It's a miracle!"

OK. The score was 7 to 7. It had been 7 to 2 in favor of Jamie's team only an inning before. This was the bottom of the seventh — the last — inning, and it was the last chance for Jamie's team at bat. "This is it," screamed an outfielder. A couple of players singled. Jamie up to bat. It's a home run!! That was Jamie's third. The other team took it gracefully. An outfielder said, "Now I'm starting to get a little busy out here." A few plays later, the game ended. Final score, 11 to 7. Jamie contentedly scratched his stomach.

Jeff Wood had to go home because his family had out-of-town company. Jamie went to Schell's Cafe for lunch. He ditched his bike on the sidewalk, not bothering with a lock or a kickstand. He ordered a hamburger and fries and chocolate milk from his mom.

"Going fishing?" she asked.

"Yeh."

"Where?"

"Down by the lumber yard."

We asked her to ask him how the game went.

"How'd the game go?"

"We won. I got three home runs."

"Hey, good."

He changed into his fishing outfit — Lee jeans, one knee worn through; Nike shoes, "cheap ones," and a shirt with no brand name visible.

We wandered down a path to find the stream. The wild grasses were four feet tall, almost as tall as Jamie. A bunch of high-school-age boys was swimming. (A twist of the Norman Rockwell scene: They wore swimming trunks.) Jamie said he fishes for trout, chubs and suckers. "That's all that's ever been caught here that I heard of." He put half a fake worm on his line ("These fish down here are so pitiful") and bit off the line. He put himself in a variety of positions — lying down, crouching, leaning against a tree, cross-legged — and didn't stay in any one for more than 15 seconds. He spent more time looking for a Y-shaped stick to hold his pole than he did using it.

Part of his restlessness was because of bugs. Rollingstone isn't part of the seven-county Metropolitan Mosquito Control District, nor a gnat control district either.

As he deftly cast, Jamie pointed out the beaver dam upstream. "Does your dad teach you about nature?" we wondered. "Nah, he teached me more about motorcycles. A lot of our friends have motorcycles, too."

A bird with an insistent song provided the only accompaniment to the rushing water. Its call was like this: "Tweet, tweet, tweet, *TWEET, tweet, tweet, tweet.*" Jamie didn't know what kind it was. "I don't pay much attention to birds."

We quizzed him about his future. He wants to be a stock-car driver, like his dad. "See, when I'm 15, my dad's going to make me a car." He wants to work someday at the Winona river terminal, like his dad. He remembered fondly the summers "when I was younger" when his dad would bring home 50 turtles and he'd keep them in pails. Tadpoles, too. He said he doesn't like big towns. Rochester would be the biggest place he'd ever live, and that's kinda big.

He said he was an average student, and pulled out a report card later to prove it. He got two A's (language and health), three B's (reading, spelling and social studies) and two C's (math and science). He was commended by his teacher for his social habits, practicing self-control, observing school rules and working well with others, but he needed improvement in listening and completing assignments.

Anyway, fishing was poor this day. "Usually you just put your pole in here and you've got something," he said. The most action he got was hook-ing a snag. He said his all-time personal best was a 5-pound carp from the river.

Once he caught a record 32 crayfish in a day. He dictated a recipe:

Jamie Schell's Crayfish

First catch 'em. You catch 'em around rocks in the middle of the summer. You can catch 'em in daytime or at night with flashlights. They swim backwards. Put a net with small holes (holes no bigger than a centimeter) in back of 'em. Poke 'em in the face with a stick. They swim backwards super fast into the net.

Get water so it's like boiling. Add a bunch of salt. Take the crayfish, like 10 at a time, and get 'em in there. They turn pretty much, you know, pure red. Grab the upper part of 'em and tear off the tail and then there are little parts on the tail you pull. The meat is under the tail. Melt some butter. You dip 'em in butter and then you eat 'em. Ever had lobster? They're just miniature lobster. I've never had lobster but I know from crayfish what they taste like.

After the fishing nonexcitement, Jamie's day slowed down even more. He stopped by the city park, which has a nice assortment of playground equipment but no pool. The preschoolers don't let that stop them from getting thoroughly soaked. They splash in water from the drinking fountain.

Jamie stopped by Jeff Wood's house (Jeff still had company) and played with his cousin in the back of Schell's Cafe. He rode around town on his bike. He named the owners of cars parked on the main street. He investigated cars unfamiliar to him. He watched bug bites swell up.

He wasn't bored. Said he doesn't get bored.

His mom, Sheri Schell, said she has always been glad she was raised in Rollingstone and is bringing up her family here. Well, she said, there was one time in her life she yearned for a bigger place; that was in high school. She went to the Catholic high school in Rollingstone (defunct after 1967) and it had no "extras," such as art or home economics.

But now the Rollingstone school goes only through sixth grade, and "I even hate to see them going to Winona for junior high. Down there are 200 or 300 kids. You call, and they never heard of your kid. We're not used to that out here.

"I like it where I'm living. I like it because I know everybody. Everybody's friendly to you. I don't know it any other way, and I don't want to. We've got lots of family here, and that's good."

The only improvement she'd consider is having a Rollingstone YMCA, not that there's a chance of that. She's always running the kids to the Y and exercising there herself. But in a few weeks, the Rollingstone Park-Rec Board is opening its summer program, with everything from tennis to a trip to the Minnesota Zoo.

After a supper at home of hot dogs and French fries, Jamie had some good farm country fun: chopping heads off chickens. He went with a friend to Dave Pollema's farm and helped catch 40 chickens and used an ax on them. He came home bloody and happy, his mom said. He also played in the creek and jumped on a trampoline. He was asleep by midnight.

—P.M.

Kaplan Bros. Dept. Store
The Legacy of Joseph and Jacob

Minneapolis, Minnesota
1981

Joseph and Jacob Kaplan. Might smiles have crossed their faces as the two teen-agers trudged halfway across Europe from Russian Poland to board a ship for a reunion with their father in America?

Might they have given each other a brotherly slap on the back, perhaps jostled each other a bit along a muddy road, had they known that the store they were to start from scratch in Minneapolis would be a Twin Cities institution 60 years later? Not to mention having something of a celebration on Sept. 28, 1981?

YOU HAD TO wonder about that as the morning sun beat down on the corner of E. Franklin Av. and 15th Av. S., and as Joseph's and Jacob's oldest customers gathered for a group picture in front of Kaplan Brothers Department Store. Joseph died in 1955 and Jacob in 1974, so we'll never know the answers. One thing's certain. The spirit of their dry-goods store lives on in the 17 old-timers who still shop there. And in the younger customers who skirt the group to make purchases on this dawn of the Jewish New Year.

The store's annual calendar needed an old look, decided Joseph's son, Steve Kaplan, so he invited folks who had been shopping at the store for at least 50 years to come to take seats on the long bench in Kaplans' shoe department for a bit of reminiscing, then a walk outside for some old-fashioned picture-taking.

People like Walter Frober, 87, who has lived in the neighborhood since 1906, 20 years before the Kaplans opened their store to customers who had come from all over the world to work in the shops, the mills, the fields and the forests of Minnesota. Frober retired from his job as a die grinder in 1963, after buying work clothes at Kaplans' for almost 40 years. Today he keeps himself busy as a senior volunteer at Mt. Sinai Hospital. "And," he says, stroking his goatee, "I plan on buying some clothes before I leave today."

Or like Andrew Handzus, 77, who used to be Frober's neighbor when he worked 48 years for the Minneapolis and St. Louis Railroad. Or like Olaf M. Bornstad, 80. "I came from Oslo, Norway, in 1926, about the same time Kaplan came from Russia. Praise the Lord!" Olaf can sling the Norwegian around — and also the Polish to Ben Ziemkowski, 86, who used to own a restaurant across Franklin. Ben's wife, Eleanor, is there, too. Her father, K.O. Aasgaard, was the cop on the block for years. "They always called him King Oscar. I don't know why," says Eleanor.

Or Len Palmer, who was a troubleshooter for the telephone company; or John Beihoffer, an interior decorator who bought his paint pants at Kaplans'; or Donna and Dorrence Weasler, who say the store never seems to change; or George and Marguerite Hagen, who still hold hands like young lovers; or Raymond Swanson, who drove truck and shopped at Kaplans' since 1926, the year it opened; or Elmer and Leona Waigand, whose grandson, Ron, also a Kaplans' customer, drove them in from Richfield for the occasion.

Or John Wicklund, who started shopping in Kaplans' soon after his marriage when he and his wife settled into an apartment at 18th and Portland. Three rooms, $5 per week.

Or Frank and Betty Justen, retired farmers from Osseo, who clothed their 10 children at Kaplans'. "Justen," says Betty. "*Just ten.* Get it?" But enough of the jokes. It's time to leave the shoe department bench for the bright sunshine of autumn.

Joseph and Jacob Kaplan. What might they have thought of such a frivolous get-together, subsisting on chicken fat, water and bread to keep a kosher diet as they huddled in steerage on their way from Liverpool to the New World?

"Now if you could just crowd together a bit more," says photographer Larry Marcus from behind his tripod. "If anyone is cold, we can get you a jacket," says Steve Kaplan.

"How about a bottle of whiskey to take off the chill?" asks an elderly wag.

"That just makes you *think* you're warm," offers another.

They sit or stand quietly as Marcus clicks away, some no doubt thinking of the past and of four-buckle overshoes and the caps with ear flappers and the good smell of wool and leather — or perhaps the Great Depression wolf at their door. Drivers on Franklin slow up to observe the proceedings, to wonder what's going on in front of the store with the paper-covered windows and fading stucco.

Across the street, a foursome of neighborhood sports stops, looks, then turns at the open door of Addison's tavern for a mid-morning eye-opener.

Finally, Marcus has finished and some of his subjects head back for the suburbs to which they had fled, while others stay on to gab a bit. Steve Kaplan tells all that they'll each get two calendars and two photos. "And if you want more, you just call me. I have all your addresses and I'll send them right out to you."

Leona Waigand pats Kaplan's arm, then says to no one in particular, "They've been nice to be dealing with since *1928*," and then she's whisked off by grandson Ron for the trip back to Richfield.

George Hagen to John Wicklund: *"Er du Norske?* [Are you Norwegian?]"

Wicklund: "No, I'm *Svenske* [Swedish]."

Hagen: "Uff Da."

"Once I was Norske," says Wicklund. "I was at a rally for Floyd B. Olson. I went into the toilet and there were a dozen big Norskes in there, all drunk. They grabbed me and said, 'Are you Norske or Svenske?' 'Norske,' I said. Sometimes it's convenient to be Norske."

Another Norske, Raymond Swanson, allows as how he gets a 20-percent discount at a downtown department store because he used to drive truck for them. "But I still shop here at Kaplans'. The quality is real good and it's still cheaper than with my discount downtown."

Then Carl Stay, still another Norske, arrives late for the picture-taking, receives condolences from Steve Kaplan. "Yah, 35-W was backed up all the way to Savage. I came damn near hitting someone who wanted to sneak into my lane. I suppose she was late for work and said to hell with everything. I didn't want my picture anyway. I'm too damned homely. I'm no chicken any more, you know." Carl is 82 years old.

"Yah, I already had my picture taken here, anyway. My wedding picture! Upstairs from here. My cousin Victor Erickson had a photo studio right upstairs, and my first wife and I had our picture taken. Over 50 years ago. I've always bought my shoes here because Kaplans' shoes have a last that's perfect for my foot. I used to pay $9.95. But now they're almost $25."

Joseph and Jacob Kaplan. What might they have thought of shoes that sold for $25 when they arrived in Chicago to find their father, Shepsel Kaplan, crippled and a new stepmother who wouldn't let the young boys stay in her house?

"When they were shut out, my father, Joe, and Uncle Jack moved on to Minneapolis in 1922 and started the store in 1926," explains present manager Steve Kaplan, who says, "We don't use titles like manager around here. When I was a kid, they were still working six days a week and alternate Sundays. They even shared a car. When Jack worked, my dad would take us in the car for a Sunday outing. It was a no-frills operation then and it still is."

No frills and lots of clothes and shoes, piled to the ceiling and stacked in the aisles. Its narrow board floors have been spliced whenever the Kaplan brothers decided to move a display table or to expand into the next building. Kaplans' offers mink-oil ointments to "protect your investment in leather," bandannas, both blue and yellow (3/$1.88), railroad caps, caps with flaps, caps without, caps for truly discriminating Ivy Leaguers.

Hand-lettered signs admonish customers to think about the store's prudent marketing policies before they go someplace else to shop:

NO FANCY FIXTURES
NO HIGH RENTS
NO CHARGE ACC'TS
NO DELIVERIES
SAVES YOU MONEY!

Iceman's togs cometh in sizes to 50, the billowy wool trousers your grandpa used to slip on over long johns ($21.99). Or felt shoes, the kind he slipped on over wool socks before he tugged on his four-buckle overshoes before he took off with his thirty-aught-six looking for a moose. Or four-buckle overshoes. Or bib overalls or flannel shirts or steel-toed shoes or clogs or joggers or thermal underwear or cowboy boots or painter's pants or NFL T-shirts.

Or gloves. Kaplans' sign outside proclaims it is the "World's Largest Seller of Work Gloves." To be more specific, furry yellow cotton gloves, furry yellow cotton mitts, brown cotton gloves, long-cuff canvas gloves, short-cuff soft tan leather gloves ($52 per dozen), blue jersey gloves, bilious green gloves, with good news printed across their furry knuckles:

BETTER AND CHEAPER AT KAPLAN BROS.
15TH & FRANKLIN
TRY US — GUARANTEED

Buckskin mitts, unlined pigskin gloves, unlined buckskin gloves, cowhide gloves, yellow plastic gloves, yellow plastic mitts, women's unlined leather gloves, lined pigskin gloves, calf-suede gloves, deerskin gloves, gloves that will hold out sandburrs, gloves that won't, some gloves with long gauntlets, some with medium, some with short.

And Kaplans' throws down its gauntlet to any merchandiser who tries to undersell them. Upstairs in the office where Victor Erickson took Carl Stay's wedding pictures, Julius Ostrow explains how Kaplans' operates. "Joe Kaplan was quite a man and not just because he was my brother-in-law. He had a theory. He always said I am not a store owner. He said my customers are hiring me to be their buyer. He set a low markup and that was it. Even during the war [World War II], when he could have made an extra buck, he never wavered. He was an unusual man.

"And he laid a foundation of service. Refunds and exchanges in *two minutes*. [The sign still hangs downstairs.] I supervised the refunds and I always told customers we're as happy to give money back as to take it in the first place. That makes customers feel comfortable. Here you never have to look at how a seam is sewed. You never have to look to see that something was right. Because you know you'll get your money back with no argument. I myself am now waiting on third-generations. Grandparents first, then parents, now children. It's very, very gratifying."

Ostrow, 73, graduated in chemical engineering from the University of Minnesota in 1932, but "couldn't find a job for love or money. So I started here as a stockboy and stuck." Lots of people stay on at Kaplans' — and long after typical retirement age. Clerk Herman Prager, 76, owned his own store in Columbia Heights before signing on at Kaplans' 14 years ago. "I gotta keep moving and the people here are very nice to work for so I stay on."

Steve Kaplan explains that customers get lots of attention because the clerks work on commission. "Some people say they're too enthusiastic. I think it's better than at the discount stores where you have a hard time finding anyone to help you."

Nettie Siegel has worked at the store since 1979, after managing clothing stores and nursing a sick husband for many years. "The management here is just fantastic," she says. "They're concerned about you as a person. If you have family matters to attend to, they understand."

Pastor Maynard Nelson of Calvary Lutheran Church of Golden Valley agrees. Nelson resigned as a Kaplans' clerk in 1957 after graduating from Augsburg Theological Seminary, but he hasn't forgotten his former employers.

"Funny," he tells a reporter over the phone, "that you should call. Just last Sunday, I told my congregation that when I was a seminary student my father died in Oregon. I informed Julius that I'd have to take a week off. I had no money and little idea of how I'd get home. The day before I left, one of the clerks gave me an envelope. The staff had taken up a collection for me and there was enough money for airfare.

"Kaplans' really cares for the people who work there. At Christmas there was always a gift. [There still is.] Kaplans' never told us what our commission was, but when we were paid, they always gave us more than we thought we'd get. When I was broke, someone would always reach in the till and give me money and say, 'Pay us back when you can.' I go back to see them because it's the only thing in Minneapolis that hasn't changed since I was a student and because they truly put me through seminary. And when it comes to being a pastor, to knowing human nature and how to get along with people, working at Kaplans' was the best course I had at seminary."

Kaplans' has every intention of continuing the tradition of NO FANCY FIXTURES . . . SAVES YOU MONEY! To that end, Steve's nephew, Ira Kaplan, 22, Jerry Kajander, 33, and Doug Nelsen, 33, are studying at the feet of master buyer Max Goldman, 70. He came to work at Kaplans' in 1955, and says prices have quintupled. "But also the quality isn't what it used to be, so the buyer gets it from both sides. I don't think any store in the country has a markup as small as ours." Max has been in the clothing business for 56 years and he has a meticulously kept buyer's book that dates from 1931.

Max has lots of time to be meticulous, according to Steve Kaplan, because he never takes a vacation.

"Whaddya mean?" asks Max. "I took a vacation in 1947. Isn't that enough?"

Joseph and Jacob Kaplan. What might they have thought, alternating Sundays at work and play, what might they have thought if they knew the tradition of hard work lives on in the establishment they started from scratch back in 1926?

—D.W.

Robert S. Graff

Here Comes the Judge

Aitkin, Minnesota
1984

S URE, WE'D be welcome in his courtroom, His Honor told us on the telephone. He promised drama, heartbreak, gentle humor, the real stuff of life, all squeezed into a few hours of misdemeanor court. "Know where the courthouse is?" he asked. No, but we'd find it. "Easy to find," he said. "It's the only one in the county." Yeh, we thought so. "Find the only stoplight in the county, take a left and there it is."

Aitkin County Judge Robert S. Graff wasn't so frisky a few days later. At 8:30 Monday morning, he looked as if he were about to film a Contac commercial. He explained that it's tough to be dignified when your nose is dripping and your throat aches. "Geez, I hate this voice," he croaked. "Usually I have such a sweet voice."

Couldn't he go home sick? No way, he said. He had 13 cases to hear that morning. The defendants, the lawyers, the game warden were all ready to go. A judge can't skip court and expect to ever catch up, he said. Graff didn't get specific, but when we checked the courtroom log we saw what he meant.

Three Twin Cities people were up on fishing violations that they had ignored since summer. A 23-year-old Aitkin man was to answer to a charge of "unreasonable acceleration." A man from nearby McGregor, Minn., was ready to explain just why he was operating an automobile on a snowmobile trail the week before.

And the case that brought snickers: An Aitkin second-grade teacher was to spend her lunch hour entering her plea to a speeding charge. What made it worse for her is her name. Mrs. Ferrari, her name is Mrs. *Ferrari!* Joyce Ferrari was charged with driving too fast at the edge of Aitkin one January evening. The city policeman's radar clocked her car at 43 m.p.h. in a 30 zone. No, not in a Ferrari. A Volkswagen.

Time for action, even though many of the defendants hadn't shown up. The ones who were there, all of whom wore blue jeans, were given statements of their rights and told they could go into the courtroom, a beautiful

1929 room with a stained glass skylight and tons of oak. The judge donned his robe and lined his mouth with cough drops. "Hear ye, hear ye," said the bailiff. The judge gave a little speech that amounted to the fact he was feeling lousy and he would give his clerk the task of reciting the charges.

The first case was the most serious. Richard Paul Schuelke of Aitkin was charged with driving while intoxicated. His lawyer, Jim Stuart, told the court that his client hadn't arrived. "I've known Mr. Schuelke the last five, six, seven years," the lawyer said, "and from time to time he's a little late." The judge said he would wait a while but added that Schuelke's girlfriend had called and said Schuelke wouldn't be showing up in court.

They went ahead with the next case. Albert Charles Hoff, a chiropractor in the St. Paul suburb of Rosemount, didn't appear either. He was charged with speeding, 69 m.p.h. in a 55 zone. He had maintained in a letter to the judge that someone had stolen his driver's license and must have presented it when stopped in Aitkin County. The judge noted that Hoff's record showed he had six prior traffic convictions, five for speeding, and therefore he would suspend Hoff's driver's license until a $33 fine was paid.

The next defendant — another no-show — was Mark Allen Mahoney of Cannon Falls, charged with driving after suspension of his license. The judge issued a bench warrant and set bond at $750.

Finally, the judge got to see a defendant. Randall Claude Turner of Aitkin was there. He was charged with driving without insurance, and the judge told him to show up the next Monday morning with a letter from his agent saying he was covered.

Then there was Bruce Wayne Thramer of Aitkin, who had been ice fishing and bought gas in Crosby and maybe there was some dirt in the gas, he said, because the car was running rough. He stomped on the accelerator for a block or so and, lo and behold, there was Aitkin Police Officer Randy Newgren to write up a ticket saying Thramer had bursts of speed up to 45 or 50 m.p.h. Thramer told the judge it wasn't *that* fast, but he did plead guilty. The judge fined him $35 and told him that if he gets another ticket, the fine will be at least double that, so watch out.

Next, the infamous case of Barbara Jo Anderson of St. Paul, charged with fishing without a license. Here's how it happened:

Dennis Lang, a 35-year-old conservation officer with the Department of Natural Resources (DNR), was spying on people who were fishing last July 24. He said he watched a family fishing from a pontoon boat for 10 minutes. He was about 250 yards away and, with the help of a 60-power spotting scope, could see their fishing lines and what they were using for bait. He said he spotted some violators and paid them a visit, ticket book in hand. He recorded: "Subject claimed not to be fishing until I explained what I had observed and I picked out the short rod and the Zebco 66 spinning rod she used. Husband, who had a license, stated she was holding fish rod for their 2-year-old child who appeared to have absolutely no interest in fishing. Husband gave me a hard time until I threatened to give him a ticket for a separate offense."

Lang said the defendant's husband had a $7.25 fishing license and could have bought a husband-wife license for only $11.25. He didn't, so Lang gave her a $44 ticket. She didn't pay. She ignored letters of reprimand. The judge issued a warrant in December. Whenever Lang gets enough warrants to make a trip worthwhile, he heads for the Cities. He didn't have enough, so he called Barbara Jo Anderson and told her a warrant was out on her. She said she would take care of things.

Is Lang the most hated man in town, as some people say? We took him aside to ask. He said no: "You might think that most of the people are mad at me, but 60 percent of the locals wave at me." How about the people from the Twin Cities, who own much of the lake property up here? "The city people say to me, 'You're just after the city guys,' but that's not true. I very often say to them that I'm glad to see them up here. That's true; I am. The local economy picks up something from them."

Then the judge heard Felix Joseph Sazenski, 66, the only defendant all day eager to tell his story. He had told almost everybody in the courthouse that morning about how he got into trouble with the law: He was looking for a friend's house, realized he was lost, tried to turn his car around and got it stuck on what turned out to be a snowmobile trail.

The judge wasn't ready to hear that. He asked Sazenski if he understood his rights. Sure, said Sazenski, and proceeded to begin his story. No, wait, said the judge. Do you understand you have the right to an attorney? Sazenski said, "Yeh, but . . . " Wait, said the judge. You have the right to a trial by jury, the right to subpoena witnesses on your own behalf, the right to remain silent.

The right to remain silent was the last thing Felix Sazenski wanted. He pleaded not guilty, asked for a court-appointed attorney and went off to fill out financial forms. The judge refused to have the county pay for his lawyer but did ask attorney Jim Stuart to stop by and talk things over with Sazenski in the hallway.

They talked it over, and then Sazenski got his chance to tell the judge what happened. He made diagrams on the blackboard of how he got on the snowmobile trail and explained whom he called to help him get the car out of the snow and told how there was some speculation that the car would be there until spring. Actually, it was there only three days (three days too long, said the judge) and was eventually removed by the DNR because it was a danger to snowmobilers.

Finally Sazenski pleaded guilty, paid a $35 fine and deposited $40 to repay the DNR for the towing. He promised to stay off snowmobile trails unless he's in a snowmobile.

"Pardon my English," Sazenski said to the clerk. "Can I get the hell out of here?" He could.

The judge told the lawyer to charge the court for the consultation, but Stuart said writing the bill would take more time than it was worth. "I just want to get back to my office," he said.

Judge Graff heard a few more cases involving snowmobiles and fishing laws. Two St. Paul people — Karen Olmstead, fishing without a license, and Lawrence Shafer, angling for fish with more than one line — didn't show up and each forfeited $250 bond. Bailiff Michael Zilverberg said of them, "Should have bought lobster. Would have been cheaper." And easier. Both defendants had been taken into custody in the Cities until they posted bond.

The judge got a break to call his doctor and get a prescription before Joseph Allen Rian appeared to plead guilty to "transporting an uncased firearm in a M.V." (That's motor vehicle.)

Rian was fined $100 and sentenced to 30 days in jail, stayed on the condition that he not hunt, fish or trap for one year or associate with people when they hunt, fish or trap. He said he didn't have money to pay the fine, but Jan. 31 would be his payday. The judge said he could pay then. Rian had to hand over his small-game and fishing licenses and then he could go.

Finally, the piece de resistance, the case of the Allegedly Wayward Second-Grade Teacher. Joyce Ferrari told the judge that she was not guilty of speeding and that she would represent herself in court. She would have to take a half-day personal leave to fight the charge, she said. "Will you have your second-graders for character witnesses?" the judge asked, trying to suppress a grin. Ferrari did not find his remark amusing.

The judge set trial for 1:30 p.m. Friday, Feb. 10.

Another thing Ferrari did not find amusing was that a big-city reporter asked her about the case. She replied, with dignity, that she would prefer the matter not get into the newspaper. It's public record, we responded. She looked pained. She said she would offer no comment.

We told her we would be at the Rippleside Elementary School the next day. Would she talk to us about second grade? Of course, she said, in a very agreeable tone.

It turned out that we spent the next day in the third-grade classroom, not her second grade, but we did see Ferrari now and again, herding children in the hallways. We checked her out with some third-graders who knew her. They like her. They didn't use words like "spotless reputation" or "unimpeachable, law-abiding citizen," but Lachele Beachem, who's 8 and had Ferrari as a teacher last year, said she was "strict but nice."

How strict? Lechele answered, "She kind of acts like a sergeant. She always says, 'I have good ears and I want to hear the lights humming' and if the kids aren't quiet, she cancels our privileges."

We didn't tell Lachele Beachem that Mrs. Ferrari was in trouble with the law. Let's keep that a secret.

~

Aftermath: Richard Schuelke, the Aitkin man charged with driving while intoxicated, never appeared in court. The judge entered into the record that Schuelke was believed to have skipped the state at 4 a.m. of the day he was to have been in court. The judge issued a warrant for his arrest and set bail at $3,000.

Barbara Jo Anderson of St. Paul, charged with fishing without a license, got to court that Monday afternoon instead of Monday morning. She pleaded guilty and was fined $130. The warrant for her arrest was canceled. Called at their home later, she and her husband, Roger, said the Aitkin brand of justice "stinks." They didn't want the hassle of pleading not guilty, driving up to Aitkin another day, losing more time at work, hiring a lawyer and arranging for their witnesses to testify that indeed she was just helping their daughter with her fishing line. It was easier to plead guilty and write a check.

Judge Robert S. Graff successfully recovered from his cold. He told us on the telephone a week later, "This is my normal voice. Melodious."

—P.M.

Judge Graff found Mrs. Ferrari not guilty because speed-limit signs were improperly posted. Three months later the judge was stopped by a state trooper for driving 67 m.p.h. in a 55 zone. He pleaded guilty and mailed in his check.

The Pitzen Family
Romancing the Rodeo

Effie, Minnesota
1981

A VIEW FROM THE GRANDSTAND — Gov. Al Quie, Minnesota's preeminent political equestrian, cantered into the rodeo arena on a white horse. Well, actually it was a dapple-gray horse.

Quie was making an appearance at the 26th annual North Star Stampede, just north of Effie. On his first turn around the arena, few in the weathered grandstand recognized the fellow carrying the state flag in the Grand Entry. So on the second pass, announcer Howard Pitzen told the crowd that the governor was there, eliciting murmurs about his fine horsepersonship. As riders broke into a serpentine, the governor lost his hat. But not to worry. The North Star Stampede is a cool and laid-back occasion, just like everything in and around Effie, a long trip from the hot, dusty, hyped-up southwestern rodeos you see on TV.

Birch, poplar and lush grass surrounded the rodeo grounds and a nippy breeze sent folks scurrying for jackets on the first day of this two-day event that Howard Pitzen began back in the '50s. Up in the crow's nest, Pitzen told the crowd they were attending the largest open rodeo in the state.

Grand Entry over, the crowd settled down to watch the first bucking bronco bolt out of its chute, then another, and another. Howard Pitzen kept a constant patter as well as announcing entrants from Effie and from Phoenix, Ariz., who had come to pound their butts for a piece of the almost $3,000 purse. And pound them they did, on angry bulls, on maverick broncos, some with saddles, some without. The arena was muddy from a recent heavy rain, and calf-roping didn't work too well, nor did women's barrel racing. Event followed event and when things didn't go so well, spectators in the grandstand who never sat on a tame nag griped about Minnesota cowboys. But Howard Pitzen hung in there, never failing to ask the crowd to "give that cowboy a hand."

If you've never been on a bronco, rodeos can become tedious from time to time up in the grandstand, as cowboy after cowboy comes out and does his thing, sometimes well, sometimes badly. It's different from watching

edited versions of rodeos on TV, where you see only the spectacular performances and don't have to smell the horse manure or listen to the bad jokes.
Clowns Hayseed Hotzler and Buckwheat Barthell had a helluva time mis-
taking dried cowpies for billfolds, rabbit urine for beer, as seasoned rodeo-
goers laughed and tenderfeet groaned.

Howard Pitzen's 20-year-old son, Fred, fixed the tedium problem in the
second hour. Fred scored a substantial 52 points riding a bull called Nip and
Sip. As he hopped off, his hand caught in the rope, the bull knocked him
down and pounded him in the groin with enormous horns. Hayseed
Hotzler distracted the bull long enough for Fred to crawl out of the arena.
An understated tension that Hemingway would have loved spread over the
audience.

"Let's give that cowboy a big hand," said Fred's father, who quickly
proceeded to joke with Hayseed.

Finally, there was a spare Pitzen bull just raring to go. "Rather than let
him go to waste, Larry Gilbertson of Effie has the itch to ride him in exhibi-
tion," intoned Howard Pitzen. Problem was, Larry had only ridden once
before, but he did a creditable job until the extra threw him for a loop, and
the first half of the weekend rodeo was over.

As folks filed out, Hayseed wondered how Fred Pitzen was doing. Hayseed had been gored in the chest in Blackduck just a few weeks before and
had lived to clown again. (Turned out that Pitzen's groin had not been
punctured, only bruised, that he refused to stay overnight in the Bigfork
hospital, that he competed the following day in the rodeo at Carlton.)

Brett Bushelle, Gonvick, Minn., sipped a cool one at the beer tent and
was philosophical about not scoring well. "They always have really fresh
cattle at Effie. Pitzen takes 'em right out of the pasture and they run like
hell. You've got to give Howard credit. He gets the biggest crowds in the
state outside of the Twin Cities. And it's a beautiful setting. It's more than a
rodeo here at Effie. It's an *event*."

A view from the crow's nest — Sunday dawns bright, as tailgaters
congregate by charcoal broilers waiting for the rodeo's second installment to
begin. The arena is drier today, the governor hasn't stuck around for another grand entry, and Howard Pitzen is hard at it by 1 p.m., spinning records
before the starting time.

"I used to be a disc jockey. Spent about two months at it. Then my
daddy told me, 'Get off that disc, boy, and get on a plow.'"

Would Pitzen mind if a visitor from the press sat up in the crow's nest
with him and assistants Cheri Harrington and Rhea Hotzler, Hayseed's
wife? "Your company carry liability insurance?" jokes Pitzen. "Sure, come
on up and make yourself at home."

The crow's nest swings and sways as Pitzen paces and worries over
attendance, lean and hungry-looking at 55, extemporaneously spinning out
his patter, which sounds different Up Here. And Down There, everything
looks different in the bull and bronco chutes immediately below. The animals stand still, tense, uncertain. Same goes for the cowboys, who lounge in

the rigging alley, rolling cigarettes, waiting for 2 o'clock and only God knows what.

"What time is it?" asks Pitzen, looking down at Cimarron Pitzen, 18, today's chute boss.

"I have 2:04," says Cheri.

"Me too," says Rhea.

Two people can't be wrong.

"I don't know about that," says Howard. "Look at all the people who get married." Rodeo humor.

The ceremonies begin, and Pitzen recites from memory "The Cowboy's Prayer," in honor of rodeoers fallen in the past year. He also offers a prayer for "the cowboy who was injured yesterday," not mentioning his son's name. Off-microphone, he points to the tin shed where he and his wife, Bonnie, lived in the '50s, before they bought their other ranch, explains that an open rodeo means that entrants needn't belong to any association, opines that the open rodeo is rodeo's backbone. Then bareback riding begins.

The bird's-eye view from the crow's nest sends prickles up the visitor's spine as Daryl Cole of Musselshell, Mont., is thrown from Firefly a few seconds out of the chute. He picks himself up and throws an aw-shucks clump of dirt at the chute gate and hobbles off.

Cheri's husband, Dan Harrington, takes a ride on Chicken Pox for a low score of 37 points. "Hmph!" comments Howard Pitzen off-mike. "She ain't bucking a-tall today." (Rodeo judges score the horse as well as the rider, and riders say they like Pitzen-stocked rodeos because his animals are usually lively.)

Down in the chute, the bronco Lone Star jumps around and kicks the slats out of the chute gate. No sense for rider Ronnie Root of Effie to mount now. As if by magic, Hayseed appears in front of the crow's nest to exchange crude pleasantries with Howard, eliciting laughter and applause from the stands. When Lone Star cools down, Hayseed disappears. So that's what rodeo clowning is all about!

Later, Ann's Special throws Scott Champoux of Effie and takes off. Troy Pitzen tried and tries and tries again to rope the bronc. "That's how he ropes calves on the ranch," says his father. Still later, a horse kicks the chute gate and gets his leg stuck. Howard supervises and gets everything straightened out.

Dan Harrington wrestles down a steer in 27.09 seconds and wife Cheri jumps up and down as the booth shakes, rattles and rolls. Terri Tellegan climbs up into the crow's nest with a movie camera to shoot her husband, Scott, who's having a terrible time with his steer. "Hustle! Hustle!" she says under her breath. Time runs out for Scott, and Terri disappears.

"The North Star Stampede has friends from all over the world," announces Howard. "Mr. and Mrs. George Howle couldn't resist and drove 2,500 miles from British Columbia to be with us today." Off-mike, he tells a rider, "Spur the hell out of that one today or all he's gonna do for you is run." And to the crowd, "Rodeo is probably the only sport where participants help each other, even as they compete for prize money."

He isn't kidding. Dave Hall of Bemidji is dragged bleeding from his bull. One cowboy props Hall's head on a saddle in the rigging alley, while another administers an ice pack and still another offers solace. First-timers get all kinds of advice from the experts once they convince chute boss Cimarron Pitzen to let them ride an extra bronc or bull. So does an urban cowboy in huge sunglasses who looks as though he never rode anything but a merry-go-round.

Four o'clock, and it's all over for another year. Fellows working the chutes are filthy with dust, the entrants' shirts are tattered and torn, their bodies bruised and broken. But talk centers on future rodeos. Howard Pitzen shuts off his mike and invites his visitor to breakfast on the morrow. Wheat cakes at his Little Montana Ranch south of Effie.

A view from the breakfast table — With its steer skulls hanging on buildings that shine silver-gray in the Monday morning sunlight, its weathered wooden corrals snaking off into infinity, its crossbred cattle grazing in the stump pastures to the southeast, Pitzen's Little Montana Ranch is almost too good to be true. Only trucks and trailers from the stock-contracting operation and the white frame house pull the visitor back from dreams of range wars, winning the West and incidents at Oxbow or down the arroyo a piece.

Howard Pitzen flips wheatcakes on the griddle as sausage sizzles in a spider, and wife Bonnie sets the big dining room table. Delvin, Fred, Troy and Cimarron sit on the living room sofa, slouch hats on, waiting for breakfast, let down after the weekend's excitement. The boys aren't a talkative lot, and three of them look stiff after two days of being bucked and dragged and gored all over the place. Delvin is 21, the oldest. He doesn't compete these days, having lost fingers and toes in a nightmare accident two years ago when a haystack tipped over in a far-flung pasture and trapped him for 26 hours in 30-below weather. Now he's following in his father's footsteps as a rodeo announcer, worrying about his grammar, but not what he has to say from the crow's nest.

Well-thumbed books fill the room's north wall, books about the Old West, books about American history, books about Communist conspiracies, Aleksandr Solzhenitsyn and Cardinal Mindszenty. The boys don't read much, but Howard and Bonnie read constantly in Western history, political analysis. Howard writes, too. And Bonnie, a schoolteacher, corrects his spelling. "Every time we do a story," says Bonnie, "I pray to Jude, patron saint of the impossible." In a 1973 article for "Western Horseman," Howard wrote: "When a man has to relocate, he must be like the coyote and learn to adapt or perish." That's pretty much the Pitzen story.

Howard relocated from Montana, where he always wanted to be a rancher, but couldn't afford it. He worked near Effie in logging camps after World War II and discovered that some land could be had for as little as $5 per acre. He bought the property where the rodeo is located and in 1953 picked up the 240-acre Little Montana Ranch for $10,000. In 1958 he married Bonnie Olney of the Yakima Valley in Washington, where her French-English-Flathead Indian and Yakima Indian family were ranchers. "But our boys don't take advantage of BIA [Bureau of Indian Affairs] programs," Bonnie says. "And that's just as well." Better than just as well, according to Howard, because "the dole has ruined more people than it's helped."

The boys gather around the table, Howard makes the sign of the cross, and everybody digs into a mountainous heap of wheatcakes, eggs and sausage.

Between bites of thin pancakes, Howard reminisced. Like the coyote, the Montanan temporarily adapted to the culture of his new surroundings. He already had the rodeo bug when he moved to the north country but figured giving up the sport was a concession he'd have to make if he wanted a ranch. "Then one day a bunch of friends were fooling around on Sunday bucking out a few horses on my place. People stopped to watch. So I figured maybe we could make a rodeo go." The next year, 1956, he and friends cleared out brush, built a corral.

"We worked from 5 in the morning 'til 11 at night. Took twice as long as it should have, because everyone stopped to gawk and ask questions. They used to say that the most exciting thing that happened in Effie was when a pulpwood truck tipped over, so people were curious about what was going on. I'm sure they thought I was stark raving mad."

Nevertheless, when the first North Star Stampede opened, a thousand people showed up and paid $1.50 to see entrants ride broncos and rope calves for $300 in prize money. And that's the way it has gone ever since. Howard was announcer from the start and eventually "slipped and slid" into the business of stock contracting for other rodeos as well. "I rode bulls and horses long enough to know that I was no rider. It takes great reflexes to be good. Some of my kids have it, some don't."

(Fred Pitzen apparently has those reflexes because he won more than $500 in the weekend event, as well as riding a bronc and a bull in the Carlton rodeo on Sunday. Cimarron came in fourth in steer wrestling, Troy fourth in bull riding at Effie.)

Life with the North Star Stampede hasn't been all syrup and sausage, however. In 1959, the rains came and the newlyweds lost $1,500. "We owed money all over," recalls Howard. "But the businessmen stuck with us." Later, when the Pitzens were buying rodeo stock, they had trouble making their $60-per-month ranch payments. "If it hadn't been for the deer roaming around here, we'd have gone hungry. But I walked into a bank in Northome one day and asked the banker for the cash to buy a string of 12 bulls. I must have hit him just right. He gave me the money on the spot. Heh, I don't think I would have done the same. Maybe the Moslems are right. Maybe everything is planned for you ahead of time."

The plan is that no one gets rich in the rodeo business, according to Howard. His contract operation charges about $4,000 to do a rodeo, of which there were nine that hired him this year. The 26th annual stampede drew about 3,000 fans, who paid $3.75 each to see Pitzen's lively animals raise havoc with the cowboys. The ranch's cattle-for-market operation is relatively small so the family income is supplemented by Bonnie's salary as a teacher in Bigfork and also by logging — Pitzen used horses to snake logs out of the woods until recently. "Whenever beef prices go up," says Howard, "I'm tempted to sell out my rodeo stock, but I never get around to it. Then beef prices drop and I'm glad I didn't. I guess it evens out."

And so it goes in the world of north-country rodeoing. Howard stands in the driveway and looks out to the pasture, where his animals reveal their Scottish Highland ancestry, a strain resistant to Minnesota winters. Readjusting as survivor coyotes do still isn't easy for Howard in some areas. "Take politics. Even the Republicans in Minnesota are too liberal for me. I guess that shows you how far out in right field I am."

Bonnie comes out to give the visitor his "press kit." A grocery bag packed with a Northstar Stampede souvenir ashtray, a jar of beets, a jar of pickle relish and a jar of homemade mincemeat. "Don't forget to tell your readers that the stampede is *always* on the last full weekend of July."

And then the visitor galloped off, well, drove actually, down the narrow road that led to Hwy. 38, the dusty trail leading back to Effie.

—D.W.

Miss Agnes Reed
Purveyor of Patrician Elegance

Minneapolis, Minnesota
1984

To FIND Agnes Reed these days takes a bit of persistence. She no longer keeps regular hours. Her customers have to sign in with the security guards in the almost-empty lobby of the Curtis Hotel. She has had
a shop in downtown Minneapolis for 57 years, including nine years in the
Curtis, but the new kids don't know her.

"That old lady who sells antiques?" a guard asks. "No, she sells dresses." "Yeah, that one. There she is."

There she is, sitting with regal bearing on an antique chair in her 12- by
16-foot shop. She can't be bigger than a size 4 and is dressed entirely in
black, from tam to shoes. Her skin is porcelain beautiful and probably always has been. The deep red polish on her nails and a flush of rouge on her
cheeks are her only color.

On display around her are antiques (not for sale) and the women's
wool jersey suits she sells for about $150.

She designed the suit decades ago, and it has served her well. Never in
her life has she sold a ready-made garment, she says. Never will.

Miss Reed (to call her anything else would be a travesty) must move
from the Curtis, which will be torn down next spring and replaced with a
parking lot. She not only has to move her shop, she also has to move to a
new apartment because she lives in the Curtis. No longer is the Curtis
operating as a hotel, and permanent residents must leave by midnight
March 31. Miss Reed says she fully intends to reopen her shop in a new
location. Where? "I haven't the vaguest idea," she says. "I have had no time
to look. I have had to do important things — records and bank work and
income taxes, plus the dentist and everything else."

She is furious that the "new" owners of the Curtis have, as she puts it,
ceased operation. "I can tell you who wrecked the Curtis," she says.
"Down, down, down, that's where they took it. It was the saddest thing.
People who have lived here for 40 years, out the door. The biggest blow
was when they took away the coffee shop. Then the Cardinal Room for

Sunday brunch. Now the pay phones are gone. Imagine!"

To pin down Miss Reed on dates is impossible. Her age is a deep secret. "Age! All women do is guess, guess, guess!" She does volunteer to pull out her old scrapbooks from her 1890s chifforobe from Belgium. The scrapbooks give some clues to her vintage, including an opening announcement for "Miss Reed's Frockery" on Dec. 1, 1926. A newspaper advertisement tells of a move the next year:

> The widening of Tenth street gave us an opportunity to secure a new and better location — so here we are. Featuring as before Frocks, Smocks, Pajamas.

She says she was born in Minneapolis. Her mother was a dressmaker, her father a food importer. She was graduated from Central High School and attended the University of Minnesota for a year. She worked in a bank before she formally got into dressmaking, although she had been making and selling clothes already in high school.

For a while she worked for others. She started with Cartwright dresses, and Mrs. Cartwright told her she was an excellent salesperson. "She said to me, 'You can make people think black is white.' I don't know that that is a compliment."

Miss Reed opened her own shop at 65 S. 10th St. in 1927 and stayed there 40 years. "At first it was the days of the carriage trade, and then hard times came. That's when rent was nothing. Nothing! Before all these awful complications in business."

> Patrician Elegance is the keynote of the Agnes Reed collection of dresses for daytime and evening. All are executed in a Sag-No-More Jersey or Silk Angora Jersey. Many have exquisite touches of wool hand embroidery. Every one is an original model designed by Agnes Reed. ATLANTIC 4831. 65 S. 10th St.

Through the decades, her customers were wealthy middle-aged and older women. Most of her customers were regulars, or the daughters of regulars. Size 14 was the most popular size, navy blue the most popular color. She adapted her classic pattern to suits, dresses, formals, pajamas, golf clothing, smocks, "everything." About 50 percent of her business was from out of town — some were customers who saw Agnes Reed suits and dresses on other women, and some were stores in seven states that took clothing on consignment.

Her business, she says, "has been just fascinating, but slow. I have just plodded along in my own way. At first, I had a few salespeople, girls, but then I carried on alone. It has been beautiful to be on a small scale. Businesses lose their charm when they get big. I've had the chance to have customers as my friends."

She talks of "Mrs. Halsey Hall, of course she's gone now" and someone else, "a stunning, big woman, beautiful figure; where have all the big women gone?" and "Mrs. Guy Thomas, who wore that model all the time" and a woman "who's gone now but she was a millionaire."

The shop was robbed several times, and newspaper accounts are in Miss Reed's scrapbook. The biggest headline on the front page of The Minneapolis Star on May 6, 1936, was "ITALY TO ANNEX ETHIOPIA." Beneath that was "Burglars Display Taste." The article read, " 'They were very discriminating,' Miss Reed said, 'and picked the more valuable embroidered dresses, scattering the others on the floor.' "

Prices were different then, she says, pointing to an advertisement:

Collegiate Pajamas in pastelle pink, blue, or yellow, are the special at Agnes Reed's Frockery this week at $2.50. These clever little Oxford cuts are made of lightweight flanelet for pretty girls in cold dormitories.

In 1956 she married Lawrence DeSomery in Reno. "It sounds weird, I know. Neither one of us had been married before, but Reno makes it sound like we were both divorced." She describes him as a great sportsman and hunter who loved the north woods. It's difficult to imagine her hunting grouse, but she says she enjoyed being in the Superior National Forest with a shotgun. Her husband hunted for more than grouse and bagged 24 trophies — "moose, elk, caribou, all but a mountain goat. That was his disappointment."

They bought a "darling little cabin" on Lake Superior, near Grand Marais. She brings out photographs to prove its charm. She loves to tell the story of the first time she saw it from the road and told the real estate man, "I'll take it." He thought she should see the inside before she signed the papers. She saw and she signed. In the middle of that night, when she was too excited about her purchase to sleep, she realized it didn't have a bathroom. "But I didn't care. It had a little house back in the woods."

Her husband worked for the state conservation department. She continued with the dress shop. "This was a hobby. We had no social life, none. I know I missed out on a lot. I didn't have the time. For one thing, we didn't spend nearly the time at the cabin we should have. I regret that. But I enjoyed my work. It was never a large-scale business, never a Harold's. But the people I met. I didn't know there was such a world. The information they dropped!"

She rolls her eyes for emphasis.

Her husband died in 1971. She sold the cabin — "it was no place for a woman alone" — and kept on with business. It has been the "travel suit" — with A-line skirt, vest, scarf and jacket — that has kept her in business. Each is cut for a specific customer and is made of double-knit, 100-percent wool. It travels well, she says. She tells of a woman whose 1946 Reed suit is now her daughter's favorite clothing.

Miss Reed doesn't do the sewing. She has hired a series of homemakers to do the cutting, and she has nuns in a St. Paul convent do the finishing. The nuns have been with her "forever. Since 1945. They're wonderful people. I love them." Which order of nuns? "They wish the name not be known."

For more than 25 years, she says in answer to our question, she has worn only black. "I think people would faint if they saw me in anything else. I couldn't get organized any other way. If you handle clothes all the time, you're not interested in a lavish wardrobe. I wear things until I'm absolutely ashamed, until they fall off."

She says she is having trouble buying materials for her business. Fabric manufacturers don't want to sell her small quantities at reduced prices. Even buttons — the right kind of buttons — are hard to come by.

Modern fashions she can do without. "I'm discouraged because everything is the same. I was at Knollwood shopping center last night. Rack after rack, all the same. You know Knollwood? A girlfriend and I had dinner there, at Bishop's, and never have I seen such a display of food. They carry your tray, and they come with coffee every five minutes. I don't think I have had a better meal in Minneapolis, outside of my own home."

Under pressure, she says she has begun to look for a new home and shop. Symphony Place has told her she may run her business from her apartment if she rents there, but she worries that a modern condominium may not suit her. "It's sad," she says, "I was going to stay at the Curtis always. We're in a state of shock. We didn't expect this. I'll survive, but when they carted the palms out of the Palm Room, some people cried. They can't take it. They can't even come downstairs and see it."

—P.M.

Miss Reed did move to an apartment in Symphony Place and runs her business from there. The Minnesota Historical Society asked her for examples of her work to include in its museum collections. She donated four suits from the late 1940s and early 1950s.

House of Breakfast
Making Everything from Scratch

Minneapolis, Minnesota
1982

Y OU CAN'T JUST drive by this place year after year. You can't just ig-
nore forever the riot of giant polka dots that greet you every morning
on your way to work. So one morning you say to yourself what the
hell and you pull up to the curb at 3733 Chicago Av. You step gingerly into
the House of Breakfast and belly up to its 11-stool counter. And once you're
seated, you can't just sit there and stare at all the choices that face you.

You're not even hungry, but you order "Potato Pancakes" because you
love 'em, even if they're out of a box. Sharon Thewaitress disappears into
the tiny kitchen and you hear zhooga-zhooga-zhooga. My God, she can't be
grating potatoes for $1.69!

She's grating potatoes. She brings a bowlful out and gives them to
Melissa Thecook, who mixes them with batter and pours three giants onto
the griddle. When they're golden brown, Sharon Thewaitress places them
before you and you hog them down. Terrific! And made from scratch!

"Everything's made from scratch here," says Melissa Thecook — chili,
barbecue sauce, hot sauce for the eggs, home fries, sugar syrup like your
mother used to make. And not only from scratch, but also *to* scratch, because Melissa Thecook and Sharon Thewaitress even make their own
matchbooks. They buy blank books and stamp the restaurant's name on the
cover. Cheaper that way. It pays to be frugal in a fragile business such as
theirs, says Sharon.

"Thewaitress" is not Sharon's real surname. Both Sharon and Melissa
"Thecook" are very private people in a very public business and they don't
want their surnames used. Nor would they say where they came from. Nor
would they permit us to photograph their faces. In fact, they hesitated to
cooperate at all because "It broke our hearts when this newspaper called
Metropolis wrote a piece on us when we were just getting started. The guy
put in all kinds of cutesy stuff and that really hurt. We're not important. It's
the restaurant that's important."

Metropolis, with its multimillionaire Eastern backer and its Harvard management, folded in 1977 after 45 issues. Melissa and Sharon have fried lots of eggs, toasted lots of toast and cooked lots of coffee since then.

It's 7 a.m. and the temperature outside is 80 degrees. Inside the tiny restaurant, it's even hotter. But that doesn't keep out their customers, who select from the vasty menu spread out on dozens of circular hand-lettered signs that overwhelm you on a first visit. There's a definite air of the '40s. The fans hum, the door to the street is open and you can hear the sounds of the city as Chicago Av. wakes up for another day of commerce. Artie Shaw's rendition of "Lady Be Good" slides out of the old radio behind the counter, where this morning's Star and Tribune reposes, magic-marked with a warning that it's a "House Paper."

House of Breakfast is the sort of place where you don't ask for a cup of coffee, please. Instead, you say slide me a cup of java. Sharon slides a cup of java at a customer, then calls "a No. 3" to Melissa, who gets busy at the griddle preparing two buttermilk cakes and two eggs. With butter and homemade syrup, "No. 3" goes for $1.09. "I Surrender, Dear" has replaced "Lady Be Good."

Melissa pours three beaten eggs onto the grill. The mixture spreads out and she shoves it into place, chops up the sausage and onions next to it with her spatula, and unwraps a slice of cheese. That's "The Tramp," which goes for $2.75, toast and jelly included. It's one of 29 omelets offered at House of Breakfast. Exotics like the strawberry-and-cheese omelet and down-to-earth numbers like the "Big Daddy," a concoction of eggs, bacon, onion and cheese. Or "The Kung Fu." Melissa says when kids eat that one they always ask her if they're going to have flashbacks like David Carradine in the TV show of the same name.

David and Lynette Patton drop by in their jogging togs. They live just up the street, but they've never been here before. "We always noticed the big polka dots outside," says David, "so we decided to breakfast here." They make their selections from the 65 informational signs hanging from everywhere, as Teresa Brewer belts out "Ricochet Romance."

Not all the signs are menu offerings.

We Serve Goooood Food. Patience is a Big Fat Virtue.
We take Pride in Our Cafe and Good Help is Hard to Find. So if You Are Here to Abuse or Mistreat Anyone Please Leave.
This Table is for 2 People. Not 1 person. Also Not for Coffee Alone. Meals Only — $1.00 Minimum Each.
Attention. If You Can't Control Your Kids DON'T Bring Them IN. We Have to Answer to Our Insurance Man.
No French Fries.
No Credit, Don't Ask.

There's even a sign on the ceiling: *Starting July 1 Minnesota Tax will be 5%. Please Note.*
Melissa says that all the signs prevent lots of misunderstanding. And

when signs don't work, she's prepared to take more drastic action. "When we started eight years ago, there was a counter by the window, looking out on the avenue. Pimps used to come in and sit and look out at their girls. So we tore it out and now we don't have the problem."

Dan Foley, a semi-regular, polishes off "The Tramp," and says, "It's just great. The quality is good and reasonably priced. Sharon and Melissa are very independent, and I like that. They know what kind of customers they want. They don't take anything from a bunch of bozos."

David and Lynette Patton finish their breakfasts. Lynette says the pancakes must be good because David is fussy and he's cleaned up his plate of Frisbee-sized flapjacks. "He won't even eat mine," says Lynette. David gets up and says, "A little breakfast place with a *big* breakfast taste." Melissa thinks that's real cute and that David should be in PR. Lynette says, "He used to be." And they're gone.

Lars Hanson, a therapist who works over on Park Av., comes in and orders two breakfasts, a "Ranchero" of three eggs wrapped around potatoes, sausage, onions and cheese, plus a short stack of pancakes. Larson, a 35-year-old breakfast aficionado who comes from North Dakota, says the "Ranchero" is the best omelet in town. "With a breakfast like this, nothing can go wrong all day."

Charlie Colden, who works at nearby Wilharm Pharmacy, comes in for one of his three daily visits before the girls close up at 1 p.m. Everett Swanson, 79, comes in every morning from his apartment two blocks away. Sharon calls his order before he gives it. "I've got so many choices, but I always eat the same thing every day — one egg, two sausages, toast and coffee. I drink my orange juice at home . . . . I worked 38 years at Minnegasco, 25 of them as credit manager. I didn't change jobs any more than I change breakfasts."

Sharon shows Everett a snapshot of her pet rabbit and his new bride. Everett digs into his sausage as Maurice Chevalier sings "September Song." It's 9:30 and the rush is over. But not for Melissa, who's back in the kitchen rolling out homemade sausages. "I don't like all that processed garbage. I used to use prepared sausage, but I was ashamed to serve it."

The girls take a short breather in preparation for the luncheon run. "When we started in 1975, we served lunches," explains Melissa. "Then we quit. But with the recession, we started up again."

The postman drops by in shorts. "He's got cute knees," says Melissa, who used to collect Robert Redford portraits, but now decorates the cafe with objets de Mickey Mouse, donated by customers and friends, and a painting on aluminum foil given them by little Faith Monson, a juvenile customer who apparently behaves herself when she drops by with her parents for Melissa's pancakes. "Once she wrote an essay about my pancakes in her grade-school class, when all the other kids were writing about their summer vacations."

Before you know it, 1 p.m. has rolled around and Sharon puts a chair in the doorway and gets to work mopping the floor. "They say we have bankers' hours, 6 to 1. But our work has just begun." After they lock up, Sharon and Melissa have lots of work ahead of them. They shop at grocery stores with coupons clipped from the Star and Tribune or cadged from customers. They have their garden beds to tend. And new omelets to dream up.

Although they refuse to talk about themselves, they love to talk about their cafe. After working for others all her life, Melissa cherishes being her own boss. She talks of how the restaurant almost went under in 1978, how she dreamed up the polka-dot exterior, then went out and painted it herself, and how business picked up immediately.

And both cherish their customers. Melissa bakes a special bread to give her regular customers each Christmas, and once she became a hero when she sent a bottle of her homemade hot sauce along with one of her regulars and his friends when they went on a fishing trip to Wisconsin. "Teddy Mondale, the vice president's son, ate in here all the time when he lived in the neighborhood."

But even with a fairly brisk business, the going is rough. On this day, a good day, House of Breakfast grossed $110. "With food costs and utilities and rent always going up, it's hard. But as long as we make money, we're grateful," says Melissa. "You see, we're lucky. We own a wonderful house. This elderly couple inherited it, and we left them a note and said we're hard-working women and $175 is all we can afford. We made a promise to St. Jude of the Impossible that if they accepted our offer we'd do volunteer work for the Little Brothers of the Poor. What can I say? We got the house and now we visit old people who can't get out." Melissa fingers her St. Jude medal.

If Melissa and Sharon are St. Jude enthusiasts, you suggest, maybe they could persuade Danny Thomas to drop in for breakfast when he's in town.

"Right on," says Melissa. "It'd be the best breakfast he ever had."

Right on is right, you think, as you pile into your car and drive down Chicago Av., your belly full of food and only five hours late to work.

—D.W.

We called Melissa Thecook before going to press with the book and found out that the House of Breakfast's real name is House of Breakfast Par Excellence and that the number of omelets now offered stands at more than 40, including one called "The Viking," which is three eggs stuffed with ham, onions, hash browns and cheese. With an omelet like that, nothing could go wrong for Hagar the Horrible.

Bill Helgeson
Barber and Rug Merchant

Tracy, Minnesota
1981

T HE PROMISE of winter whistles down the back street as the customer
from Minneapolis hustles into the toasty warm shop and settles down
into the barber chair. Barber Bill Helgeson takes a clean barber cloth,
performs a veronica with the grace of a matador and says, "Good afternoon."

It's 9:05 a.m., but Bill likes to keep his customers off balance whenever
possible. Once noon hour is over, according to customers who've been
dropping in for the past 55 years, Bill usually greets everyone with a terse
"Good morning."

As Bill snip-snip-snips the fringe around his new customer's shiny
dome, he talks of how he came to Tracy in 1926 from a barbering job in
Glenwood. "It was seasonal in Glenwood, so I came here to work for just
five months. And I'm still here."

Is he glad he stayed?

"I don't know."

Bill snips and the dusty-sweet smell of talc assaults the customer's nostrils. Tall bottles of green Pinol Skintone Lotion, yellow Hess Coconut Oil
Shampoo, Lucky Tiger tonic, Amber Lime tonic, Three Roses tonic and
Glover's Imperial Sarcoptic Mange Medicine recall the days when every
self-respecting shop had a foot-high stack of Police Gazettes and every barber had patter to bewitch the frightened child, bemoan the national debt,
bedevil the only Chicago Cubs fan in town who dropped in to have his
judgment besmirched. Bill has a patter of his own:

• Shoes. "You've got to have good shoes if you're in a business like
this. I'll bet you nine out of 10 people who come into this shop have shoes
that don't fit right. One of the barbers in town wears cowboy boots. Cowboy boots weren't made to stand in. They were made to *sit* in."

• Toupees. "I sell a lot of them, but mostly to people from out of town. I
did sell one to a fellow from Tracy. He worried about what people would
say. I told him: 'Listen, it'll take eight weeks to get the top piece. Mean-

while, you grow yourself a mustache. Then when the top piece comes, I'll fit it for you and shave your mustache off. You'll go out of here and people will say what did you do with your mustache? They won't even notice anything else.' He didn't believe me, but he did it and it worked."

• The Old Days. "In the old days, they played cards in the back of the shop, and they sold moon in the basement. Used to be three wooden shelves stacked with bottles that said 'Body Rub.' Those shelves would be full on Monday, empty by Friday. That's lots of body rub. That's before I owned the place."

• His electric-powered tricycle. "It works real good, but when I first got it I couldn't make it all the way to work because I didn't have a long enough cord."

• His customer's head. "When the light shines on your head, it looks like an angel's halo."

• Barbering as a profession. "I like my job well enough, but if a guy had brains he'd get a job that had a retirement program. There aren't any paid vacations in this business. When the shop is closed, the income stops. Still, I can't complain. The town has been good to me. We have a nice home, and I put both daughters through Mankato State."

Bill the Barber makes his final snip on the Minneapolitan's fringe, sweeps his warm hand across the shiny pate and asks the eternal question: "Sir, have you ever thought about buying an ear-to-ear carpet?"

The visitor passes up the offer, pays Bill $3.50 and regrets not asking for the shampoo at $1.25, followed by a four-bit tonic.

"I'd like to barber for two more years," says Bill. "Then I could say I barbered for 60 years." Sixty years? Just how old is Bill the Barber?

"Thirty-nine years and some months."

That adds up to 77 years, which is just about right, considering the customers who start filing in to get their ears lowered. Howard Erickson, 68, settles into the chair. He looks like Maurice Chevalier in work boots.

"Good afternoon," says Bill. "Look what the cat dragged in."

"He's got no manners," says Howard to the visitor from the Cities. " 'Course if he didn't insult me I wouldn't know what to think." Howard's been coming to Bill the Barber's since he was a kid and enjoys needling Bill just ever so slightly, wondering if Bill's electric tricycle can get up to the speed limit, wondering how many bales of hair Bill has cut, wondering this, wondering that. Bill just goes snip-snip.

This is really a narrow building. How narrow?

"It's eight feet, six inches," answers Bill.

"Easier to say eight and a half feet, Bill," says Howard. "I remember when Bill was open on Saturday nights. We'd come in here and get our hair cut, then sit around and chat. At closing time we'd stand here and watch Bill sweep up the hair. All colors."

"Believe it or not," says Bill. "Once I cut five pounds of hair off a woman's head. It was when women started getting their hair bobbed. This woman comes in and lets down her hair. It hung to the floor. As soon as I reached for the shears, she says 'I can't do it' and ran out. She came twice before she finally got up the courage. I took one snip and the tears just rolled down. I weighed it later and it was five pounds. Fellow at a national barber convention said he'd cut off four pounds once. But nobody ever told me they'd cut five."

It's Gus Wendland's turn. Gus comes dressed for the occasion in a blue suit coat, white shirt, red tie, green work pants with belt over gray wool pants with belt. He remembers the time when he was a kid and his dad took the family out on a bobsled and one of the horses dropped dead. "But I don't remember how we got home."

In comes Clarence Harnack, 82, Bill's neighbor. Bill won't get five pounds off Clarence's head. Clarence, says Bill, "should have slept further down on the pillow." As Bill clips Clarence's fringe for the second time this month, a photographer comes in and starts snapping pictures. "Clarence," says Bill, "if you're gonna have your picture taken, maybe you better think of having some hair on your head."

Clarence has caught that pitch before and so tosses it back ever so gently. "Well, no. I guess I better leave it the way it is."

Then the visitor from Minneapolis hustles out into the cold, the wind nipping around his lowered ears, wondering if Bill's mustache trick would work for him. Would people really say, "What did you do with your mustache?" Or would they say treating his affliction with Glover's Imperial Sarcoptic Mange Medicine must have worked pretty well?

—D.W.

Bill Helgeson hung up his clippers in August 1984, which means he got his wish and made it through his 60th year as an ear-lowerer.

Alina Schroeder
Interpreter for the Deaf

Minneapolis, Minnesota
1983

ALINA SCHROEDER is expressive, no doubt about it. Even when she's talking with hearing people, her face and hands give strong clues to what she's saying. But you should see her communicate with the deaf. Her eyes seem to triple in size. See that eyebrow going up? She's starting a sentence. Forehead wrinkled? She's puzzled. And her hands! Her hands make it clear why sign language is called poetic.

Schroeder is the city of Minneapolis's interpreter for the deaf. Her hearing is normal, and she changes spoken words to sign language and vice versa. Whenever she is "signing" for the deaf, she also mouths the words in an exaggerated fashion for lip-readers.

When a deaf man who witnessed a crime viewed a police lineup, Schroeder was with him. When a hearing-impaired woman talked with her alderman about cable television for the deaf, Schroeder was there. She's in the tax office, city council chambers, jail, public health office, pet licensing department — wherever her hearing-impaired clients need her to deal with city officials.

Perhaps because her parents are deaf and her husband is hearing-impaired, Schroeder is strict about keeping confidential her clients' names and situations. She and other certified interpreters for the deaf pledge to uphold a code of ethics. No gossiping, it says. No adding or subtracting from what the deaf person and the hearing person are telling each other. No personal opinions, like, "Watch out, this guy's a crook" or "Sounds overpriced to me." Just translate the information and let people make up their own minds. Deaf people, she stresses, can make their own decisions. They have the right to "hear" everything.

Ethics also mandate that the interpreter copy the moods of the hearing person who is talking and the deaf person who is signing. If the hearing person sounds excited, the interpreter should sign with broad, animated gestures. If the deaf person is angry or happy or sad, the interpreter's voice should convey that. Likewise, boredom should be passed on.

"When I'm interpreting for a boring professor who talks in a monotone way," Schroeder said, "my goal is to have the deaf person fall asleep about the same time as the rest of the class."

Sometimes it's difficult not to get emotionally involved in the deaf person's predicament, she said. Doctors' and lawyers' offices can be tough. "You try to be as neutral as possible, really not there, especially in sensitive situations," she said.

Delivery rooms can be joyous. Schroeder missed out on that one. She went all the way through birthing lessons with a deaf couple but was out of town when the baby came.

Occasionally, it's best to refuse an assignment. She told of a female friend who was sent to a clinic to interpret for a deaf man. What she didn't know was the man was scheduled for a vasectomy. Assignment declined.

Schroeder, 30, hadn't intended to interpret for a living. Her degree is in education. What she wanted to do was teach art. No jobs. She was a certified interpreter for the deaf, and she got her current job three years ago. The closest she gets to art now is to volunteer as an interpreter at the Minneapolis Institute of Arts. Her dream job is to teach art to deaf children.

The city job is 20 hours a week, at about $10 an hour, maximum pay per year, $10,500.

She said, "I'm obviously not in it for the money. I enjoy it, I think I do it well, it's different every day, it has lots of opportunities. I've met Eugene McCarthy and [Walter] Mondale and I got to introduce my mother to Muriel Humphrey."

And isn't it satisfying to help the deaf?

"Yeh, that too, I suppose, but it sounds so patronizing. This was a skill handed to me on a silver platter. The skill and the understanding came from growing up with it, from being this kid in the store with my father and the clerk saying to him rudely, 'Are you deaf or dumb or something?' I don't know if I was more hurt or angry or embarrassed."

She was born in The Netherlands and grew up in a trilingual home: Dutch, English and sign language. Her father was deaf at birth, as were some of his relatives. Her mother apparently lost her hearing when she was born; the forceps left blood spots around her ears. All four of their children can hear.

Alina Schroeder remembers when it dawned on her that her mother was deaf. She was a little tyke, and they were out shopping. She called down an aisle to her mother, and her mother didn't respond.

In Holland when the Schroeders were there, hearing-impaired people used the "oral method" of communicating — using lip-reading and what residual hearing they have. However, even skilled lip-readers get only an estimated 20 to 30 percent of what is said. "A lot of it is guessing," Schroeder said. "If you say a few words, any words, in the morning to a lip-reader, the answer is likely to be, 'Fine, how are you?' "

When her family came to the United States in 1956 (Alina was 3), the family found much more of what's called "total communication" — signing, lip-reading, hearing aids, the written word, whatever works.

Part of Schroeder's job is to write a monthly newsletter for the deaf. ("Newsletters are big for these people, for obvious reasons.") It's sent by teletype to anybody who wants it and lists such things as:

Dayton's wants a part-time signing Santa. The Minneapolis Public Library has free noon talks about gardening on Wednesday and will provide an interpreter. The Guthrie has interpreted performances of "A Christmas Carol." Ditto for the Children's Theatre's "Cinderella." Minneapolis declares a snow emergency. ("We all get that kind of information from radio or TV. They don't.") Bread of Life Lutheran Church for the Deaf has a discussion on stress. A workshop is scheduled on "family violence in the deaf community."

Deaf people love the teletyped newsletter. One sent her a message: "Thanks for the TTY News. I pleasure to heard about it." Don't knock the grammar, Schroeder said. Imagine using English you've never heard. Plus, keep in mind that "pleasure" and "enjoy" are the same in sign language.

She said deaf people traditionally have been reticent to send letters because their written communication tends to be faulty. A service offered by the Deafness Education and Advocacy Foundation is "bilingual translation service" — helping hearing-impaired people write letters to insurance companies, credit-card companies, etc.

Another of Schroeder's functions is to get across the idea of what helps the hearing-impaired.

"There are 20,000 hearing-impaired and deaf people, just in the Twin Cities," she said. "You look surprised. Everybody's surprised at that number. You know why? Because people don't *look* deaf. They don't have canes or wheelchairs or something to remind you of their handicap, so you think they don't need help. But they're cut off from so much information."

She said people would be more sympathetic to the problems of the deaf if they kept in mind that they too may someday lose their hearing: "Handicapped people, you know, sometimes refer to a nonhandicapped person as a TAB — *Temporarily* Able Bodied."

—P.M.

Alina Schroeder is the mother of a brand-new baby boy, Benjamin. She reports his hearing is fine: He wakes up to the slightest noise.

The Fredrickson Family
Scourge of the Diamond

Lakeville, Minnesota
1983

HOMER PURDY of Golden Valley called Neighbors a few weeks back. Purdy worked for years as a salesman and got around the country quite a bit. He told us we should beat it out to Herman Fredrickson's place in rural Lakeville because Fredrickson had all kinds of good stories to tell us.

So we beat it out to Dodd Blvd., six miles south of downtown Lakeville, to see if Homer Purdy was pulling our leg. He wasn't.

One of the reasons Herman Fredrickson has so many stories to tell is that he has so many relatives. His father, Nels, came from Denmark to settle the farm that Herman and his wife, Eleanor, still live on. His mother, Emilia, came from Norway. Once Nels and Emilia got together, over a 30-year period they managed to produce 18 children — 14 boys, four girls. When Herman was born, they wanted to call him Enoch, sort of a play on the Norwegian phrase *mer enn nok*, meaning "more than enough."

"But they called me Herman and had one more after that."

Herman sits bib-overalled in the office across the road from Fredrickson Lumber and Construction Co., which he started 30 years ago. He employs 15 people, 13 of them Fredricksons.

He smiles from behind steel-rimmed specs, puffs on a cigarette and gets going on his passion, baseball. He started playing in the Dakota County League with the big guys when he was 14 and didn't put his spikes on the shelf until he was 47. He pulls out a postgame photograph taken in 1929. It could have been a scene from the old song, "Yohn Yohnson's Wedding."

Arthur Fredrickson was there, Herman Fredrickson was there, Walter Fredrickson was there, Soren Fredrickson was there, Otto Fredrickson was there, Edwin Fredrickson was there, Joseph Fredrickson was there, Nels Fredrickson was there, William Fredrickson was there, Axel Fredrickson was there, Martin Fredrickson was there, and Fred Fredrickson was there, too. There they stood, in their woolen striped uniforms with "FB" emblazoned across their chests.

"FB," explains Herman, stood for Fredrickson Brothers. "Of course they called us lots of other stuff, too, like Full of Bull." The FB team broke up as the Great Depression deepened, but the brothers scattered out to play in several Dakota Country League teams. Herman played second base and outfield for Eidswold and has lots of good stories to tell. He remembers creamery picnics highlighted by ball games that drew as many as 2,000 people, or the Fourth of July picnic sponsored by Eidswold's two churches. "Oh, we had cars lined up on both sides of the road and running way out of town."

Not that the surroundings were very elegant. "We made our own diamond, skinned off the grass with shovels, built our own dugouts. We had bleachers that seated about a hundred people and the rest had to stand. Then we'd take up a collection to buy new uniforms. I paid two bits for a pair of used baseball shoes. Dale Quist played for Dundas. He hit a ball out to me and I scooped it up and got more alfalfa than I should have and just couldn't get rid of the ball. Whenever I see Quist's mother in for coffee at Northfield, she kids me about that one."

And then there was the unassisted triple play Herman made with a broken thumb. "It probably sounds like bragging, but it happened so quick I didn't know what was going on. We were at Elko. I was playing center field because of my thumb. A guy hit the ball over second base. It looked like a safe hit, so the runners on first and second started running. I caught the ball right over second. I touched second after doing a somersault, then touched the guy heading back for first." Herman recalls he batted .500 that year.

Herman kept playing until 1958 and took some razzing about that. "Fellow came back to town for a visit. He asked me what position I was playing. I said catcher and second base. 'Gosh,' the fellow said, 'you must be faster than ever, Herman.' "

After 1958, Herman concentrated on his sense of humor, on cultivating the home place, on building his business. Herman likes a joke as well as the next man, probably better:

• "At a family reunion, my sister told people that I was a Ph.D. I only went to high school for two years. She said Ph.D. stood for post-hole digger. Our company builds pole buildings, you know."

• On working for the Lord: "The pay isn't so great, but the retirement program is *out of this world.*"

• "There was this old Norwegian who never went to the doctor. Finally his wife hounded him and hounded him and finally he went for a check-up, but he wasn't happy about it. 'What seems to be your problem?' the doctor asked. 'Vhen did ay ever say ay had a problem?' said the Norwegian. 'Ah, well,' said the doctor, 'maybe we should start with your family's medical history. When did your father die?' 'Vhen did ay ever say may fodder vuss dead?' 'Oh,' said the doctor, 'do you mean he's still alive?' 'Yah, heece still alive. Heece 104 yeerce old. An' hee yust married a turdy-yeer-old voman.' 'My goodness,' said the doctor. 'At 104, why would he want to marry a 30-year-old woman?' 'Humph!,' said the old Norwegian, 'vhen did ay ever say may fodder *vanted* to get married?' "

• "Walt Dziedzic, one of your aldermen, he played for Orchard Lake. He was one of the hardest hitters I ever played against. And there was only one pitch Dziedzic couldn't hit — low and behind him."

• "We had a preacher named Von Fischer at Christiania [Lutheran] Church. My neighbor said that was like putting sauerkraut on lutefisk."

• "My wife, Eleanor, subscribes to a magazine called The Farmer's Wife. I occasionally take it to the toilet with me. So then I tell my wife I've got the farmer's wife in the toilet . . . . "

Enoch, Herman, *MER ENN NOK!*

And Herman loves his farm, which his father homesteaded in 1882. "He paid $5 an acre, I guess it was. One day when I was a boy, we were walking in a real nice field of oats. Dad said, 'I grubbed this land all by hand and I hope one of the boys will take it when I'm gone.' I made up my mind right then and there. Now, when I feel blue, I get in my old Chevy and drive to the end of the farm. It's just like medicine for me."

Of the 18 children brought up on the farm, seven sons and three daughters are still alive. Most stayed in the neighborhood. Sister Elizabeth ended up in Auburn, Wash. And two or three brothers took off and settled way off in Northfield, Minn., 14 miles away. Herman had a stroke last year and takes it easy. His brother Edwin, 82, works the morning shift at the lumberyard; brother Art, 66, takes over in the afternoon.

Last summer, the Fredrickson family had a reunion at the Elko ballpark. There were 460 family members there, enough to field a nine-team softball tournament. Herman Fredrickson played second base and his team took second.

Enoch, Herman, *MER ENN NOK!*

—D.W.

Ed. Zunde
Tale of a Latvian Tailor

Minneapolis, Minnesota
1983

THE FADED sign is unprepossessing. It hangs over the little lawn at 1126 University Av. NE. and simply says ED. ZUNDE — TAILOR. But the reporter's waist has expanded, even though his ankles haven't, and he has this Great Idea. So he parks his car and enters the old house where Ed. Zunde, Tailor, holds sway.

A tall, gray-haired man stalks out into the waiting area and greets his visitor, who explains his Great Idea. He explains that since he started buying cheap off-the-rack trousers with 40-inch waists, the circumference of his pants legs seemed to expand disproportionately.

"Yah," says Ed. Zunde, Tailor. "You look like you got pajamas on. HO, HO!"

Well, says the reporter, could a tailor take in the legs or would he just have to grow bigger ankles? And if the tailor could, how much would it cost?

"Ooh, let's see. Aah, ooh," he says, pulling here and tugging there and f-f-f-f-f-ing with his chalk. "Oh, yah, I take in waist just a bit, too, and shorten cuffs. Ooh, about $9."

And so it is that a reporter, looking as if he walks the streets of Northeast in cheap, gray pajamas, hires a tailor whose grandfather was tailor to the family of Nicholas II, last Czar of All the Russias. As the reporter watches, the tailor rips blind stitches, cuts, sews and presses, finishing the job in 45 minutes. And then, between answering the phone, serving customers, cutting and stitching, he speaks of the tailor's trade, of his earlier life in Europe and how he loves his life and work in the New World. No charge.

Although Zunde "gets by" in Latvian, Russian, German and English, his English syntax isn't impeccable and sometimes he has trouble with "th" sounds and long vowels, sometimes with finding the right word, after a generation in the United States. But he makes up for such minor lapses with irrepressible enthusiasm and wit and a booming laugh that makes harrowing experiences sound like picnics.

Zunde sits in a darkened room before his Chandler Mark 52 machine, a bright ray of light directed at his big thick fingers, which deftly trace his intentions on the shoulder of someone's sports coat. He speaks in rapid bursts, then thinks, then bursts again.

He was born 62 years ago in Riga, Latvia, where his father ran a tailor shop. "Our family was from Sweden. But my grandfather, he was tailor for the czar, the last czar before the revolution. My grandfather died in revolution time. Did you see in the paper? The Russians are causing trouble for the airlines? Then they [the Russians] turn around and tell us it's America's fault, that the U.S. was spying. What stupidity! We got satellites to do that now. HO, HO!"

Zunde says that as a kid he wanted to be an engineer, but then the Russians came in 1940. And then the Germans came and chased the Russians out. Both were bad, according to Zunde, but the Russians were worse. "The Russians, they come in and JING, JING, JING! They break the glass panels and take my dad's fabrics, and then they took all the machines but one. That's Russian work for you. My dad wanted to fight them, but Joe, his Polish tailor, said don't fight to my dad. They got the *guns*, Joe said.

"The Russians, there's something cruel about them." He tells of the political classes the Russians introduced into his school's curriculum. "The new teacher told us the Russians came to help us little starving countries. One boy jumped at that. He said, 'What the hell you talking about? It's the Russians who starve.' You know? The boy, he was only 16, a good student. Teacher got him kicked out of class right there. The boy was never heard from again."

The Germans "liberated" Latvia in 1941. "Shoo-er," says Zunde. "They were rough on the Poles and the Baltic peoples. But at least the Germans didn't take your machines. They let you work."

Zunde pauses from his own work to show the reporter an old book depicting Russian atrocities in Latvia. "Here, here's a picture of the president of the Latvian Boy Scouts, Gen. Goppers. They even murdered him." Zunde shakes his head and quickly adds that he has nothing against Russians or Germans as people. "Lots of Russians live in this neighborhood. Good people, my friends. They hate the Communists like I do. And many Germans help me when the Americans were bombing us [in the work camps], and we had to get out. But the Fascists and the Communists . . . " Zunde, Tailor, shakes his head again. He says he never votes party, but always for the man.

"The only thing I belong to is the Boy Scouts. When I was a D.P. [displaced person] and they ask what party I belong to, I said, 'Just Boy Scouts.' HO, HO!" He shows his Russian army draft card, something he never had to use because the Germans drove the Russians out in 1941. "But I kept it, in case they ever came back."

The Russians did come back, for good, but Zunde and his wife, Velta, and baby daughters, Zinta and Gunta, were shipped to Germany, where he worked at forced labor in a tank factory, then in a bakery ("I got my first taste of cognac there"), then as an interpreter.

"When the Americans got closer, they let us take bicycle and get out of Frankendorf. The Nazis said if the Americans ever catch us, they kill all of us with the *knife*." Zunde runs his index finger across his Adam's apple and says HO, HO! "Finally, American Jeep with machine gun approach the town. American soldier motion me, see? My wife said, 'Don't go.' I said, 'I go.' He had the gun, I a little English. The soldier said, 'Where is the burgermeister?' I answered and he said, 'What nationality you are?' I said, 'Latvian.' And the guy with the gun said, 'Hey, I am LITHUANIAN!' And then he gave me American chocolate, and my wife said the Nazis are stupid."

There followed four years of displaced persons camps for the Zunde family. Traveling from one to another, Zunde did his first tailoring for pay when he made a pair of trousers for a fellow Latvian who in return hauled the Zunde family's scanty belongings in his horse-pulled wagon to a new camp. Zunde doesn't complain about the camps, because there was always work to do, and he ended up setting up a tailor shop to repair U.S. 3rd Army uniforms.

Then, in 1949, the Zunde family fortunes changed. Ray Petersine owned an incubator factory in Gettysburg, Ohio. He needed help and went to the old Latvian Embassy in Washington and looked over the lists to see whom he might sponsor. Zunde smiles. "He picked us! Later he told me that he was impressed that I listed myself as a tailor. Also, he said he liked our names, Edgar, Velta, Zinta and Gunta Zunde. HO, HO!" So the family moved to Gettysburg, and Zunde worked for $40 a week installing insulation in chicken incubators. One day, Petersine's daughter went shopping at Jack Cornell's fancy clothing store in nearby Greenville. Cornell told the woman that he was looking for a tailor. The woman said there was a D.P. tailor working in the Petersine factory. Cornell expressed interest, and she brought the news back to Gettysburg.

But Zunde was reluctant to leave his benefactor. "You know? Ray Petersine, he said to me, 'Edgar, you want to work at your trade. This is a free country and you're free to go. What you can do for yourself, you better do for yourself.' And then Ray Petersine helped me move our things. This still touches me." Zunde taps the reporter's knee for emphasis, then brushes a bit of moisture from behind his spectacles.

Zunde worked in Greenville for 10 years and visited Minneapolis in 1958. "Here, I like it. All this lakes and birch and spruce. It's like Latvia. And so many Latvians here. I could not believe." So in 1961, he made the big move, not in a wagon this time, and set up in the old house on University Av. He says life has been good to him in America. He sings in the choir of a Minneapolis Latvian church, he's active in Boy Scouts, he has a log cabin up north. Behind him, in his sewing room, are boldly stroked watercolors of the mountainous forests of Latvia that he paints from his mind's eye.

Zinta and Gunta have left the nest and he and his wife were recently divorced. The tailoring business isn't what is used to be, either. "I think this trade will be missing before long. When I came there were three tailors in neighborhood and a boot maker. Now only me. HO, HO!"

Zunde used to make suits from scratch, but nowadays there isn't good enough natural fabric around to make it worthwhile, so he keeps busy altering clothes. He has no argument against polyester, which he pronounces "py-laster." He mentions well-known judges and lawyers who buy used clothes and hire him to make them fit. "Here, see here. A young man bought for $5 this tuxedo at a rummage sale. I make it over for him for $65, and he has a wonderful thing. A real bargain. I learn this from my father, who altered clothes to fit any fashion."

Judy Rumchik of Cambridge, Minn., comes in with a pile of wool blazers and skirts. She's lost weight and wonders if Zunde can help her out. Ooh, aah, shoo-er. Rumchik discovered Zunde through a friend who used to live in northeast Minneapolis. "I heard," she says, "that he [Zunde] was a neighborhood fixture, so here I am."

Zunde tells her to come back in three weeks for the altered clothing. In comes Phil Becker, 27, who has a scrap-iron business in Minnetonka. Is his leather jacket ready? You betcha. Zunde has lined the jacket with real sheepskin, cut from a vest that someone else forgot to pick up years ago. It's a perfect fit, and Becker is pleased. And even more pleased with the price Zunde quotes. $32. "I hope," says Zunde to Becker, "this keeps you nice and warm." Becker leaves.

"Maybe people say, 'Ed. you could charge more.' What's more? I don't lose in any way. I say if I make an honest, decent living I'm happy with that. That fellow, he's a nice boy, he's got a job, he's doing something."

Zunde has miles to stitch before he sleeps, a wedding dress, another tux due for a wedding on the following day. So the reporter pays him $9, changes back into his reworked trousers and steps out onto University Av. with a spring in his step, like Esquire's Man of the Month, after a lesson in good citizenship from Ed. Zunde, Tailor, a man who knows where he's been and likes where he is.

—D.W.

Ed. Zunde, Tailor, died in February 1985.

Debby Schneider
Contest Winner Extraordinaire

Bloomington, Minnesota
1983

Highest-Paid Writer: In 1958, a Mrs. Deborah Schneider of Minneapolis wrote 25 words to complete a sentence in a competition for the best blurb for Plymouth cars. She won from about 1,400,000 entrants the prize of $500 every month for life. On normal life expectations (age 75), she would collect $12,000 per word. No known anthology includes Mrs. Schneider's deathless prose.

—Guinness Book of World Records, 1983

IT WAS 25 years ago this month that Debby Schneider made the big time for completing the phrase, "I'd be money ahead in a new '58 Plymouth because . . ." Every month since, she has gotten a $500 check in the mail.

Besides being $150,000 richer and doubling her age, what has happened to Schneider? Well, she drove Plymouths for many years but has switched to Pontiacs. The two children who were babies in diapers when she won the contest are now a doctor and a lawyer. She has won a mess of other contests. She specializes in positive thinking, runs an outfit called "The Center for Positive Power" and is making a series of tapes about programming the subconscious mind. Some things don't change; she and her husband, Allen, live in the same Bloomington house where she penned her prizewinner.

And just what were the 25 magic words she wrote for Chrysler Corp.?

She's not telling. She never will tell, she said. Her children will find the answer in her safe-deposit box after she dies, but meanwhile only she and her husband and probably someone at Chrysler know for sure.

(Can't you just see each departing Chrysler president solemnly taking aside his successor and whispering Debby Schneider's sparkling words into his ear?)

Schneider had to sign a contract with Chrysler promising not to reveal her entry. In the decades before she won, sponsors used to publish winning entries. But companies were bombarded with complaints from also-rans who maintained that their ideas were identical or better. Entrants demanded duplicate prizes, and the sponsors had to spend a wad of money and time to dispute the claims.

"If Shakespeare himself had written those 25 words, they would have been picked apart," she said.

She was told she wouldn't see her entry splashed across Plymouth ads, and she hasn't. About the only use of the winning words comes when she and her husband playfully toss a few into a conversation. No one has picked up on it, she said.

It was a heck of an entry, she maintains to this day. Every word was right. Every angle was studied. She test-drove Plymouths, read every pamphlet that Plymouth published, pored over newsletters on how to win contests. She knew Chrysler Corp. had featured highway safety in its sales campaign for Dodges, so she included a safety reference in her Plymouth entry. She practiced writing phrases with contrast, humor, alliteration, balance and flow. She made sure that what she wrote about Plymouths was applicable to no other car. She thought it all through.

"I tuned out the competition and told myself I had an excellent chance to win," she said. "I do that whenever I enter a contest. I don't think about the millions of other competitors. I think it's self-defeating to let doubt enter your mind.

"Anything I do, I do with total commitment. It's my life style."

She mailed in an entry one week, and a new, improved version the next. She sat back to wait. While she was waiting, Pillsbury notified her that she was a finalist in its national Bake-Off. Her party-cookie recipe brought her $100.

Then she got the $500 a month, plus a '58 big-finned Plymouth. The next day, she got a $55 check as winner in a National Safety Council contest. And shortly thereafter, she placed among the top 20 sandwich makers in the nation.

The sandwich entry shows how her mind works. You've got to understand, she said, that she can *imagine* using her senses. She can "smell" Arpege when she wants to, even if the perfume isn't around. She can "hear" a drill when she sets her mind to it, "taste" a lemon. With her sensory skills, she visualized the sandwiches she used to have as a kid at summer camp — a concoction of bacon, honey and an English muffin. She wanted some color so she mentally added lettuce and thin slices of orange. It was the year of the Sputnik so she stuck in toothpicks with olives at the ends. She called it the "Sputnik Special" and won the contest.

Her children began to think she could win any contest she entered. They wanted her to name the Cocoa Puff twins so she could win a train set for them. She explained it would be extremely unlikely for her to win, but she'd give it her best. Much to her surprise, she won the trains for them.

She said that part of the reason her Plymouth winning is still the largest on record is that such contests went out of vogue. The scandal about the

"$64,000 Question" hit in 1958, the same year Schneider won her pot of gold, and sponsors backed off from big-money promotions.

When her children were in school, she went back to college and got another bachelor's degree in teaching and then graduate certification in learning disabilities. She taught in the Bloomington school system for seven years. She was burning out and schools were being closed, so she became a travel agent for 10 years. A primary benefit of the job was being able to see much of the world. When the airlines were deregulated, she found herself putting in a lot of time and effort for few dollars, so she quit to study for a master's degree in psychology. Now she's a part-time counselor and also conducts workshops and teaches community education classes. "The thing I most want to do is to help people realize their own potentials," she said.

She kept getting calls from family members and friends asking her to send them some positive power. "I obviously can't give them my eight-week class over the phone, so I thought about what I could do to help give them the power to reprogram their minds. 'Tapes!' I thought."

Schneider has produced a series of 10 tapes, including "Power through relaxation," "Contest-winning power," "Power over procrastination" and "Power through effective communication." She sells them for $10 each from the Center for Positive Power at 8828 3rd Av. S.

Her positive thinking has changed her life, and it can change yours, she said. This from the world's highest-paid writer. Before Debby Schneider, the person holding the title was Ernest Hemingway. "Sports Illustrated" paid him $30,000 for a 2,000-word article on bull-fighting. That was a paltry $15 a word. She's already gotten $6,000 a word. And she expects to live a good long life to push up the figure. She's a positive person.

—P.M.

The Owens-Vann Family
Up from Slavery

Minneapolis, Minnesota
1982

PREFACE — After Nancy was born a slave in 1841, her South Carolina master sold her away from her mother. First she worked as a house girl, then in the fields. Sold again at the age of 11, she was put in the fields by her new owner. She told her grandchildren years later that when she couldn't produce enough work, the new master hanged her naked from the barn rafters and whipped her.

Nancy endured.

She married Thomas Rivers and bore him a son. When they were sold apart, she married Charles Owens and bore him 11 children; some were sold, some died young and some survived into the 20th century. One of her sons was Charles Hamilton Owens. After the Civil War, the Owens family moved to Dallas, Texas, then to Sapulpa, Okla., where one of the family married into the Vann family.

The Vanns trace their heritage back to Simon, an African sold at an American slave market in the dim past.

In the 1930s, many members of the Owens and Vann families left the maelstrom of the Oklahoma dust bowl for the verdant promise of California. Others migrated to the factories of Detroit, still others to Minnesota and 16 other states of the union.

But they kept in touch. In 1978, they staged a reunion in Los Angeles, at which time they voted to meet two years later in Tulsa, just 15 miles from Sapulpa, where so many of the older family members were born. At the 1980 meeting, those assembled voted to meet up north, in Minneapolis.

The Neighbors section heard about the reunion from a neighbor of Beulah Wright, co-chairman of the 1982 reunion. We called Beulah, told her we were used to three-hour, Sunday-afternoon Jell-O and hot-dish reunions, and asked her if we could drop by to observe a more elaborate mode. Beulah said, "Sure, come on over. And bring your appetite."

This is how the Owens-Vann family reunion went:

Day 1, a Thursday, at 6 p.m. — There's lots of hugging and kissing in the back yard of Ben and Inez Crushshon's new home in north Minneapolis. It's cocktail hour before the roll-call dinner when the Minneapolis committee will find out how many people have made the pilgrimage. Folks walk onto the lawn, tentatively, having come from the Leamington, where an entire floor has been reserved for out-of-towners. Ben Crushshon directs them to a table that holds liquor, beer and soft drinks, encourages them to help themselves, then moves on for more handshakes.

In the kitchen, women crowd around the stove, fret about the menu, talk to beat the band. Beulah Wright's daughter-in-law, Joann Wright, says, "We're trying to get to know each other. It's something people should do." Annie Ross, 64, sits across the table looking stoically at nothing in particular. Annie still lives in Sapulpa, where she works as a domestic. Annie rode the Greyhound for 14 hours to be at the event.

Robert Blackburn, 32, flew in from Los Angeles, where he works as a car salesman. "I didn't have time to go to the first two reunions. Now I've got plenty of time." He loves the clean air in Minneapolis and wonders about property taxes. "On the way from the hotel, someone showed me apartments for low-income people, people on welfare. Compared to Watts they look like luxury places."

Leonard Pierson, co-chairman, sits at a typewriter and takes down people's names as his fiancee, Sharon Robinson, a Hennepin County social worker, just stands there, amazed at all the people hugging and kissing. "I've never been to a family reunion. It's so exciting; they really know how to make it work. One thing's certain. It hasn't dissuaded me from marrying into this family!"

Howard and Bertha Swingler organized the first reunion in 1978 and were hosts at the roll-call dinner at their Los Angeles home. Bertha's looking forward to being "just a guest" this time. Howard, a former boxer who married into the family, gets a big hug from Inez Crushshon and then worries that economic hard times will cut into attendance. Troy Foster, a Tulsa water-department employee, drove to Minneapolis. So did Robert Owens, who works at a Chevy agency in Tulsa. "It's my first reunion," says Robert. "I came to see people I've never seen. And the country. I really like it here."

Archie Ray Goff, who moved to St. Paul from Tulsa in 1964 and married into the family, asks Robert Owens if he knows the Goffs in Tulsa. Sure enough he does. Ted Owens, a Tulsa telephone-company employee, says the Leamington reminds him of the Mayo Hotel in Tulsa, where the second reunion was held. Goff says he worked at the Mayo when he was a kid. "I ran the dog races, a gambling game." The fellows nod and smile.

A bunch of women crowd around a picnic table. Mary Foster, Tulsa, is a three-time attender. Joyce Owens, Merced, Calif., says this one's her second. Elizabeth Norton, Tulsa, didn't even make it to the one in her hometown: "I was on the 11-to-7 shift at St. John's Hospital." Deloris Lewis, a math teacher from Detroit, is making it No. 2. She's looking forward to visiting Hubert Humphrey's grave, which is part of the tour scheduled for the morrow.

Cochairman Beulah Wright arrives, with peach cobbler, chicken casserole and a bundle of nerves. She's 39, a big, abrupt woman in a flowered dress. She shakes some hands, hugs some hugs and disappears into the kitchen.

Geneva Johnson came from Sapulpa. Her son-in-law, Archie Goff, chides her about finding her a new husband in the Twin Cities. "I've got one who's ready, Geneva."

"You take care now. If his mind is made up, mine might not be," says Geneva, who fans herself and says it's as hot in Minneapolis as it is in Oklahoma.

Corinne Lobster, a friend of the Owens-Vann family and chief cook for the event, appears and shouts, "You come on now and get your food." Right on. Tables on the lawn are heaped with fried chicken, barbecued chicken wings, green beans, peach cobbler and hot rolls that float an inch above their pans. Mounds of food magically disappear, and Corinne Lobster is in her glory.

Dinner ends and Leonard Pierson asks the group of 90 people to crowd together to get their weekend marching orders. "Beulah Wright will now give a prayer. Without prayer we can go nowhere."

"*That's right*," says someone in the crowd.

Beulah steps up and gets rolling. "Thank you, thank you, O God. . . . Let peace and happiness be among us. . . . We're nothing without You (*murmurs of assent*) . . . . Bless us. Give us the happiness a family should have. . . . Bless those who have gone. (*Bless You, Lord.*) Amen. (*Thank You, Jesus.*)"

Then there's talk about family, about how to get back to the Leamington. And by 11 p.m., the lawn is empty.

Day 2, 8:30 a.m. — Beulah's at it in her Park Av. kitchen, scrambling eggs and frying bacon purchased in wholesale lots. She's wearing a T-shirt that says, "There are two kinds of people in this world. OKLAHOMANS and those who wish they were." Corrine Lobster is cooking up a big kettle of grits, and Esther Jivens works on hash browns for breakfast for the folks who'll soon come from the Leamington.

The kitchen's steaming and so is Beulah because the grandkids who stayed overnight are pretty rambunctious. Before you know it, she grabs Orlando in one hand, Burvis in the other, and marches them to opposite corners of the dining room. Soon there are kids facing all four corners. "Now you stand there," says Beulah, "and be QUIET!"

They stand there, quiet.

Beulah spreads out newspapers on the back lawn and prepares plates of breakfast for the kids, who file out meekly to chow down. They talk about all the fun they had the day before watching HBO at the Crushshon residence. "Then we went to the hotel," says 8-year-old Burvis. "We were really getting down, but then we had to come to sleep here."

A van pulls up to the curb out front and a flock of people pile out and into Beulah's living room. The table groans with food. Cottrell Owens needs biscuits. "I've got my rice, but I need biscuits." He gets them, more of the feathery ones whipped up by Willie Mae Webb.

There's talk of family history. Robert Blackburn isn't certain when his grandpa moved to California, but thinks it was about 1948. "No," someone says. "That was in 1938." Dust bowl times. Addlissie Brown of Compton, Calif., remembers Oklahoma. She would like to move to Minnesota because it has snow and cold, just like in Oklahoma.

With breakfast over, folks pile into cars and vans for a tour, which includes the state Capitol, Hubert Humphrey's grave and Betty Crocker's kitchen. By now, the reporter, used to the typical three-hour, Sunday-afternoon, Jell-O and hot-dish reunions, is exhausted and heads back to the office. He didn't make it to the evening banquet in the Leamington's Michigan Room. Nor did he attend the final two days of the reunion.

Day 3 — A big picnic at the pavilion in Theodore Wirth Park.

Day 4 — Worship services at New Bethel Baptist Church and a 2 p.m. farewell dinner at Ames Elks Lodge on Plymouth Av.

Aftermath — Beulah Wright ended up in the hospital after her relatives went back to California, Illinois, Michigan and Oklahoma. When she got well enough to talk, Neighbors visited her in her room.

Was it worth all the effort, Beulah? "Oh, yes. I'd do it all over again. But don't write 'Beulah.' Write the whole Minnesota committee and our friends who helped with the food."

Beulah said the whole affair cost between $3,500 and $4,000, that the most heavily attended event was the picnic, which drew 150 people. And what of 1984? "We discussed where we'd meet, and I guess we're not going to meet in a city. We're going to take a cruise on an ocean liner." That fits in very well with a quote that appears in the frontispiece of a historical booklet published by the Owens-Vann family in 1980:

> *Far better is it to dare mighty things, to win glorious triumphs, even though checkered by failure, than to take rank with those poor spirits who neither enjoy much nor suffer much because they live in the gray twilight that knows neither victory nor defeat.*
> —Franklin D. Roosevelt

—D.W.

Paula Leu
Her Motto: 'Never Give Up Hope'

Anoka, Minnesota
1984

WHAT'S STRIKING is how matter-of-fact she is.
The cancer, she says, has been found in her spine and her skull, her shoulder and leg, this arm, this hip. She explains she can't put pressure on this leg because a tumor on the hip bone is pushing against the sciatic nerve. She used to weigh 130 pounds at 5 feet 6; now she weighs 97.

And her voice — has the cancer somehow made it harsh?

"Oh, no," she says, grinning. "I was at a track meet yesterday and I was yelling so much that I'm hoarse."

Paula Leu, 18, is a track coach now. She used to run herself. In fact, she was one of the best girl runners in the state. She was expected to be a basketball star, too. While a sophomore at Anoka High School, she had already placed 12th in the state in cross country. Last year, as a junior, she won the 800-meter run in the state meet with a time of 2:13.

This year she's been waiting at the finish line, cheering on the others. Her teammates this year in cross country, track and basketball elected Paula their captain.

She has proven herself in more than sports. Tuesday evening she graduated with honors from Anoka High with a 3.5 grade-point average and a bent toward math and science. Several weeks earlier, at an awards assembly, she received the Principal's Award, one of four that Arthur Dussl has handed out in his 12 years at the school. He said he gave it to Paula not *in spite of* her cancer, but *because of* it.

"The quality of our character can be measured by how we handle adversity," Dussl said. "Paula has been our greatest teacher."

When trouble invades our lives, he told the students and staff, "Let's close our eyes and see this girl walking down the hall, and let's be the stronger for it."

⁓

Paula Leu, people say with admiration — she's the one who showed up for school every day she was not hospitalized or too sick to move. She's the one who wouldn't allow anyone to carry her books until she absolutely had to. She's the one who put jittery guests at ease at the open house in honor of her graduation.

She's the one whose most negative answer to "How are you feeling?" is "Oh, I'm a little sore." She's the one, exhausted as she was, who consoled the little nephew who climbed up on her wheelchair to announce, "I got an owwie." She's the one who tells her family, "There's always hope — if not for me, for someone else."

Some testimonials:

Karen Brown, an English teacher at Anoka High, described Paula as the teacher's dream — smart, dedicated, wanting to learn, mature, humble. Paula's standards are high, always have been, always will be. Brown said, "There are no gifts for Paula in terms of grades. She wouldn't allow you to lighten the load for her."

Other students with perfectly healthy bodies came up with a multitude of excuses, but not Paula, Brown said: "If she missed two weeks of school when she was hospitalized, she would demand to know what she had missed and would make up every speck of it."

She said Paula wrote a term paper while prone on the davenport at home.

When Paula recently got her senior photos, taken before chemotherapy robbed her of her blonde hair, she gave one to Brown. Looking at it, then at Paula, Brown felt herself losing control and her eyes tearing. Paula comforted her. "Come on, Mrs. Brown," she said. "You're tough."

Brown says she is not a religious person but thinks that "something, I don't know what" has touched Paula. "If it hadn't been the disease, it would have come out some other way."

Gretchen Olson, a 17-year-old at Anoka High who runs the mile and two-mile, said Paula's support and coaching showed. "She made me run better. She knows how to run; she has the techniques. But more than that, she expected each of us to do well, and so we did."

Most of the girls concluded that if the cancer had hit them, they would have accepted tutoring at home and would have hidden from the world, Olson said.

"Not Paula. Other people avoided the subject. We pretended it's not happening. But she wants to tell us all about it. She says, 'If there are questions about the cancer, just ask me.' She said that a couple of times . . . . I think she's still hoping to get better and I think she can. If anyone can, she can."

Jane Van Dusen and Eda Jones, two of Paula's nurses, describe her as gracious and stoic and more worried about how her cancer is affecting her family than she is concerned with her own pain. Dr. Loren Vorlicky said, "She's been an inspiration to a lot of sick kids."

Kristi Kropp, a former Anoka High runner who is now a student at the University of Wisconsin, said, "As far as talking to Paula on the phone or getting her letters, you wouldn't know she's sick. She's interested in *my* running, how *I* am, how *my* life is going. She keeps telling me how special and tough *I* am. It's hard to get her to talk about herself. She wrote last fall and told me, 'You probably know that I have cancer. Sometimes I get really scared, but I'm trying; I'll fight through it.' "

∽

Her medical problems began in December 1982, when she had abdominal pain and trouble breathing.

"They finally found I had [an ovarian] tumor, a benign tumor about 14 pounds. The strong muscles in my stomach held it in, but it was pushing on my lungs."

The Sertoli-Leydig tumor is extremely rare and hardly ever malignant. It was removed and judged benign. Paula was told the danger was past.

Last August, she went to a doctor because she had a pinched nerve in her leg. He also took another look at an arm she had broken earlier. X-rays showed a strange spot on her left shoulder. "They went further and further with tests and found I had cancer," she said.

The cancer had spread throughout her body. One of her doctors, Robert Haselow of Methodist Hospital's radiation therapy department, said she has many dozens of tumors. With her permission to discuss her case, he flipped through her chart: "Right hip, left hip, left shoulder, behind the eye, the bone of the neck, the low back . . ."

To put it simply, the cancer is eating her bones.

As rare as this kind of cancer is, so is her spirit, Haselow said. While many cancer patients, including young people, become highly angry or deeply depressed, Paula has accepted the fact she has cancer and has decided to fight it with everything she's got, he said.

She began chemotherapy the first week of school last fall. She lost her hair in November.

"My doctor and nurse were surprised it stayed as long as it did," she said.

She got a wig but "looked like an old lady," so she stuck it away in favor of caps. In the same month she lost her hair, she and her boyfriend broke up.

"That didn't have anything to do with my illness," she said. "I didn't have time for a boyfriend."

Paula has gone through a series of chemotherapy treatments and last week finished another round of radiation. The primary goal is to reduce her pain. What she and her medical team hope for is to put the cancer into remission.

"The chemotherapy is working," Paula said, "but not as fast as we'd like." The "we" is prominent when she talks about fighting the cancer. It's like a team sport, with her as captain.

"The cancer has spread some," she said. "It's spread to the other arm. They're doing radiation, and we're hoping that'll take care of it."

Will it?

"I don't know. We don't know," she said thoughtfully. "I have no idea. I don't know what to think."

That's as negative as she gets. Mostly she talks about her motto: Never give up hope.

Asked why she agreed to talk about these things for a newspaper article, she said, "I want to help other people appreciate what they have, not to take for granted what they have, including health. I wish I would have appreciated that stuff when I had it."

Her sickness, she said, has had some benefits, including an increased appreciation of her family and her friends and "the things that I've got that haven't been taken away from me. I can feed myself, I can talk, I can see, I can hear. My brain functions normally. The cancer could have affected my body in other ways. What I have I appreciate."

∽

Paula is the second youngest of nine children — seven daughters and two sons. Her parents are Phyllis and Art Leu of 4075 165th Av. NW., Anoka. He's a toolroom superintendent for Litton Microwave, and she was a school secretary until Paula got sick and needed extra care.

What does her family think has made Paula so strong?

Her sisters said the Leus are positive thinkers. "That came from Mom," said sister Liz Voss, 26. "We make up our minds and we do it."

And where did Mom get that attitude? Phyllis Leu said, "From my mother, I guess. She was a strong person."

The Leus have expected their kids to rise above bad situations. Don't let the little things get you down, they say.

Paula points with pride to the accomplishments of her siblings. Grace was class valedictorian, Mary was a college cross-country runner, Walt went to the state gymnastics meet, Patty's marching band played at President Carter's inauguration. . . .

The Leu family, gathered from all parts of the country for Paula's graduation, says she is no superhero. She has had her bad bouts with the cancer. But the worst they can point to, it seems, is her spells of crabbiness, lasting several days at most. Of course, there have been tearful sessions, they admit. But they won't talk about them. That's personal.

An example of Paula's positive thinking concerns a new drug that lessens her nausea when she's getting chemotherapy. She used to throw up every half-hour for the eight hours she was getting the treatment. With the new drug, she vomits maybe once an hour, and she says that's "a lot better than before."

She doesn't talk about religion unless asked. Then she says the shock of cancer made her turn more to God: "I needed help; I couldn't do it on my own." Hers is a strong Catholic family, and "now I'm not just going to church and letting my mind wander. Now I listen."

She also listened intently during graduation ceremonies last week. The standard graduation phrases — "This turning point in our lives" . . . "The object is to live and love and be ourselves" — took on new meaning. Paula and other honors graduates got their diplomas after all the others. She was shivering during the outdoor ceremonies. She didn't ask to be moved up in the program or to leave before the recessional.

In a fall at home several days before graduation, Paula broke her arm and hurt her hip. Until then she had gotten around with the help of a crutch. She doesn't complain of pain, but her family knew on graduation night that she was hurting by the way she got skittish when anyone got too close to the arm.

When Paula Leu's name was called and her sister Linda Leu wheeled her up to the stage, there were cheers and a spontaneous standing ovation from other graduates and the members of the audience.

"Thatta way to go" boomed a male voice. "Love ya, Paula" a girl yelled. Paula beamed.

She won a scholarship — $500 from Anoka High School to "an outstanding graduate who has distinguished herself academically and has set an example for others." She is enrolled at Anoka-Ramsey Community College for next fall and wants to prepare to study physical therapy. After she got sick, she decided on a career in health.

The angriest that people have seen Paula Leu was when she learned last fall that her cancer was announced over the Anoka High public-address system. She didn't want that kind of attention.

"But in the long run, I was glad they did it," she said. "Because everyone knew the truth, and there weren't totally unreal rumors. At first, it was hard because everyone knew and they didn't know what to say. But then, they saw I was the same person as before."

—P.M.

Paula Leu died at home June 25, 1984, less than a month after graduation.

Bohemian Flats
Neighborhood of Squatters

Minneapolis, Minnesota
1984

DONNA LIND has worked 15 years at the Hennepin County Historical Museum, and she called to say that she hadn't "ever seen anything like it." Neighbors is always interested in what people have never seen anything like, so we rushed over to the 30-room museum at 2303 3rd Av. S., to interview Lind, its executive director.

Lind explained that one of her projects this year was to do a four-part slide-presentation series on Minneapolis neighborhoods. "We have a terrific collection of photos in our archives, and I decided that the first neighborhood we'd do would be Bohemian Flats."

On the face of it, one wouldn't think Bohemian Flats would be a big box-office attraction. The Bohemian Flats neighborhood of squatters, you see, was condemned more than 50 years ago to make way for a municipal freight terminal under the old Washington Av. bridge, on the Mississippi's western shoreline, just across from the University of Minnesota. Remnants of the settlement lingered into the 1960s.

But Lind went ahead with the project, sent publicity to the media and contacted Holy Immanuel and Prince of Glory Lutheran and St. Cyril's Catholic churches, where Slovak heritage and language are still emphasized. On March 11, Lind set up her slide show titled "Bohemian Flats: Growth and Demise of the River Flat Settlement" in the museum's auditorium and waited for some Bohemians to show up.

"I've *never* seen anything like it," said Lind. "There were so many people lined up, they couldn't get into the auditorium, which seats 90. So we showed it twice. I told the people who couldn't get in for the first showing that they should look around the museum, but they just stood outside the door for an hour and waited. I guess they weren't so interested in history as they were in *their* history." After the first hour-long show, Lind and her assistant, Millie Gershone, herded another 90 people in, but there were still folks left over, so she promised another showing two weeks later. "About 200 people showed up for that one and there were *still* people we couldn't accommodate, so we're having another showing. This time we'll have it in the auditorium of the Government Center, next Sunday at 1:30. Can you make it?"

You bet, Donna.

∽

Sunday, April 1. By noon, people were walking under the gleaming towers of downtown Minneapolis toward the Government Center, towers their immigrant parents and grandparents would never have dreamed of when they came from Czechoslovakia to a rough-hewn Minneapolis that offered employment in the sawmills, the flour mills, the cooperages, to a Minneapolis that had offered inexpensive living below the Mississippi River cliffs since 1869.

Their descendants came from the city, from the suburbs, even from rural Wisconsin; they came in Vikings jackets; they came in pin-striped suits; the old, the middle-aged, the young. They came to renew childhood acquaintances; they came to see where Grandpa lived. They came for emotional and spiritual reasons as much as they came to see photographs of the tiny thrown-together houses where they and their ancestors had lived, in the days before some of them could afford a camera, in the days when they snaked their firewood and even building materials out of the muddy Mississippi, days when they dreaded the spring floods, days when they didn't realize they were poor.

> The houses in the pit, viewed from above, resembled black scorch flecks in the bottom of a huge kettle. Nils had often wondered how human beings could endure living down there. . . . He looked down the row of little houses, at the tiny front gardens enclosed with picket fences, and at the chickens and ducks, yes, even geese, poking about in them. Nils's eye followed the long stair he had just come down. Obviously there were oceans and whole continents lying between this place and the one up above, even though only a bridge separated them . . . a low house squatted on its haunches. It looked as though it had come scooting down the cliffside, heading straight for the river; and then, having hooked itself fast just in the nick of time, had remained there. He could see that the curtains in the little windows were spotlessly white.
>
> — From Ole Rolvaag's "The Boat of Longing"

In the auditorium, folks line up at the plat map and point out the spot where they lived. They shake long-forgotten hands. Mrs. Mike Gabrick Jr. of Minneapolis has her son, Robert, in tow. Robert came in from Somerset, Wis., and brought along his sons — Brad, 18, and Ross, 15. They'd come twice before, but there was no room in the auditorium. Millie Gershone said she sold 12 memberships already and now she's hawking the spring edition of "Hennepin County History," which is devoted to the Flats and one of its early Bohemian residents, a man named Francis New, born Frantisek Novy, a stonemason who wrote letters back to his homeland.

John Kovach tells a reporter that his father, Mike, a foundry worker, bought his home on the Flats for $200 in 1908. John, 75, avoided the lung disease that killed his father by working as a currency buyer for Midland Bank. "Be sure to mention all the help we kids got growing up there: the Children's Gospel Mission, the Salvation Army, University Baptist Church and Ed Curry at the Pill House." (John called later to say that we shouldn't forget how the Presbyterians at Riverside Chapel opened their swimming pool to the kids on the Flats.) When the auditorium is almost full, Lind gets up and greets the folks. She tells them how this series was to deal with four neighborhoods, but how the extra showing of Bohemian Flats has cut the series down to two. And then she starts the slide show to oohs and ahs, as the slides flash on and off the screen.

"The first squatter on the Flats was a Dane, who settled there in 1869. Subsequently, the area was called the Connemara Patch, Little Lithuania, the Danish Flats, the Cabbage Patch. After our first showing, someone said it should have been called Little Venice because of the spring floods. This show deals with the period between 1910 and the late 1920s, when the people from Czechoslovakia made up the majority of residents. Since the first showing, I've met all kinds of wonderful people who lived on the Flats, and they've given me their oral histories." She tells them how John Stanko, a retired foundry worker at American Hoist and Derrick, meets with his old buddies for breakfast once a month to reminisce about the Flats. "John says we should call the Flats 'Little Vascek,' because that's where most people came from in Czechoslovakia."

John stands up in back and takes a bow.

The slides flash on, successively showing winter, spring, summer. Early photos show a barren environment. Later, when the neighborhood's population had grown to 500 people, trees had grown up to provide shade and the city finally got around to installing two fire hydrants along Mill St.

> In 1917, George Sefcik paid $22.50 per year for the land his house squatted on at 106 Mill St. "In the event of the flooding of the premise by reason of erection of the Government Dam or Condemnation proceedings by the U.S. Government against this property then this lease shall be null and void and terminate immediately."
> — From a ground-lease contract, donated to the Hennepin County Historical Museum by George Sefcik

Several slides show the railroad bridge dominating the skyscape and the old Washington Av. Bridge, from which folks from the rest of the city gawked at the little neighborhood going about its business. "Yeah," volunteers a member of the audience. "On Saturdays, people would be on the bridge going to the football game and we'd call up, 'Hey, mister, throw down the pennies.' And they'd throw down the pennies.''

*The train ran across the river and to the University. It went right
past Northrop Auditorium. When a coal train stopped on the bridge,
three kids — named Brownie, Monkey and Hruby — climbed up the
high pilings, jumped onto a car and tossed coal over the side onto the
flats. And the neighborhood divided it up, evenly, for the winter ahead.*
— From Lind's interview with John Kovach

In the spring the floods came, and folks nod when Lind reminds them
how they had to move in with friends on the Upper Flats, about 15 feet
above river level, or climb the 79 steps that led to relatives who lived "up on
the hill," the place to go once one achieved success in the New World.
"When the floods came," Lind asks, "what did you do with your furniture?"
"We didn't have any," shouts a wag, and then folks argue about
whether the water ever actually got into the little parlors of their youth, but
agreed that it always got into the crawl spaces, where it would rattle the
Mason jars that Ma had filled for the winter from her tiny garden.

*The room she ushered [Nils] into was a veritable doll parlor. The
ceiling, distressingly low, almost touched his head. All the objects
seemed to be scaled to proportion: A cot did service for both bed and
sofa . . . the table was diminutive; and the chairs looked as though they
were never intended for grownups. But the room was as tidy and at-
tractive as human hands well could make it.*
— From "The Boat of Longing"

Lind smiles when she remembers how the original text of her show
said something about the women pounding their week's washing white in
the Mississippi. "They straightened me out on that. When they were kids,
the river was filthy, full of tar and oil."
"Yes," says John Stanko. "And raw sewage."
The show was originally scheduled to last an hour, according to Lind,
but it lasts longer every time because everyone wants two cents' worth of
the anecdotal action. "Oh, there's our house," says Paul Garay. "At 72
Cooper. And the Romad house at 74, and the Kisells' at 76 and the Medvics'
at 78."
Lind takes notes. "Oh, see here," says Lind. "An automobile. Does
anyone know whose it is?"

*Mike Bozonie's father worked as a mason and helped build the
high steps to one of the buildings at the university. He figured that the
plan was all wrong, that it wouldn't come out right. So he told the
foreman. The foreman told him to mind his own business. So Bozonie
called Devre Olson, the contractor. They checked it out and Bozonie
was right. They didn't give him money. But they gave him a huge*

Lexington touring car that was almost as big as his house. It was one of the first and one of the fanciest cars on the flats.
— From Lind's interview with Mike Bozonie

A big guy identifies it, and Lind moves on to another slide of a shady stretch of houses, pointing out that everyone had a fence to define the property lines and to keep spring-flood flotsam out of the yards.

"And to keep our ducks and geese and chickens *in*," adds someone.

(Later, Anne Michalik Yurik, sporting a big button that said "JA SOM SLOVAK DAJ MI BOSK" — "I'm Slovack, give me a kiss" — talked about the geese. "We had a neighbor whose geese would get out. They'd come right into our house and lay eggs on my mother's feather comforter. At least the eggs didn't break.")

Lind tells a story about Mrs. Krestes, who had seven cows on the Flats and delivered milk, door to door, in pails. "But when her husband delivered, he just led the cow to the doorstep and asked the housewife how much she wanted and milked the cow on the spot."

Christmas began on the evening of December 24 and dinner was not served until the stars came out. In many homes a space was set for the family dead because it was felt that they were present on special occasions. Before the dinner was eaten families partook of holy bread, brought from the church, which they dipped in honey.... As the sun was setting and before the church bells rang for the evening service, young girls who wanted to be married began to sweep the kitchen floor. When the first chime of the bell was heard, they would run outside with the sweepings and look about for a man. The name of the first man a girl saw would be the name of the man she would marry.
— From WPA-Hennepin County Historical Society book project, "Bohemian Flats"

The show ends at 3 p.m., and Lind invites everyone into the adjacent jury room for chatting, but not before Susan Melovsky Mihalko, who was born on the Flats 84 years ago, tells how she operated a grocery, what things were like. And not before a woman gets up and says, "We had a good time down there, didn't we?"

Back out under the gleaming towers, people make their way to the parking lots where there's not a Lexington touring car in sight. Minneapolis had come a long way since the days when these people, as kids, didn't know they were poor, since the Minneapolis Tribune editorial that appeared in 1931 after the original Bohemian Flats were no more, read:

Thousands of Minneapolis residents will regret the passing of Bohemian Flats.... There humble people living in humble homes seemed to have created a little world of their own, quite detached from the city's general atmosphere. There a police officer was seldom summoned. There old-fashioned church bells called the people to worship in tiny churches. There were picket fences with little gates giving into tiny yards, flower boxes in windows; usually careful attention was given to keeping neat and clean every inch of home-owner's land. There lived a people who contributed to the American melting pot of many nations. Over their heads roared the traffic of a busy city quite unheeded and apart from their scheme of life which seemed to radiate a contentment and tranquility most charming.

—D.W.

Rick Roseberry

Small-town Gumshoe

Wadena, Minnesota
1982

I shook the rain from my trench coat and walked into the Wadena Post Office. I was looking for the town's private eye. It was about 11 o'clock in the morning. The sky was gray. So was the post office.

A clerk behind the counter looked up. "Rick Roseberry?" I asked. Probably an alias, I said to myself. The clerk poked a thumb toward the back. Roseberry was sitting on the steps, waiting for me. He was pretending to watch Wadena school kids take a tour of the place.

"Peg Meier?" he asked. I nodded. We shook hands. His handshake was firm, but he wasn't one of those bozos who like to break a lady's hand. I respected him for that.

Roseberry led me into the courthouse basement. It was a big room, painted government-green, with two tables and some chairs the only furniture. He sat me down at the big table and walked over to the coffeepot on the smaller one. He poured us each a cup of mud, black. The mug he gave me was plain. His had an American eagle and the word "Rich" on it. Rich, eh? Something was out of whack. He had said his name was Rick.

He asked what I was after. I said a story for the newspaper about what it's like to be a private detective in a small Minnesota town. He said OK, but I couldn't use his real name or the fact that he works part-time for the post office. The words hit me like a pile driver to the solar plexus. I said no deal. Either we tell the suckers who read this paper everything or we tell them nothing.

He didn't say a word. He drank his java. I watched the dimple in his chin. A good, solid dimple. Not one of those offensive, tiddly dents. He was wearing a black shirt, the collar arranged real neat over his black herringbone jacket. I noticed he wore shoes. Clever, I thought.

Finally he spoke. He said he'd have to make a phone call before he could decide if he would talk to me. OK, I said evenly, get on the horn. He got up and left the room, leaving me behind to take a gander at the Pioneer Journal shopper. I read the whole thing before he got back. He must have been gone 10, 15 minutes. I wondered if the room was bugged.

"OK," he said as he came back into the room. "Let's give it a try." He didn't explain the phone call; I didn't ask.

He pulled a cigarette from his deck of butts, tapped it a few times and lit up. I shot him some questions, starting with the name. He said Rick Roseberry was his real name. People like to make it Rosenberry or Raspberry, but it was Roseberry.

He said he was born in Laurel, Miss., and had wandered around the country some. He took two years of college in California, then worked for a police force in Los Angeles County, in the detective division. He said, "See, in L.A., I was involved in every kind of crime." He meant crime detection, I figured. "We handled every kind of crime on the books, except illegal transportation of Japanese women into the United States." He wasn't joshing. Said that really was a criminal offense. Outdated, but on the books.

He had a family, a wife and three kids, and life in the big city got hard: "I got tired of the rat race, the dog-eat-dog environment. I had to get out." Roseberry became police chief in Oslo, Minn., 25 miles north of Grand Forks. His wife is from Grand Forks. They stayed in Oslo two years, then he took a job as deputy sheriff in Minnesota's Marshall County.

In 1979, he came to Wadena to be a sergeant in the police department. He worked the graveyard shift, he told me as he played with his cigarette in the ashtray. The job didn't go so hot. He got only one weekend off in five. Nothing was going on in town. "Open bottle, DWIs, barking dogs. It got old real quick. Once you get a taste of the big-city crime, it's hard to get excited about barking dogs."

As a reporter for a big-city daily, I knew he wasn't just whistling Dixie.

He quit the job, he told me. He got another one as a part-time postal clerk (he beat out about 50 guys who were after the job; times are hard) and he began his private-eye biz.

I asked how he could make a living as a private eye in Wadena, population less than 5,000.

He can't, he said, looking me straight in the eye. I believed him.

Most of his work comes from outside Wadena County. He said he works all over the state, from Duluth to Owatonna, from Moorhead to East Grand Forks. The closest other private eye he knows of is in St. Cloud. Lawyers hire Roseberry to investigate in criminal and civil cases, he said.

Like what?

"Surveillance," he said, dragging off another cigarette.

Surveillance?

"Yeh."

He told me later that jealous women have hired him to track their husbands. He also interrogates prospective witnesses and delivers confidential legal papers for law firms.

"Murders? You investigate murders?" I asked him, point-blank.

"Not here. Assault with a deadly weapon, yes. Murder, no."

I asked if he uses fake names and disguises. He said he does. He sometimes wears glasses, carries a cane, grays his hair. When? When does he do that? When he's following a person and the person may be getting wise, he said. "You might sit next to the subject you're following and if it happens too many times a day . . . " He didn't finish the sentence. I caught the drift.

He said he makes about half his income from his J & R Private Detective Agency (J is for his wife, Judy; R is for Rick. Judy answers the phone.) Besides working for the post office about 25 hours a week, he makes a few bucks teaching karate in Wadena two nights a week.

He wants to stay, he said. "A big city is nice, but not for a married man with children. If I was single and just had myself to look after, I'd like to go back to L.A. You can't beat a small community for raising a family. I enjoy the pace here."

I couldn't stop him on the topic. He kept going, building up steam. "Lakes are only a matter of a 15- to 30-minute drive. I like to fish with my boys. I like the fact that the crime rate is low. We don't have that noise, the jet noise, the traffic. Once in a while you hear an ambulance siren. That's about it. Helps the inner tranquility."

If he'd have his druthers, he'd work full-time as a private investigator. "It's a fascinating life, challenging," he said. "In order to be good at it, you need confidence in yourself. You need to be a good salesman and a good actor."

I checked the clock. It was getting late. I said, "Take it easy, kid." He gave me a grin and wished me well. I got up my courage and asked about the name on his mug. Well, I asked, which is it? Rich or Rick? Rick, he said, contritely. His wife bought him the mug and couldn't find one that said Rick, so she settled for Rich. That's the whole story, he swore. For some reason, I figured he was shooting straight.

That was about all I was going to get from him. I stood up and buttoned my coat. Together we walked the block to the Uptown Cafe. He had coffee; I had chicken soup. We wished each other luck.

Nice guy, Roseberry. I wondered if I'll recognize him if I see him again.
—P.M.

Rick Roseberry skipped town. It was tough, but we managed to track him down in East Grand Forks, Minn., where he runs the Double-RR Bail Bonding and Private Detective Agency. The J for Judy in the old J&R name got left behind in Wadena. They're divorced.

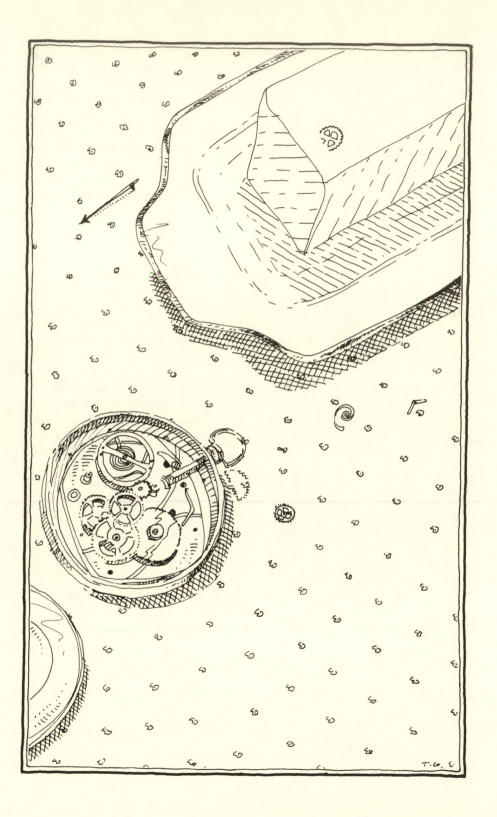

Frank Nicolay
Dean of Clock Repair

Minneapolis, Minnesota
1983

THE JEWELERS EXCHANGE BUILDING at 627 1st Av. N. is a solid, old-fashioned building. It's the sort of place where you pass up the spiffy elevator to walk up marble steps, to all six floors, gliding your hand along a shiny wooden railing as sturdy as the day the building opened in 1914.

And when you reach its fifth floor, you'll find a solid, old-fashioned man who has been working at the same location 63 years. Some folks around town call Frank Nicolay the best clock repairman in the business; Bloomington antique clock dealer Irv Moss calls him "the Dean."

A year ago, Neighbors ran a story on Al Uglum, a south Minneapolis clock restorer who works out of his basement. The next week, Frank Nicolay called the paper and asked why no one ever wrote about the Jewelers Exchange. Nicolay said that he's been there for nigh onto two-thirds of a century, that he'd seen good times and bad, that there was a real story in the building where so many jewelers and watchmakers have plied their trade.

Why not, indeed? Neighbors made its way past the new Faegre's and the new Loon, then past old Jim Gianoulis's barbershop in the lobby of the Exchange, then climbed the stairs, noting signs for jewelry outfits like Lundquist Jewelry Co., Martin Jewelry, Joseph Lukic Co. Neighbors thought it would get some history of the building from its oldest resident and then beat it.

Neighbors had another think coming.

Frank Nicolay, 79, sat in a high-ceilinged room amid a riot of brass clock movements, old electric Westclox kitchen clocks, 400-day anniversary clocks under their glass domes. With a tick-tick here, a gong-gong there, everywhere a chime-chime, here and there a ping-ping, the interview began. Nicolay sat at his work table, a physician in brass, peering through his eye loupe into the guts of a German chime clock. Nicolay has a big face topped with wispy white hair. His blue slacks had a sharp crease, his blue shirt was crisply pressed and his blue tie was choked up around a neck showing the folds of age.

"I remember my first venture into this business," he said, turning a screw that caused delicate strike and chime governors to spin almost invisibly. "I was just a little kid and I took a $1 watch apart at the kitchen table. When the mainspring blew, little parts flew all over the room. One part landed in the butter. I got a swat that sent me six feet."

The swat came from his father, Peter Nicolay, a German immigrant who settled his family in north Minneapolis and went to work as a sheet metal worker. After Frank made it through his second year at North High, he heard that George Kelly and Harold Scharf were opening a clock- and watch-repair business in the new Jewelers Exchange and needed an apprentice. "They asked if I wanted it. What does a starving kid say to that? Of course I wanted it. So I went to work as an all-around flunky for the astounding salary of 12 dollars a week. A lot of people nowadays would laugh at my income, then and now. But I've done all right. Nowadays, it's what you earn that's important. To me, that was the last requisite. I wanted to know what I could learn. George and Harold were darned good teachers."

Tiny washers, nuts and springs slid out of the clock, drifted onto the table as Nicolay recalled 1920, when he'd hop the streetcar to deliver work to the carriage trade on St. Paul's Summit Av. and to Minneapolis's lake district. "But the upper crust doesn't come down here anymore. Guess they're afraid of the area. One woman wanted me to accompany her down on the elevator. And if you live long enough, they all forget you." Nicolay admitted that he was robbed once. While he was working, someone sneaked into his back room and stole $500 worth of repaired watches. "You know, when you're bearing down on your work, it isn't always easy to hear a footpad."

"Footpad." That's the kind of word that Frank Nicolay loves to use.

But he doesn't worry much about footpads and other assorted hooligans who may lie in wait in downtown Minneapolis. He drives in from Crystal five days a week and works about seven hours a day, even though the carriage trade doesn't show up as regularly as it used to.

The phone rang and Nicolay grumped his way through a conversation, then hung up. "That was a fellow who wants me to check over his grandfather clock. Lives in a fancy apartment on the Mall. I thought I'd lost him through neglect. But he said, no, you worked on the clock 12 years ago and you're the only man I want to work on it. That makes you feel sort of good."

He said business is slow from time to time and that makes him wonder if it's worth it to drive in. "And then all of a sudden, it'll pick up. People will rediscover me. They'll call and say, 'Are *you* still there?' I'll say, 'Yes.' They'll say, 'Oh, I didn't think you'd still be there at this late date.' And then I'll say, 'Just try me.'"

Nicolay worked on the chime clock without even looking into it and told how he caught onto the repair business and finally became a partner. "We split the rent three ways, 12 dollars apiece." Today he pays $160 per month for two sizable rooms. "It's all I want to pay. But this is a good building." He looks at the open window fronting on 1st Av. "When they turn the heat on, it's bountiful."

"Bountiful." Another word that comes from the word hoard of Nicolay's fertile brain.

Eventually, Nicolay had the business all to himself as the other companies in the building came and left and were replaced by new jewelers. "A lot of people in this building don't even know me. I guess the old get older and the young get new ideas." Nicolay is perfectly happy with older ideas. "I used to sell new clocks. But I don't anymore. I don't like the quality of the new stuff, and I'm not so hungry I have to sell it." He picked up a substantial brass movement and pointed inside at a brown doodad. "See that? For 3 cents more they could have used brass. But I guess it's nylon. . . . You take Seth Thomas. They used to make great clocks. But you know their motto."

Not really, Frank.

"It's 'America's finest *name* in clocks.' Notice they don't say anything about finest *clocks*."

Frank Nicolay was on a roll. "I don't blame people for buying cheap throwaway watches these days. Years ago, the big jewelry stores in town preyed on poor young girls, clerks maybe making $15 a week. The girl who worked at Kresge's would bring in her watch to the big store. There was always the guy who told her what was wrong. He was always a nervous type. He'd put in his loupe, look at the watch and start talking and writing stuff down. He'd do an entire *litany* of what could be wrong. Any honest jeweler would have just said I'll clean it and adjust it and you can have it next week. But no. He'd say come back and pick it up in three months because he knew it would take her that long to save up the money to pay for the repairs. So when the [throwaway] watches came along, I don't blame people for buying them."

Nicolay said he likes to charge people what he figures they can afford to pay. "I'll give poor people the work as long as I'm eating. I take pleasure in a job well done. Of course, I'm not averse to getting paid once in a while." He and Mabel, his wife of 42 years, "a local gal," are comfortably fixed as long as a long illness doesn't assault either. "Medical charges are ridiculous. I believe it's the biggest problem facing the country today. For years I traded with this pharmacy in our neighborhood. The price for my heart medicine kept going up. So I called around to other pharmacies and found out I was right. I called the guy. I told him I'd traded with him for years, but now I was going somewhere else. I told him it was all right to make a fair profit, but he was gouging. I wanted him to know that."

He carefully placed the German chime movement into an ultrasonic transistorized cleaning unit, his concession to technology, and recalled the days when movements were cleaned with potassium cyanide. "I breathed it for years and survived. I hope I'm favored with being able to keep on with my work. You know, it takes *strength* to loosen these tiny screws. It's amazing."

When Nicolay isn't loosening screws, he's gardening, dining out with

Mabel, visiting relatives. Not long ago, he flew to Oregon to visit a grandson. "It was my first flight. When I found out you can't get hurt flying, I decided to. You can get killed, but you can't get hurt. I like that."

Police sirens wailed down on the street. That, Nicolay figures, has scared off some of his fancy customers. "Are you too holy to listen to an Irish joke? Well, Pat and Mike come from Ireland to New York City. They're standing on the street when two squad cars go by, sirens blasting. Mike says to Pat, 'Pat, Pat, they're moving Hell and two loads have already gone by.' "

Moving. Will Nicolay ever move out of the old Jewelers Exchange? "A while back, two young fellows came in with clipboards and they asked me all kinds of questions about how much it would cost me to relocate my business. I told them the next time I relocate, it's going to be in a really undesirable spot. I'm going to retire on a feet-first basis."

Then Neighbors left the building with lots of notes about Nicolay and a few about the Jewelers Exchange. Back at the office, an almost-fresh copy of the Minneapolis Star and Tribune reported that: "Some of the major property owners on 1st Av. N. in Butler Square have sent a letter to Alice Rainville, city council president, calling the city's attention to 'the crying need for immediate action in the Block E and D sections west of Hennepin Av., specifically from 5th St. through 7th St.' The group specifically recommended that the city 'take immediate steps to condemn and clear the Block E section [between 6th and 7th Sts.] of present buildings and utilize the land for temporary parking.' "

Tom O'Meara has owned the Jewelry Exchange for seven years. He said in a later telephone conversation that he's talked to city planners and his building isn't going down for a good long while, that the Jewelers Exchange tradition is still very much alive. Sixty percent of the building is still occupied by jewelry-related businesses. So Frank Nicolay won't have to worry for the present.

That should please Nicolay, the man who gave new meaning to the word "crotchety," the man who doesn't know what "temporary parking" means.

— D.W.

Detour on Hwy. 12

Return to Rural America

Highway 12, Western Wisconsin
1983

PART I, **The Road Not Taken:** Gloom pervaded the little dining room in Eau Claire, Wis. The year was 1940 and Uncle Floyd Amundson, the host, said, "Kid, if you'll stop playing with your food and if you'll clean up your spinach, I'll take you to The Cities and show you the Christmas toy display at Dayton's." Within seconds, the player with food licked his platter clean and asked for a second helping of spinach. But Uncle Floyd never kept his Dayton's promise. Normally, Uncle Floyd was a wonderful fellow, but apparently the mere prospect of making the trip was more than his usually infinite patience could bear.

See, if you lived in Eau Claire, Wis., there was only one way to drive to "The Cities." That was along Hwy. 12, which compared favorably to a cowpath, but not to today's Interstate Hwy. 94. The player with food never did make it to The Cities until he was at college in the '50s. And then it was still a long, tedious process whenever he wanted to partake of such cultural offerings as the Aquatennial, the Ice Follies, the Alvin burlesque theater, Excelsior Amusement Park or when, in rags, he had to refurbish his wardrobe at Nate's on Washington Av.

Part II, The Road Taken: So he'd rise early, polish up the St. Christopher medal on the visor of his roommate's '41 Buick, then slide into the procession of bumper-to-bumper Macks and Autocars and Internationals out of Chicago, slouching toward The Cities on that narrow concrete ribbon called "12." By the time he got to Elk Mound, Wis., he wondered if he'd make it to all those fabulous bargains before Nate closed his doors in the evening.

But the towns eventually slid by — Menomonie, Knapp, Wilson, Hersey, Baldwin, Hammond, Roberts, Hudson, then across the river to Mecca, The Cities. After graduation, he remembered those tedious trips to the fleshpots of Minneapolis with affection, but was happy for I-94 and the effortless trips brought him by progress, even though it came after he graduated in 1958 and moved out of the region.

Part III, On The Road Again: Last May the Wisconsin Division of Highways started tearing up I-94 between Menomonie and Hwy. 128. Westbound traffic was once again routed onto good old 12. On Aug. 5, he and photographer Art Hager traveled the 16-mile stretch, a strip out of his past, where soybeans grow right up to the roadside; where cows gaze out, close enough to slobber on your fenders if you stop; where old roadhouses of his youth still beckon with signs proclaiming Pabst and Blatz; where you can almost read the tombstones in cemeteries speckled with arbor vitae.

The trip turned out to be fun and exciting, if bumper-to-bumper traffic threading its way through the eye of a needle can be judged fun and exciting. Or if a Volvo Turbo 6 tractor-trailer rig trying to crawl up the tailpipe of the Chevy you're riding in can be judged fun and exciting.

One fellow who thinks the five-month detour is fun and exciting is Greg Corrigan, 37. He and his sister, Monica Bauer, bought Knapp's Knapp House two years ago. This comfortable spot has been feeding and watering locals and travelers since 1928. It got started by dispensing doughnuts and gasoline. But for years it's had a full menu, a pleasant barroom and Sunday buffets that offer more than 100 items, ranging from Amsterdam onions to kumquats. Corrigan said that summer is traditionally the Knapp House's slowest time, but not this year. "July was great. We've added breakfasts to our menu. We went from serving 20 pounds of hamburger at lunch every week to 60 or 70 pounds. This summer we doubled our beer sales. Do you know that people come all the way from Illinois to go tubing on the Apple River? And they stop here for carryout beer."

Corrigan believes most travelers don't mind the detour because it's relatively short. "I think people welcome the chance to see a small town close up and to get out close to nature and smell the roses." (In spots you can also smell the cow manure, which smells pretty good after days in the office.) "And some people are pleasantly surprised to come into our place and see that it's a modern restaurant with the same things city restaurants have. Their faces seem to say, 'By golly, Knapp is in the 20th century.' "

Possibly one tourist wouldn't agree that Knapp, population 419, has reached the heights to which Western civilization is capable. "She came in and asked where the McDonald's was in town. Another woman had apparently never been off a freeway. She told my wife, Jackie, that she couldn't believe how big those black and white cows were close up."

Noon rolled around and cars began pulling into the parking lot bearing Minnesota, Illinois, Ontario, Missouri and Texas license plates. Art and Jerry Lou DeBernardi of Foley, Minn., were returning home from a vacation in Door County, Wis., and stopped for the soup and sandwich special. Jerry Lou said, "It's kind of nice in a way, to get off the freeway," and Art added, "Driving freeways is all right if you want to make time. But I still say I like to go the old way, drive through the towns. I like to stop in cafes and hear the people talk."

More people made their way into the big dining room. An older man cloaked in seersucker and draped in flowing white locks probably wasn't a

Dunn County farmer. Tom Hitschell and Tom Bear of St. Louis hunkered down to a home-cooked meal. They were on their way to a convention of the American Theatre Association in Minneapolis. Hitschell, a theater professor, said "This is beautiful country. Even with this detour, it's nice. I don't mind it at all."

Out in the barroom, longtime employee Florence Hyatt mixed drinks and told the nostalgia tripper that he should call on Mike Carlin to see the special detour T-shirts Carlin had printed up for the occasion. "They're really neat. I know I'm going to buy one." Sure enough, Carlin was dispensing more gas than usual this summer at his Union 76 station. And T-shirts, too. He said he'd sold about 75 of them to locals and workers from the I-94 construction crew.

A smoky mist hung along the dark green hillsides that shimmered in the blistering heat. Hay cured in windrows along the roadside, and cars sped along, almost bumper to bumper. Not many folks tried to pass and most slowed a bit at a green sign that said "Wilson, Pop. 155," then sped up when they realized the Wilson loop was several blocks off to the right of Hwy. 12. It was time for a bag of popcorn, so Hager pulled off 12 and drove to the very heart of Wilson, a sleepy town whose edges were curling up under the sun. Wilson has five bars — Ken and Dee's, the Wilson Nite Club, the Poplar, the Round Oak Inn and the Legion club. One for every 31 men, women and children in town.

Dee and Ken Kongshaug can't complain about business, they said, but the detour has nothing to do with it. They've owned their little bar for 22 years and neighbors are pretty good about patronizing them. "The detour doesn't give us any business," said Dee. "It's a pain in the . . . ah, don't quote me on that." Apparently the detour doesn't hurt Dee's and Ken's business. But it's hard this summer for the local elderly to negotiate getting on and off Hwy. 12, which they've treated as their personal driveway since I-94 came through a quarter-century ago. "One good thing," said Dee. "Accidents aren't as bad as they predicted. There've been very few."

A competitor, Jim Reich of the Wilson Nite Club, agreed. He said he heard that the highway department predicted 40 deaths during the detour. "But there've hardly been any." He also said the detour hurts his tavern-supper club business. "I'm waiting for the detour to be over with. The tourists are going too fast to stop. And people around here don't like to compete with the traffic. There are more cops on duty now, and that's another reason for them to stay home." Dick Wendt of the Wisconsin Division of Highways said later he couldn't figure out how the 40-deaths rumor got started. "Certainly not from our office. Redoing a stretch of road like that wouldn't be worth even *one* death." He also said the rerouting onto Hwy. 12 was made because history has shown it's better to use a highway that was built as a two-laner rather than taking a one-way road on a freeway like I-94 and making it one lane each way. "When someone gets on a road like 12, they're psychologically prepared to travel in one lane." Reich added that there have been accidents despite precautions by his agency.

"But from what the police say, the detour is working better than they anticipated."

Reich's wish for the detour's termination will be fulfilled Oct. 15, when paving on the I-94 westbound roadbed is supposed to be completed. But the detour will be opened again next May when work begins on the eastbound lanes. Greg Corrigan said that some of his repeat tourist customers say they just stay on Hwy. 12 through Baldwin and until they have to join the four-lane rat race beyond Hudson. But Neighbors had lingered too long on the nostalgic ribbon and had to leave the rustic paradise for the speed and efficiency of I-94 as soon as possible.

Turning off the primrose path of dalliance onto Hwy. 128, they ran into trouble in paradise. A travel trailer had upended, pulling up the pickup that pulled it, pulling down an electric line at roadside. Eighteen-wheelers stacked up behind the tangled mess as volunteers directed traffic. Margaret and Marvel Lee of Columbus, Wis., had been heading for a Good Sam Club camping bash in Winnipeg when Lee's trailer hit some grooves in the asphalt and he lost control, flipping the whole works halfway out into the road.

A fine kettle of asphalt, the trailer ruined and all! But fellow campers Margie Bean and Bea Schomburg of Madison, Wis., assured the Lees they'd stick by them until all but the asphalt grooves were ironed out. "We're sure," said Margie, "they'll be able to bunk with someone once we get to Winnipeg."

Apparently, traveling 16 miles close up to rural America, close up to those cows, makes people more neighborly than usual.

—D.W.

Greg Bodin
A Strong Arm, a Soothing Voice

Robbinsdale, Minnesota
1982

W HEN HE was a seminary student, Greg Bodin was assigned to work as a hospital chaplain. He didn't much care for hospitals, especially their smell, and he found himself hoping for an easy load.

"What I wanted was to work on the floor with the patients having tonsillectomies, and we'd sit around and eat ice cream and everyone would go home in three days," Bodin said.

Of course, it didn't turn out that way. On his first Friday night at North Memorial Medical Center in Robbinsdale, four people hurt in a car crash were brought to the emergency room; two died and two were taken to the intensive-care unit. Before he had time to catch his breath, he was called to the bedside of a man having a heart attack. The man died. Then Bodin's beeper went off, and he was called to baptize a dying newborn.

Instead of going to the nursery, he ran in the other direction — to the men's room. He sat on a toilet, teary-eyed and exhausted. "What do I say to these people?" he asked himself. He wondered if he could spend a lifetime hiding out in the hospital bathroom. He questioned whether he was fit to be a pastor.

He began to pray: "Lord, if You want me to go to the family of that dying baby, You've got to give me strength. I don't think I can do it."

He did it.

Recalling that night, Bodin says now, "I don't know how many people have great spiritual experiences in the bathroom, but I did. It probably was the best thing that ever happened to me. I was at the end of my own strength, and I gave up trying to do it myself."

∽

If you're ever near an emergency scene in the Twin Cities, look around for Bodin. At 6-foot-7, he's easy to spot. "He's the big, hairy one over there" is the way people tend to identify him.

He's at fires because he's chaplain to the Minneapolis Fire Department.

He's at shootouts and suicide attempts and he makes death notifications because he's chaplain to suburban police departments in Hennepin County. He coordinates about 20 pastors who serve as volunteer chaplains because he heads the Emergency Chaplaincy Corps. He rides ambulances and he holds patients' hands in the emergency room because he's a chaplain at North Memorial hospital. His full-time job is at the hospital ($17,000 a year); the other jobs are volunteer. All are nondenominational.

Most of his work is listening, not praying. He's been in situations where he doesn't even mention God.

"I listen for clues, subtle or direct," he said. "If someone says, 'Hey, I don't believe in God,' then I'll say, 'That's fine. I want to be here with you and be helpful and supportive, if you want.'

"A crisis situation is not a time to push religion down someone's throat. These are vulnerable and hurting people. I'm entering people's lives when they're really in pain."

Some of his work is with people in physical pain. More is with people in emotional pain. Even at the hospital, he ministers to relatives and friends as much as to patients. He doesn't pretend to be a social worker or psychologist, but he's had training in both fields and uses them extensively.

"It's not just all God talk."

∼

Counsel a fireman who is depressed over marital problems. Inform a family that their young son, who has cancer, has just committed suicide. Visit a man in intensive care who had open-heart surgery. Spend some time with a woman who lost her husband to a stroke several days ago. Refer a rape victim to a counseling group. Hang around the emergency room because accident victims are on their way. Hear a man who lost his house in a fire say he's grateful that no one was killed but he's upset that he has lost his "possessions and photos and dreams." Help calm a woman whose husband is on the living-room couch while paramedics work to save his life.

Not a happy kind of job, most of us would think.

Bodin isn't sure how long he can stay with it. A clue is that the two men who had the North Memorial chaplain's job before him lasted three years each before they went on to other things. At 28 he's younger than they were, but he's not sure youth provides staying power.

He said, "Right now I love my job. If I ever get to the point where I didn't feel for these people anymore, then it's time to leave."

It would also be time to leave if he feels too much. There's such a thing as too much sensitivity, he said. People don't want to be pitied; they want to be heard. They don't want a bawling minister; they want a strong arm and a soothing voice.

He's learned to try not to make assumptions: "I don't know what they'll need from me. Or even *if* they'll need me." One of his biggest surprises was from the mother of a young man who had committed suicide. The mother was completely unemotional when Bodin appeared at her door to give her the bad news. She calmly told him, "Well, he's been trying to do it for years, and he's finally done it."

Another time he underestimated the immediate reaction. He was with a young father who lost two children in a fire. The distraught man grabbed Bodin by the shirt. Bodin put an arm around him and got him off to a private place in a neighbor's apartment. In a rage, the father picked up a table and flung it across the room. He pounded the walls. He lunged for Bodin. This was a time when Bodin's size helped. He put his arms around the man, squeezed him tightly and held on until the man's anger turned to grief. He sobbed in Bodin's arms.

As much as Bodin deals with people in shock, he works with them later when they're mourning. He makes it a point to check in with people several weeks after their tragedy.

"Sometimes if I can stick with families long enough," he said, "I can see the good parts of life." For instance, he's still friends with the parents of the baby who died his first night at the hospital. He is close to the family of a little boy from Starbuck, Minn., who had his arm bitten off by a bear. Bodin said, "I spent the evening with his father, still in his farm clothes and covered with his own son's blood. That kind of experience can bond people together."

⌒

When he started as a hospital chaplain, he wasn't good at being able to leave his job behind him. "I'd carry the heavy weight around with me. Their experiences brought so much pain to me, too. I sometimes would try to think of myself as the Wounded Healer, or Super Chaplain."

He forced himself to learn to take half a day off here and there, to go home and walk the dog ("Snuggles"), to go running or to play softball when he thinks he's going to burst, to see a silly movie like Bill Murray's "Caddyshack" rather than "Elephant Man."

In order to remember that ministry includes such happy occasions as marriages and baptisms, he is an associate pastor of Trinity Covenant Church in Crystal. He said, "When working with a lot of darkness, it helps to be with laughter."

Last Sunday the pastor and many men from the church were on a fishing retreat, and Bodin preached to the left-behinds on the theme of "Fishers of Men." He told the congregation, "If a fisherman makes too much noise, he scares the fish away. If a Christian is witnessing too loud, you scare people away." He also said, "We don't need to be fast talkers; we need to be good listeners."

⌒

Bodin and his wife, Cindy, have gone through two grievings of their own.

A year ago March, she miscarried at 3½ months. They didn't want their loss to be impersonal, so they named the child Adam. This spring her second pregnancy was going well, they thought, and the baby was due in April. In March the doctor thought she might be carrying twins and did an ultrasound scan. Not twins. And something was wrong. Doctors told the Bodins the baby couldn't live. "We went from the thought of two babies to one to none in half an hour," he said. The baby girl was born dead March 3.

Bodin said, "They left us alone with her for half an hour. We just looked at her and held her. She had cute little black curls, and long legs and big feet like her dad. We named her April Joy because she was supposed to be our April Joy."

Their pastor asked Bodin if he wanted to say something at her funeral. "No," he said. "Today I'm not a minister; I'm a grieving father."

He had done a lot of reading and counseling about grief, but he surprised himself with the depth of his own. His sobbing surprised him. Maybe the death of his babies had a purpose, he said. Maybe his pain can be converted to help for others.

The Bodins have signed up for adoption with Lutheran Social Services. "That gives us hope for the children we want, and we may try again ourselves," he said. "Meanwhile, we look forward to seeing April and Adam again some day."

∾

A 29-year-old man was injured in a motorcycle accident and died in the emergency room less than half an hour later. It was up to Greg Bodin to go to the house of the man's girlfriend and tell her.

"This doesn't get any easier," he said afterward.

Often he's confronted with people in emergencies who are trying to be brave. There's too much of the big-boys-don't-cry attitude in our lives, he said. And too much Christians-aren't-supposed-to-grieve. "That's a bunch of baloney," Bodin said, using one of his strongest negative words. "Saint Paul said, 'Don't grieve like those who have no hope.' He didn't say, 'Don't grieve.' "

Sometimes someone will ask him, "Can you pray for him?" Bodin responds, "I'd like to. Why don't you tell me a little bit about him." Not only is the prayer more personal, but it helps the survivor's grieving process. "Some ways to grieve are better than others," he said. "I try to help their grieving go in a useful direction."

He also tries to keep this in mind: "Even Christ didn't heal everyone. I have to remember to say, 'Lord , I'll leave the rest to You.' "

—P.M.

Greg Bodin did not tire of his chaplain's job: "I'm still loving the people and the things I'm doing." Good news: His wife gave birth to a healthy baby boy, Karl Gregory Bodin, on May 20, 1983, and they were expecting another child in 1985.

Lanesboro
Such a Pretty, Friendly Town

Lanesboro, Minnesota
1983

JUNE 8, 1983
Dear Ruth:
Just a note to tell you I've decided we should change our vacation plans for the summer. Let's forget about the trip to Europe. Let's go to Lanesboro instead. Let's forsake the cruise on the Rhine for a paddle down the Root. Let's cancel our reservations at Hotel du Turenne on the Ile de la Cite. Let's pitch our tent in Lanesboro's Sylvan Park, where there's a little bandshell featuring entertainment every summer weekend. Let's forsake French National Railways and take a walk along the abandoned bed of the Milwaukee Road.

Hold on now, don't get your dander up. I realize you've been looking forward to Rome and Venice and Paris. I realize we honeymooned in those glamorous spots just 13 years ago this summer. But after three days in Lanesboro I've gotta get back there soon, and I want you to come along.

I made the trip early Monday morning, driving in from Winona on Hwy. 43. Holsteins grazed on the lush green hillsides, hillsides greener than Ireland's. Yellow limestone quarries punctuated that green every few miles, as did white mailboxes, like Sven Sveen's a few miles out of town. I swooped up and down the undulating highway, catching a glimpse every few miles of the beautiful Root River winding its way toward Rushford. Willows hung over blue-green waters, which rested in wide, placid pools before turning corners into swift rapids. I took a quick right and descended into the town where the first business opened up in 1868.

The weather was perfect, Ruth, and at 8 a.m. the sun was already beating down on the brick and stone buildings, some ornate, some austere, along the main drag. I guess the town never got around to modernizing its storefronts, many of them put up in the 1890s. Not much aluminum siding and ugly plastic on Parkway. Nor did I get the impression that the well-kept buildings have undergone an expensive restoration project that turns some towns we know into instant Disneylands. I thought to myself, here's a town that goes about its business, doing the essential things it takes to stay alive, taking its beauty for granted. No big deal.

The Champs Elysees is fine, Ruth. But the 50-year-old White Front Cafe, operated for the past 13 years by Art and Olive Haugen, has its charms too. I stopped by for scrambled eggs, under the shadow of a tall bluff at the end of Parkway, the main drag. The eggs came moist without my asking. And coffee was 27 cents, unlimited refills. Waitress Verna Berg said it was "a good leader." Glancing at the inexpensive menu items, I wondered where the followers were.

Farmers Jim Ostrem and Dewey Hungerholt breakfast most mornings at the White Front. Jim told me that he'd retired his corn acreage under the PIK program and for silage had planted 6½ acres of popcorn, which the government allows. Jim and Dewey contemplated this year's silage heating up and popping the roof off Jim's silo. At another table, old-timers Joe Enright, Alvin Peterson, Ed Gatzlaff and Oscar Olson took their morning coffee. Enright, an Irishman, retired as manager of the municipal liquor store and now sells gravestones. Why else would an Irishman hang around with old guys? Years ago, they said, all but one of the farmers on Irish Ridge were Irish. Just one Norwegian. "But he finally went into the woods and hung himself, that's no lie," said Oscar Olson, who also told me he got a conservation award for strip cropping before he retired. "You sure, Oscar, that you don't mean strip-teasing?" asked Enright.

Ruth, my love, how can you beat conversations like that?

And where in Paris can you buy fresh Copenhagen and Hall's Mentho-Lyptus cough drops or get a real malted mixed on an old Hamilton Beach three-beater? At noon, I stopped by for lunch and ate the best Swiss steak since Mom and Dad closed their restaurant. You want something a bit more chic? Of an evening, we could cross the street and sup at Lanesboro's answer to trendy — the Bent Elbow, run by Mary Pierce. Regional artists hang out there; it has lots of weathered wood and tile, a fireplace, hanging plants and a salad bar.

I intended walking off the calories on Monday afternoon, taking the state trail across the downtown railroad bridge. The Milwaukee Road bed runs along the Root and before I knew it I was at the stone dam built a century ago by the pioneers. The green water rushes over the dam's moss-covered lip, turns white in the fury below. Two kids were down fishing in the pools beyond. I reclined on a concrete pier and took the sun for an hour or so, listening to the rush of the water, wondering what I ever saw in the Cote d'Azur, with those oil tankers lurking half a mile out from its stony beaches.

I roused myself and hit the trail again, walking past dense underbrush sparked by wild geraniums, pink and fragile. Shards of bluff rock bestrewed the trail, and the spicy odor of undergrowth stung my nostrils. The rush of the dam receded in the distance, but I could hear a dog bark in town. Soon I came to a marsh that had tried last year to be a cornfield. I clambered up a steep bank and found myself on Oxcart Rd., leading to state Sen. Duane

Benson's farm. When Benson was elected, folks said there'd probably be a four-lane highway built to his stock farm. It never happened, and the hair-pin curves are such that you sometimes feel as if you're walking in tight circles. (So much for the trip from Berchtesgaden up to Hitler's hideaway.) How Benson hauls his wide-beamed Angus steers out of there to market is a mystery to me.

I realize, Ruth, that we can't just hike a vacation away. Last March, Don Chaapel finished restoring the town fire hall built in 1886. Now it's called The Outpost, which is well-stocked with rental equipment and locally made crafts and antiques for sale. Manager Jo Miller told me The Outpost will provide instruction in rock climbing, guide service and will rent us canoes, inner tubes, bicycles, tennis rackets. In winter it sells and rents skis and snowshoes for gliding or tromping along the Milwaukee Road trail. It will also offer programs in wilderness survival technique according to demand. It's first-come, first-served for equipment, unless we call in advance. The Outpost is open from 8 to noon at its bait shop on the Root, 12:30 to 5 p.m. at the downtown store, Mondays through Fridays. On Saturdays it's open from 10 a.m. to 7 p.m. and on Sundays from 11 a.m. to 5 p.m. If we want to call, the number is (507) 467-2158.

On Tuesday, Arland Elstad, 66, gave me a tour of the Lanesboro golf course, built in 1927 after being designed by Willie Kidd, the Scotsman who served as club pro for many years at Interlachen Country Club in Edina. Arland is proud of the beautifully maintained course, and rightly so. He was president in 1967 when club members put in their own grass greens. Arland, a grandson of pioneers, said it's tough to keep a course going in such a small town, where a few people pay only $125 a year for family memberships. "But we manage," he said, "by doing lots of the work ourselves." Anyone from anywhere can walk on the course at any time and play nine for $4.25, all day for $6.35. And with only 65 paid memberships, Ruth, getting a tee time shouldn't be as difficult as at St. Andrews in Scotland.

Arland had a caution, however. The course is as hilly as a roller coaster and there are no carts for rent, so be prepared for lots of exercise. You'll also be happy to know that Lanesboro Golf Course does not condescend to women. The women's tee-offs show little favor to the fairer sex, and you'll have to loft your drive over a big oak tree on Number 1 if you expect to par that hole. Back at the White Front, Norman Storhoff recalled when he picked sweet corn on what's now the golf course. "Ten cents a day. But then ice cream only cost a nickel, so I could take every other day off."

Remember 13 years ago, Ruth, when we sat in suburban Munich's Nymphenburg Park and fed the pond carp? On this trip, we can evade Dick Guindon's acid-tipped pen because the Department of Natural Resources operates the largest trout hatchery in the state just outside Lanesboro. Hatchery supervisor Darrell Hanson, whose grandfather and father before him ran the place, told me that the spic-and-span hatchery turns out 2 million trout a year, which swarm about artificial ponds before being released into some of the best trout streams in the state. Like Duschee Creek, which runs through the DNR grounds. We can take guided tours there on either Tuesdays or Thursdays if we call two weeks in advance: (507) 467-3771. But we'll have to check our fishing rods at the gate.

When a day of strenuous exercise is over, Ruth, you can head for one of three antique stores. I'll head for a libation at the American Legion club, on the second floor of an old stone building that once housed a milliner and her eight seamstresses in the days before folks ran off to the cities to buy ready-made dresses and hats.

As yet, there aren't any hotels or motels in Lanesboro. Jack Bratrud, Minneapolis, recently bought the old stone Thompson building on Parkway and has plans to restore it to its original conformation and call it ''Mrs. B's Historical Lanesboro Inn,'' with 10 rooms and a restaurant downstairs. Bratrud told me that his financing is guaranteed and that soon Lanesboro will have a bed and breakfast.

Until then, we don't have to worry. Sylvan Park is a city-owned park just a short walk from the business district. Tent sites rent for $3 and camper sites for $5. It features a trout pond, stocked with surplus from the hatchery. Also tennis courts and playground equipment. In case you get rambunctious or long for Rome's Borghese gardens, we can make the steep climb from the park to the top of Church Hill. Lanesboro Leader Editor Charlie Warner said not to worry about mosquitoes because still water can't hang in the bluffs that surround the town. He lives in a brushy area out in the boonies and can't remember more than four bites all last summer.

Sounds great, eh? We can always go to Europe, Ruth. But once Arthur Frommer discovers the Root River region and publishes ''Lanesboro on $5 a Day'' . . . well, don't say I didn't tell you about it first.

Your Loving Husband,
the rural Halliburton,
Dave

—D.W.

Despite the letter, my wife and I went to Europe that summer anyway. But whenever we're in southeastern Minnesota, we try to make a stop in Lanesboro, one of Minnesota's prettiest, friendliest towns.

Mary Watkins
Murray's Powder Room Attendant

Minneapolis, Minnesota
1984

IT WAS EARLY evening on St. Patrick's Day, and everyone having fun at Murray's Restaurant had been having fun for quite a while. People were four deep at the bar. The piano player was taking a break, and the customers were singing "My Wild Irish Rose" a cappella and ever so mournfully.

Into the women's bathroom came a 50ish woman, paper shamrocks pasted to her cheeks and green bows tied in her hair. "Are you Irish?" she asked Mary Watkins. No. That didn't stop the customer. She put big, sloppy kisses on both of Watkins' cheeks and smacked a shamrock onto Watkins' forehead. "Thanks, Honey," Watkins said, smooth as silk.

Watkins, never nasty, said later, "You see it all here."

For 38 years, she has held the title of Powder Room Attendant at Murray's Restaurant & Cocktail Lounge, 26 S. 6th St. She said St. Patrick's Day is crazier than the average shift — especially this St. Patrick's night, when a full moon presented a double whammy.

But over the course of a year, Mary Watkins is privy to almost everything in a privy. Some of the city's most powerful women tell her their problems. She hands tissues and hand lotion to old ladies in minks and to girls in T-shirts. She's nursemaid to pregnant women who feel woozy and psychiatrist to women whose romances have soared or soured. She hears every side of every argument among the help; even the male waiters and bartenders demand her ear when she emerges from the bathroom.

She sees and hears it all, but she doesn't tell. "Sometime it's like a confessional almost. What goes on here, stays here." You can't worm much out of her.

The job description wouldn't attract many applicants, but Mary Watkins loves her work at Murray's. She says people need her. They send her postcards from England and California. They remember her at Christmastime. They give her an affectionate pat on the way to a stall. They know her name, even when they meet her on the street. The clean-up part in the bathroom is easy, she said as she wiped out a sink, but it's the dealing with people that can get rough.

"Funny thing," she says. "When people have a couple drinks, they get moody sometime. I don't say much at first. Sometime they want to talk, sometime they snap at you if you talk."

The women's room has toweling on a roll now, but Watkins keeps some hand towels around to mop sick faces. That doesn't happen much, though: "Just every once in a while I get a sick one. The girls are learning to drink better." Used to be, back in the days when Bernie Bierman coached the Gophers, she would get five or six sick fans a night. Her goal was to keep drunks standing or sitting: "Don't let 'em lay down or they'll pass out on you. Then a man or something has to come in and get 'em." She doesn't miss the sickies but she does miss the glory days of Minnesota football: "I don't think I'll live long enough to see the Little Brown Jug come back."

She and her late husband didn't have children, and a favorite part of her work is being with the little girls. Regular patrons know they can send sleepy or ornery kinds in to Watkins to be entertained in front of the mirror. "You know Mr. McReavy, the undertaker up Northeast?" she said. "He had two little girls who used to come in and play with me. One of the daughters came in years later and said, 'Remember me? I want you to see my little girl.' The tears came and I couldn't hold them back."

She dropped a few other names — generations of the Egans, the Barbeaus. But if any of them ever told her their problems, you won't learn them from her.

Most of her tales, even those without controversy, come without names attached. Like the love story of the woman — "a pretty, red-haired girl" — who three decades ago spent time at Murray's. One day she announced to Watkins, "When I get my vacation, I'm going to spend two weeks on the end of the bar." That she did. One of those days, a male admirer said to the woman, "How about lunch tomorrow?" and pretty soon, according to Watkins, the two were going steady and then married. Now they bring their children to Murray's.

Her previous job was as a waitress at a Nicollet Av. barbecue. It was in 1946 when she heard that Murray's Red Feather, then at 18 S. 4th St., was looking for a female attendant. She decided to try it. She liked it.

⌒

Murray's has a different attitude than most restaurants about its help. It's family-run. (The third-generation, 22-year-old Tim Murray, is now in place; Watkins said of Tim, "He's a nice little guy. I knowed him before he was.") Murray's employees are almost like family. Most can stay as long as they want. The average length of service is decades. Sometimes patrons complain that the waitresses are slow or aren't much to look at. Other customers say the old gals give great service; they've got the routine down pat and can handle anything.

There are plenty of the admiring kind of customers — people who like *knowing* the waitress, bus-boy and bathroom attendant; customers who say to the hostess, "How's your daughter?" and to the waitress, "How are you doing after that surgery?" Much of Murray's clientele is older people, who don't mind if lunch runs an extra 10 minutes. If on a Saturday night, they have time for an extra few pieces of Murray's famous garlic toast, that's fine.

Owner Pat Murray, however, won't accept the idea that his older employees are slow. He said, "You work smarter with experience. I'd match Gussie [Lewandowski] against any 25-year-old waitress in town. She's been with us on and off for 50 years, and she's about 70 now. I've been working this dining room for 22 years and I have not seen Gussie slow down, and I've got three or four more like that."

He's got a waitress who's been at Murray's 37 years; two "bus boys" for 24 and 20 years. "When you look to conserve costs, the last thing I look for is people costs," he said.

But back to Mary Watkins, whom he describes as "as sweet and lovely a person as there is," Pat Murray said he has never heard a bad word about her from a customer or employee, and he doubts his parents, the founders, did. As far as he's concerned, Watkins can have the job as long as she wants. When she no longer does, he may well be interested in finding a replacement. "It's a nice service to have." He thinks Murray's is the only place in town still with a powder room attendant.

Cheryl McDonald, 26 years old and the dining-room manager, said a large share of the employees are earning above union scale. At one point or another in their careers, someone in the Murray family decided they deserved a raise and that raise has stayed with them. "It's hard to know if all their policies pay off professionally, but they are humane," she said.

According to McDonald, Watkins is the world's most generous person. When McDonald's baby was born, Watkins tucked bills in McDonald's pocket and said, "This is for her bank account."

Occasionally younger customers don't understand about bathroom attendants, McDonald said. "They say to me, 'What's that lady doing in there?' I blame it on their rearing. I explain she's there as a service to keep the ladies' room clean and in order and to be like a mother to them."

∽

Watkins' husband, Art, was a professional musician who died 12 years ago. She had a woman friend live with her for 20 years, "but she passed away and now I'm alone with my little dog, Baby."

Baby, a cockapoo, is treated well. "Baby won't eat nothing but chicken," Watkins said, so every Sunday Watkins bakes a chicken "for me and Baby."

Of all the friends Watkins has at Murray's, few can say they've seen her home. One waitress who has said, "It's beautiful, very beautiful. She's an excellent housekeeper, and don't ask how often I clean my house."

Mary Watkins is opinionated. She listens, then she speaks her mind. An employee tells her she's wallpapering a bedroom, and Watkins will say,

"I hate wallpaper. Wallpaper is for bad walls, and all my walls are nice." A restaurant friend says she's mad at her husband and she'll get some sympathy and maybe Watkins will go so far as to call the guy a crumb, but she'll remind her marriage is sacred and they'd better simmer down and work at staying together.

A devout Catholic, she never, never uses profanity. Bartender David Moon said, "As the song goes, never a discouraging word. Work in a restaurant is a high-pressure job. Waitresses are screaming, bartenders are mad, tempers flare. Mary does a lot to offset ill feelings. She's the safety valve here."

She spends her own money for supplies — tissues, lotion, Tampax. She used to have lipstick and perfumes, but women today carry them in their bags. Besides, about 10 years ago women began stealing her supplies. "The old-timers never did anything like that," she said, outraged. "Now you come back, and your mirror and tray and everything will be gone."

Watkins works Mondays, Thursdays, Fridays and Saturdays, usually from 5 p.m. until closing. She used to work six nights a week, but her doctor recommended cutting back to four. Her sister-in-law, Mildred Watkins, (they married brothers), works Tuesdays and Wednesdays. "If one get sick, the other always carry on," Mary Watkins said.

Murray's will be closed for a month this summer for extensive remodeling. The new place will have a bigger, fancier powder room. But, ladies, be careful when you look for Watkins. The men's room will be where the women's is now.

⁓

Mary Watkins skillfully avoided answering two big questions: age and money.

Pat Murray told us how much Watkins is paid. About $4.50 an hour, plus tips. He couldn't be specific on tips, and Watkins didn't want to. She did say that fewer than half of the women tip now. "The last 15 years, not like it used to be," she said.

And age? She finally gave in. She was born in 1904, she said. Unbelievable. It's true, she insisted. She'll be 80 on June 20. "God's been very good to me," she said.

—P.M.

Bill Perry
Heeding the Call

Minneapolis, Minnesota
1984

B ILL PERRY sat at his desk in a downtown Minneapolis office and remembered the first time he felt God's call to the ministry. "I was 13
years old and all alone. I opened Dad's desk drawer, took out a Bible
and gave a sermon to the empty house."

Last year, 33 years later, Bill Perry was ordained a Baptist minister.

He might have made it to the pulpit sooner. His father was the Rev. J.S.
Perry, D.D., a preacher at Peace Baptist Church in Birmingham, Ala. His
mother, Martha Elizabeth Perry, held a degree in Christian education and
taught religion courses in Birmingham and at state and national Baptist
conventions. His late uncle, Dr. T. DeWitt Bussey, was president of Birmingham Baptist College. "I attended school there and at Miles College. But then
my life took a turn. My mother insisted that all her children learn to play an
instrument. I took up keyboard. When I was 4, I was singing and playing in
churches and at church conventions."

After college, Bill Perry hit the road as a professional entertainer, singing gospel and pop with the likes of Lou Rawls, Sam Cook, the Rev. Gate-
mouth Moore.

"I sang with Mahalia Jackson, the Rev. James Cleveland, Aretha Franklin. And I sang at the White House for President Jimmy Carter." Perry
appeared on the Johnny Carson, Merv Griffin and Mike Douglas shows,
played the big houses in Las Vegas, New York, Los Angeles and Washington, D.C.

By 1965, he was playing an engagement at the White House restaurant
in Golden Valley. "That was where the Lord started dealing with me very
specifically. I felt the urge to get off the road. I made an agreement with the
Lord that if He would give me a job with roots, I would give Him the rest of
my life. One night, on break, I went to the bathroom. There, I met some
people I had seen in the audience. They worked for Northwestern Bell —
Bob Peterson and John Innes. I'd seen an ad for a job as communications
representative for Bell. I didn't know what that involved so I asked them.

Bob Peterson said, 'Why don't you apply? Use my name if you like.' "

Bill Perry did that, got the job and went to work in the marketing department. For six years he worked 8 to 5 at the telephone company, then played at the White House until 1 a.m.

"You see, I still had a real battle going on inside me. Despite my commitment to the Lord, I wasn't sure what I wanted to do. I had people applauding me every night. That's hard to give up. But the Lord came to me one night and He said, 'Perry, we made a deal. You said if I gave you a job with roots you'd give this up, give your life to me. What's your problem?' "

Not a man to renege on a deal, Bill Perry tickled nightclub ivories for the last time on New Year's Eve 1972. He worked his way up at the phone company. In October 1983 he was named manager of the customer relations department. He has a big office, looks the part, a can-do man, a big man in a tailored suit.

~

Bill Perry's phone rings. It's the Metropolitan Council. They're busy with International Trade Center proposals and their phones don't work. Bill Perry gets on the case. He dials, he talks, he smooths things out, he contacts the repair people. And he talks to them in the honeyed cadences of a corporate communicator.

That done, he returns to his spiritual autobiography. "When I left the White House in Golden Valley, my life really took a change. You see, the Lord has a way of coming into our lives when He can use us. But material gain versus giving of yourself completely weighs heavy. You look at what the Joneses are doing and it's difficult to give up what you're doing. I looked at my life. People all over the country had told me I was great and that was good. But what you have to gain, the Lord told me, far outweighs what you'll be giving up."

Perry's cadences slow down, then pick up. He stops, he starts, the words flowing out forcefully, pulpit style. "The Lord spoke to me many times, once on the Crosstown. I was driving along and I drew a blank. I didn't know where I was . . . which direction I was heading. The Lord . . . you see . . . was trying to tell me something."

Soon after the Crosstown experience, Bill Perry was named minister of music at Greater Sabathani Church in south Minneapolis and became active in church affairs. "But you can go to church every Sunday and it doesn't mean a thing. The Lord didn't really get me to accept my calling until 1980, the year my wife, Elizabeth, developed a chronic illness. She had a blockage of the sweat glands and broke out in terrible boils. Our doctor told us there was nothing he could do, so we went to the Mayo Clinic. The doctor said he didn't know if they'd ever find a cure for Elizabeth but gave us two medications and sent us home."

Bill Perry leans toward his guest to drive home the point. "Ten miles out of Rochester. I had a gospel tape playing. I started to sob uncontrollably. Suddenly, I said, 'Yes, Lord, I hear You.' You see, the Lord was saying to me

'I've given you everything you asked for. Must I take your wife from you before you'll heed your calling?' As we drove on, I was holding onto the wheel as if it were life itself. When I got home, I felt *different*.

"Even then I tried to run from it, but the next Wednesday night I felt an urge to go to prayer meeting. We'd just organized our Macedonia Baptist Church, so I went. July 18, 1980. I was playing a song, 'He's so real in my soul today, He has washed all my sins away, Jesus's love just bubbles over in my heart.' I began to sob. I got up and announced that night that the Lord had called me to preach and that now I had to yield to Him."

So 30 years after Bill Perry preached to his father's empty study in Birmingham, Bill got down to brass tacks. He and his wife affiliated with a Denver nondenominational study group. "I studied, became involved with the indwelling of prayer."

On Nov. 20, 1983, he was ordained at Macedonia Baptist Church. Now, besides directing the church's five choirs, he preaches once a month at Macedonia and delivers guest sermons at other churches. "I preached last month at Colonial Church in Edina. A man came up to me afterwards and told me that that day was the first time he ever wept during a church service." No one should be ashamed of that, according to Perry, because every human being has an emotional side. People holler and shout when a Viking drops a pass in the end zone. Why shouldn't they express an emotion in church?

He teaches adult classes every Sunday and counsels the lonesome, the forgotten and the people who teeter on the brink of salvation. "Recently, a young woman called our house from a phone booth on Lake St. She wanted to talk. Well, I like football and it was a playoff Sunday. I didn't see much football, but when the woman left she looked happier than when she came. But, remember, I don't have that effect. The Lord was working through me. I have nothing to boast about."

And what of his wife's chronic illness?

"The Lord has arrested her affliction. . . . Oh, yes, she takes her medication. But the Lord chose that medication to do His will. We call it 'arresting' because we know the Lord is using this [disease] to maintain our attention. If it completely went away, I wouldn't have the same need to follow Him."

The phones begin to ring and it's time for Perry to return to corporate communications, but not before he tells us that the smoky nightclubs are a distant memory, that recent secular music appearances include playing the piano at friends' parties. But most of his performances are in service to his God. For instance, Perry and his friend Tom Tipton performed on nationwide television at the Crystal Cathedral, in Garden Grove, Calif., on the Sunday in 1982 that their friend Dr. Robert Schuller opened it.

The interview was over, but not before Bill Perry invited a reporter to attend Macedonia Baptist Church the next time he was asked to preach.

∾

The Macedonia Baptist Church, at 3801 1st Av. S., doesn't look much like Robert Schuller's Crystal Cathedral. But what once was an insurance company building is now joyful on a nippy March morning, the spiritual home for this young congregation of about 350 Baptists. It's a friendly place where newcomers are warmly welcomed by the congregation's sisters and brothers. It's 10:45 a.m. Families greet each other, take their places in the newly painted auditorium, which comfortably seats 275 worshipers. Sun streams in through plain glass windows. Up front, a drummer adjusts his snare drum. In back, a little kid stands in his pew so he can see what's going on. Ushers in black suits and white gloves greet worshippers with the program for the day. The organist unlocks his keyboard. Across the stage, pianist Gary Hines, son of a respected Twin Cities jazz vocalist, Doris Hines, sits down and begins to play. The organist and drummer join in. Stragglers in the spacious lounge areas hurry into the auditorium. Eight deacons and deaconesses stand in a row, facing the congregation. They will be up there, off and on, for almost two hours. During that time, music will be continuous.

Now the choir is lining up. Clad in deep brown robes, with white scarfs descending from right shoulder epaulets, the singers march down the central aisle slowly, precisely, in a one-step. The Rev. W.J. Perry replaces Hines at the piano. The choir lines up behind the pulpit, where they'll be for the entire service. Perry plays the piano with one hand, his other thrusting heavenward, in short jerks. He also sings, sometimes a soft counter melody, sometimes a powerful rumble that cues the choir: "FORGET about yourself and concentrate on HIM!"

Now the deacons and deaconesses are clapping and the entire congregation sings to a mournful beat. Hallelujah. The choir stops, but the organ and piano continue as Deacon Forrest Green welcomes the worshipers. "How good God has been to Macedonia . . . . "

"Oh, yes," say several members of the congregation.

" . . . Remember when we had only one piano, remember when we pushed it in here? Now we have two pianos and two organs."

"Oh, yes. Uh-huh. Oh, YES."

Although the service at Macedonia has as many rituals as the Church of England, it's a service where folks aren't afraid to participate. At first, the give and take makes the reporter uncomfortable, but soon his innards are stirred in a strange and happy way.

Deacon Dwayne Harris reads Scripture, Sister Barbara Smith leads the congregation in extemporaneous prayer: "God is able . . . . Anything we ask Him . . . He can do." Murmurs of assent. Sister Smith builds to a fortissimo, then slides into pianissimo, saying, "And when we've done all we can and we can do no more, Lord, we ask You to make a home in Your kingdom." Amen, amen.

Worshipers continue to file in late and folding chairs must be set up. That's the way it always is, according to the Rev. Perry, who pounds out a lively tune. The choir stands up and Perry chants, "I'M GOING ON . . . . I've been lied on, cheated, talked about, mistreated. But I feel like going on . . . . C'mon chilluns," and the choir lifts its voice in song. The new congregation secretary is introduced, and Deacon Ercell Chadwick explains that the newspaper is here for a story "and everyone should act just the way they usually do." Deacon Green reads down the list of ailing members, exhorting those in good health to pray for their brothers and sisters. The Rev. G.L. Anderson, senior pastor, makes announcements and observations. Anderson's observation is actually an extemporaneous sermonette, delivered with spirit and skill. He mixes Bible passages with personal experience, not to mention humorous asides: "Macedonia is playing basketball against New Hope [a St. Paul congregation]. Let's pray for New Hope." The Rev. Anderson sees Tom Tipton sitting in the back and wonders if the congregation could impose upon Tipton for a song.

There's an offering, then a young child is welcomed to the congregation. Then it's prayer time. The Rev. Anderson says, "The only way for the world to get on its feet is for the church to get on its knees." People come forward and pray. "Prayer," says Anderson, "is not just to ask for things, but to fall before His celestial throne and thank Him for being good to us. He *has* been good to us. The Lord never promised us a light load. But He *did* promise He would always be there." One woman is moved to tears and Reverend Perry's wife gets up to comfort her.

The choir sings again, watching Reverend Perry, his free arm moving up and down like a piston. Soloists Myra Anderson and Claudia Ashly make a joyful noise unto the world and ushers pass out fans. "Man," says The Rev. Anderson, "cannot be saved unless by preaching. Reverend W.J. Perry will bring us the words of the Lord today. The preacher needs your support, so please say amen."

But not before Tom Tipton sings "It Is Well With My Soul."

W.J. (Bill) Perry, the phone-company-executive-turned-preacher, is at the lectern, a white handkerchief folded in his right hand. What he's about to do, you don't learn in homiletics class. "It is WELL with my soul! Can YOU say the same this morning!?" Amen, amen. "I like JESUS because He's so PERSONAL. He don't have to bless ME for YOU. Oh, the SPIRIT OF GOD IS HERE THIS MORNING!" Amen, amen. "We'll get a few formalities out of the way and then we'll let the spirit of the Lord take over.

"People from the [Star and] Tribune are here this morning. The reporter told me earlier that he didn't know if a photographer could make it because she was downtown where they're blowing up a building. I told him not to worry! I told him the Lord would bring a photographer." He looks down at photographer Stormi Greener, who clicks away.

"Next week, I'll be preaching in Birmingham [Ala.], at Peace Baptist Church. I'll be able to stand where my daddy stood and proclaim the Gospel. The Lord was able to take me from nothing and make something out of me." Amen, amen. The congregation bows for a short prayer and then Perry reads from Acts, where Saul breathes murderous threats at the disciples before his conversion. And then he's off and running on the theme that you can change all sorts of things on your own hook, Christian friends, but you need the Lord to help with spiritual changes.

Reverend Perry's cadences are as dramatic as his well-told story of Saul's encounter with the Lord on the road to Damascus. "Saul . . . didn't realize . . . didn't realize . . . the force he was dealing with. All Saul could finally say is 'I . . . am . . . experiencing . . . a CHANGE!' Saul was blind three days:

"No food . . . "

"Yes," echoes the congregation.

" . . . No water . . . "

"Yes!"

" . . . Just . . . GOD!"

"Yes! Yes!"

Reverend Perry wipes his brow and tells his audience that whatever they want to change from, the Lord will help. He nods his head rapidly, smiles a glad smile. "He'll let you dance for Him." He does a four-bar softshoe dance. The floor behind the lectern rumbles. The congregation says hallelujah. "The Lord didn't say we strive *for* perfection, but we should strive *to* perfection. Because if you get too perfect, honey, you'll be doing the Lord's work." He takes the congregation up with him, then slows down, then asks a rhetorical question with a twinkle in his eye. The answer is obvious. He moves away from the pulpit and down the aisle, then back. "If I never preach to you again, I want you to know that Jesus CHANGED me. When Jesus makes a CHANGE, you can say like the words of the song 'Use me, Lord, in Thy service.'" He sings ". . . I'm willing, Lord, to run, hallelujah, all the way. Let's see the hands if you want to run all the way." Hands go up around the auditorium.

After an hour and half, you wait for Reverend Perry's vocal cords to give way. But then he chants the conclusion to his sermon, calling for "a change, A SPIRITUAL CHANGE! Yea, Lord, yea, Lord," softer, softer. And then he stops. Abruptly. He leaves the pulpit and a woman in white comes with a cape to drape his shoulders. He sits down, moist and exhausted.

The Rev. G.L. Anderson is up. He tells his flock that because Reverend Perry is such a recently ordained preacher, "Macedonia should be very, very proud of him."

Amen, amen.

—D.W.

Soon after this story appeared Bill Perry left Minneapolis to become assistant pastor and minister of music at First Baptist Church in Birmingham, Ala., where he also works in management at South Central Bell. Home at last!

Adrian's and the Loon
From Neighborly to Trendy

Minneapolis, Minnesota
1982

EDITOR'S NOTE: Neighbors reporters Peg Meier and Dave Wood both hail from Wisconsin, Land of 10,000-plus Taverns. So we thought it would be meet and right to unleash their reportorial talents on two drinking establishments in Minneapolis: the Loon Cafe, which is downtown at 500 1st Av. N., and Adrian's, a 3.2 bar at 4812 Chicago Av. Meier is considerably younger than Wood[1], so she was assigned a nocturnal trip to the Loon, and Wood was sent on a dawn patrol to Adrian's. Here's their report.

The Neighborhood

ADRIAN'S: (Wood) The business district at 48th and Chicago was coming alive when I walked over from my house at 10 a.m. on Saturday, a half hour before the bar opened. Customers queued up at the two branch banks within a block of each other. An ominous old helmet glared out at me from the display window at Vet's Salvage Diving. The clerk at Square Dance Heaven/Polka Paradise was waiting for customers in search of colorful costumes celebrating a rustic Terpsichore. The Shenandoah Pharmacy announced a clearance sale. One store was closed, but the black-and-white sign that announced a generic "Tax Service" held promise that its doors will open next spring when the neighborhood once again does battle with the IRS.

The Loon: (Meier) I went to the Loon about 8:30 on a Friday night. The trendy bars in the neighborhood, including those at Butler Square down the block, had attracted so many people that I couldn't find a parking place. I

---

1. Meier: I'm 36, he's 46. My big goal in life is to write a footnoted newspaper story. With only a bachelor's degree and three credits toward a master's, I have unrealistic aspirations of someday becoming a scholar. David Wood, Ph.D., Bowling Green University, 1969, is sick of footnotes. Don't expect any from him.

circled a few times, gave up on free parking and pulled into the lot across from the Loon. "Two-fifty," said the young attendant. *"Two-fifty?"* He knew right away I was out of my element. "Yes ma'am," he said.

Ma'am? Ma'am! At my age, I'm going to be too old for this place, I figured. (Incorrectly, as it turned out.) Outside the Loon, I met my friends — three young people, in their 20s. They volunteered to help this old woman crash the bar scene.

The Decor

Adrian's: I opened the door at Adrian's at 10:30 and there stood owners Jim and Barb Scott patting out Juicy Lucys behind the shiny mahogany bar lined with red and yellow ketchup and mustard squeezers. Jim, 27, bought the bar four years ago, when he was a business student at the University. He married Barb a year later. Laura came along just 11 weeks ago, and she was sleeping peacefully in a bassinet on a Formica table along the north wall.

Adrian's is clean to a fault, but not botanically fancy. The north wall is decorated in bright green. The south wall behind the bar is decorated in a tasteful montage of Pee-Wee P-Nuts, Blue Diamond Smokehouse Almonds, Salmon Sharpies, Porkie Bacon Rinds, Scherer's Pickled Turkey Gizzards, Magic Chef Pork Hocks and a spotless grill hood.

Adrian's seats about 75 people, and in its cavernous back end there's plenty of room to stand around and watch customers play electronic games. A middle-aged guy came in the back door, walked past Jim and Barb, said, "I'll see you later, " and disappeared out the front door. "He comes in at least eight times a day," Jim said as he slid a thick slice of cheese between two hamburger patties, then crimped the edges. A Juicy Lucy, ready for the grill, if a customer should happen by.

The Loon: Decor? I couldn't see decor, for all the people. It was wall-to-wall humanity, as crowded as a bathroom at a Vikings game at half time. Anyway, Friday night is the Loon's busiest time, and this Friday night it was packed, by my standards, anyway.

"Oh good, it's empty," said the young man behind me, not kidding, so it must be even more jammed some Friday nights.

Lots of customers were in their 20s, but a goodly share were in their 30s and 40s, even 50s. Many were in three-piece suits and crisp Oxford shirts. They had come to the Loon after work and hadn't cleared out yet.

A friend of mine who cuts hair for a living has spent many a Friday evening here, wearing her pin-striped suit and carrying a borrowed attache case, in pursuit of the middle-aged professionals who frequent the Loon. She has good teeth and hair, and that's important here.

The younger ones, their callipygous (get the dictionary) bodies in designer jeans, come downtown mid- or late-evening, and they were thronging in by 9 p.m. Later came the sophisticates, looking as if they had just come from the Guthrie.

But back to decor, I went to the Loon for lunch a few days later when the place was not so packed, and I noticed there *was* a decor.

Co-owner Jim Robertson told me then that management wanted to have a bar with no stained glass and no ferns. Management succeeded. Instead, it chose neon pictures for the wall (one of a hamburger, another in pink/lavender that says EATS) and, near the windows, non-fern plants (fig trees and corn plants, to be specific).

A handsome pattern of cattails has been hand-stenciled on the walls. The booths are old, the hardwood floors wavy, and the place seems old and friendly. Bottles of Grey Poupon mustard join the traditional Heinz ketchup and French's mustard. No squeezers here.

The Clientele

Adrian's: Jim, who bought the bar four years ago, didn't figure it would be wall-to-wall humanity on this beautiful day, but 74-year-old Sylvan Millwood, the night clean-up man at nearby Pepito's, dropped by for a beer before going home to install storm windows. Another guy came in, after dropping off a broken storm window at Anderson's Hardware. He was a Lutheran and didn't want his name used here. CPA Michael Carr, a recent arrival to the neighborhood, came in with a new faucet from Anderson's, ordered a burger basket and a Coke. He pondered a chart on the refrigerator listing 16 volleyball teams sponsored by the bar. He wondered if they sponsor a basketball team. Jim said yes and he'd check to see if there was room for another hoopster.

By noon the place was busy with University of Minnesota students who grew up in the neighborhood. Suburbanites with a fondness for Juicy Lucys. Middle-aged guys like Emmert Wanquist, who lives 20 blocks away, but comes on weekends "because you can't find a corner like this anywhere else in Minneapolis." And daily regulars like Vern Lowe, a retired salesman; Arley Olson, a truck driver, and Tom Jenks, a city employee. When these guys arrived, they made mandatory trips to the bassinet to admire little Laura before Barb took her home. When Tom walked in, Jack O'Connor described him as "one of Mark Dayton's few private contributors." Tom said, "Humph!"

Jack asked where his beer came from. Jim Scott explained that Leon was in yesterday and left money to buy Jack a beer. The regulars ostensibly came to Adrian's to watch the World Series, but they broke off into conversation groups and cribbage games. Bill Irvine, operator of the Parkway Theatre next door, told me between pegging that his "Gallipoli"/"Breaker Morant" double feature for $1.50 was going great.

Later on, Ruth Johnson dropped by. She comes on Saturdays because she and her late husband, Herbert, always did. She chatted with Norma Finseth, known to the gang as "Our Queen," and to Clayton Finseth, known as "The Grinch," for arcane reasons too complicated for me to understand.

The Loon: It's easy to meet people at the Loon. We grabbed a booth that happened to open up, and all evening long people who were standing next to the table started conversations with us.

Paul Scalisi, a graduate student in hospital administration, said that during the summer he came to the Loon on Friday evenings "to find girls who have swimming pools for me to spend Saturday afternoon with." His goal this night was to get a few phone numbers of women he might like to get to know.

"I never have gone home with a woman I met at a bar; that's not how I operate," he told us. But he likes meeting women here. He said the energy level at the Loon is high, the people are fun and friendly and the food is good and inexpensive. He's from Boston, and he's been disappointed with Twin Cities night life. Until the Loon.

Claudia Lucht, 26, is from New Hope and drives a fork-lift truck for a living. One reason she likes the Loon is that it serves the kind of wine she likes. "Most bars don't serve Liebfraumilch, only Chablis," she said. "Chablis gives you such bad breath you can't stand to talk to anyone, and no one wants to be near you."

Annette Hudok, 31, of Crystal, said she and her friends usually go to the 494 strip for weekend action, but "somebody talked us into coming here and we liked it. It's a friendly place, and we're party people. . . . More people are starting to come back downtown."

Now just to prove there are guys around here in their 40s, let me tell you about Dennis Filas, a 42-year-old architect and structural engineer from San Francisco. He's in town on a project so secret that he wouldn't talk about it. He would talk about how the Loon is like a lot of places he goes to in California.

Big shots come to the Loon, I'm told. People like George Steinbrenner, Ralph Lauren, Richard Simmons and Hulk Hogan[2].

Plus local surgeons, defense attorneys, dancers and actors. Not to mention punk-rockers and stewardesses, oops, flight attendants.

The bar's owners say the clientele and the atmosphere have put the Loon in Esquire magazine's list of the top 100 bars in the country, to be published in the December issue.

Conversation

Adrian's: Jim Scott said nothing about Esquire or even the Viking Report because his customers were too busy talking about such things as: *Sports talk.* The NFL strike and last night's Richfield-Burnsville game, where Vern Lowe's grandson, Chris, starred at right defensive end. *Culinary talk.* The sinus-clearing chili sauce made by Karl Efverstedt's wife, Sara. Who has the better Juicy Lucy, Adrian's or Matt's, the place on Cedar Av. that originated the cheese-stuffed burger?

History. Jack O'Connor, a former College of St. Thomas psychology professor, loves Eugene McCarthy's sense of humor. "Remember when George Romney said he'd been brainwashed? McCarthy said a light rinse

2. Meier: Hulk Hogan is a professional wrestler who was in "Rocky III."

would have done the job. God, that's great. Or when asked why George McGovern wasn't as bright a speaker as *he* was, McCarthy said you can't expect a metaphor from a Methodist." *Urban gentrification.* Pepito's recently added valet parking, and there was talk of a Mercedes and Porsche invasion of the neighborhood. *And just a little bit of sex.* Salty Al Sorlie told me he was working as an apartment-building caretaker. "Yeah," said Jack O'Connor. "Taking care of all those widows." Al's riposte: "Humph!"

The Loon: Some people had serious conversations about Reaganomics and Japanese cars and which teams are in Sports Illustrated's top 20 and which list the Twins belong on. (Not complimentary.)

Other snippets of conversation: *The language.* "When a guy says 'Ish,' I want to pull my hair out. It's OK if a girl says it, but when a guy says it, it's like fingernails across a blackboard." *Hair:* "It was such an awful haircut that I was crying. I mean crying!" *The opposite sex:* "That one looks four-times divorced." "I'm in love with two women already tonight." "He looks like he just emerged from Dayton's Boundary Waters department." "Guess who's my type?" *The media:* "Pat Miles has almost New Wave hair, and I don't care for it. Next week Dave Moore will have a safety pin through his nose."

The Drinks

Adrian's: It's 3.2 beer, beer and more beer at Adrian's. From 50 cents a glass to 80 cents a bottle to $2.75 for a big pitcher of Schmidt's. If your taste runs to Heineken's, that comes to $1.35 per bottle. No one at the bar seemed to wonder what these Dutch guys in an Amsterdam brewery think when they get an order for 10,000 cases of 3.2 beer to be shipped to some place called Minnesota.

Retired railroader Glen Jorgenson came in with a Mason jar of peppery tomato juice canned by his wife, Ruby. Folks pour a shot of it into their beers, drink, smack their lips. The juice was wonderful.

The Loon: It's Christian Brothers vodka with freshly squeezed grapefruit and orange juice, for screwdrivers and salty dogs — $1.95 each. It's Beefeater gin and Johnnie Walker Red Scotch. It's Brandy Alexanders, grasshoppers, banshees and Frangelica Mulchs made with Haagen-Dazs ice cream, $2.95 each.

The Loon sells a lot of beer (Michelob and Michelob Light on draft, everything from Budweiser to St. Pauli Girl Light or Dark by the bottle), barrels of white wine and extraordinary amounts of Cold Spring mineral water for $1.25 a bottle.

La Cuisine

Adrian's: Adrian's menu offers 22 items, not including Red Baron pizza. That's lots more than the Willows in the Hyatt Regency. Nine items are permutations on the basic burger, which sells for $1.25. One favorite is the "Lurtsie Burger," a cheeseburger with bacon that sells for $1.90. Folks argue about how and when it got its name. But it most certainly involves a long-ago visit by Bob Lurtsema³. Those with adventurous palates might prefer the BBQ beef or corned beef or a burrito or something really pricey, like the shrimp basket for $3.50.

Back by the games, Craig Klausing, John Wentworth and The Mysterious Lady from Golden Valley, who wore designer jeans but refused to give her name, dug into their burgers. Craig came over from St. Paul and said he likes Adrian's because "you don't have to fight off the ferns." John prefers the Lurtsie and said he "wouldn't know a quiche if it bit him on the butt."

The Loon: The best-sellers are the Burgerloon (a large hamburger on nice light or dark callipygous buns) and served with fries or fresh fruit (grapes and cantaloupe when we were there), for $4.55, and a choice of chilis (Pecos River Red, Rufus Valdez World Championship Chili and Pinto's Famous Diablo), $3.95 for a big bowl and $2.35 for a cup. There's always a soup of the day and Minnesota Wild Rice soup. Appetizers go like wildfire — breaded cauliflower for $1.95, a side order of fresh fruit for $1.75. Spinach salad for $3.95. No quiche to bite you on the butt.

—P.M. and D.W.

---

3. Wood: Oh, what the hell? I'm not that sick of footnotes. So I'll try my hand after being out of the groves of academe for years. I spent a week phoning Bob Lurtsema to find out if he remembered visiting Adrian's, and when I finally caught him, he said, no, he knew the area in south Minneapolis, but he couldn't recall ever stopping at Adrian's for a goldfish-eating contest, one of several theories about how the burger got named. I doggedly asked another question: "Robert Evans of Twin City Federal, the man who gave me your number, said that he'd never heard of Adrian's either, but that your nickname is 'Lurtsieburger.' Is that true?" Lurtsema replied, "Yes, that's so. My friends call me Lurtsieburger because I'm not good enough to be first string, but I'm not all that bad." He hastened to add that this interpretation should cast no reflections on Adrian's Lurtsie Burger. So it is with regret that I must report that dogged, exhaustive research has uncovered no findings for any future study of the Lurtsie Burger Conundrum, a question that will no doubt plague researchers for centuries to come.

Mary Jo Copeland
Feeding the Poor

Minneapolis, Minnesota
1984

MARY JO COPELAND slices metaphors off her imagination the way some folks snip celery into a kettle of soup. She called Neighbors last week and said, "There's fertile soil out there. What we need is someone to plant the seed."

Let's unravel that figure of speech. The fertile soil she referred to is the Twin Cities church community. The seed she wants planted is her idea that street people need free lunch lines to help them through their terrifying lives. The someone to plant the seed? Well, she figured Neighbors might do the job if it had the space.

Neighbors had the space, so on Dec. 28, we made our way to Catholic Charities' Branch II Drop-In Center, at 1201 Hawthorne Av., in the shadow of the Basilica of St. Mary, which pays its rent. Its big glass windows were coated with ice, but inside it was toasty, except around the chilly edges, and folks were helping themselves to coffee, old doughnuts and peanut butter sandwiches, donated by such companies as Byerly's, Lunds, McGlynn's and Sherman Bakeries, the European Pastry Shop and Mr. Donut, or purchased with United Fund money. Copeland sat in the center's office and explained that she got her idea for the lunch line last summer.

"I figured just because the people who come here are poor, they shouldn't have to eat just doughnuts and cold sandwiches all the time. They should be able, once in a while, to eat just like your family and mine. So last July, I started calling all kinds of churches, Catholic and Protestant, it didn't matter. I asked them to bring their own home cooking down here. I asked them to come themselves and interact with poor people, to touch them.

"Visitation Catholic Church on Lyndale was the first that stepped forward." See how Copeland uses a metaphor? Churches don't usually *step forward*. But, in her poetic view of the world, churches do step forward.

"They brought homemade chili, milk, fruit. It was beautiful. Some people tell me that I'm enabling people who come to the branch to blow their

GA [general assistance] checks on liquor. But the way I see it, there's no room for blame or shame. Caring and sharing is what I'm interested in. I tell them 'I'm not trying to change your lives. I'm trying to be your friend.' You know, you can't be a beacon if your light doesn't shine."

Copeland, 41, lives in north Minneapolis. When she's not volunteering three half-days a week as an advocate and crisis counselor at the drop-in branch, or when she isn't hustling churches to participate in the lunch line, she spends time with her husband, Dick, a buyer for Gateway Foods, and eight of her 12 children. "Four children are gone from home now. Thank God for that," she said, laughing. Copeland laughs a lot. She also weeps for life's fallen.

"When I was young, I wasn't a wanted kid. I'd come home and just hope that my mother would give me a hug. . . . So when people come into the branch, I go out and hug them. It's a gift God gave me. You see, people coming in here and interacting with people is just as important as the food they bring."

When the clock on the wall said 11 a.m., the center was crowded with young and old, and it was time for Copeland to go out and do her thing. She had a big hug for a young man in an old coat. "Harold, how are ya? Better? Good! You looked sort of down the other day." Then she ran over to two old-timers. "This is Jim and this is Russ. This man is from the Star-Trib. . . ." Jim and Russ said something about this being "hobo heaven" and Copeland said someday they'd all be together in real heaven.

"Elmer, you got a new coat!"

"It's the one you gave me last week," Elmer said.

"Oh, yeah, that must be one of the coats from Visitation Church. Great!"

The frosty door swung open to 12th St., and members from Colonial Church of Edina, a Congregational church, trooped in. They bore a noon luncheon for 350 people. Edina, eh? What will they serve? Clear turtle soup? Vichyssoise? Pate Forestiere?

Nope. Good, honest steaming vegetable soup made with their own hands. Vegetable soup with chunks of beef floating about in it. And cheese sandwiches . . . And cunning little Christmas cookies with fancy frosting, the kind that take a long time to make. Copeland kissed the women from Edina, who had made this trip before. Hosts Kris Brehm and Mary Ellen Rockewell lined up the fancy cookies for serving. Their friends, Nan and Bob Edlund, fussed with the soup-ladling arrangement. Their guests sat on the frosty edges of the center, smoking, talking and smelling aromas emanating from the serving table. Old men played cribbage in the middle of the room. A young man walked in with the previous night's vomit on his fatigue jacket and joined the ragged line beginning to form an arm's length from the soup kettles.

Bryce Cannon, 62, sat at a card table, wishing he hadn't chosen Minneapolis as a place to stop for the winter. He said he doesn't come to the center to eat, but "the cockroaches drove me out of my room" at a hotel up the street. Cannon said that he figured Copeland is "quite a woman, quite a woman."

Ronald Holloway, a towering man, figured the same. "What Mary Jo's saying makes a lot of sense. And what she says comes from her heart."

"Oh, you dear heart," said Copeland, hugging him around the waist.

"You're the dear heart," said Holloway.

The soup was ready to be served, but branch administrator Joan Connors had a presentation to make. Copeland didn't know it that morning, but her name was given over the airways as WCCO radio's "Good Neighbor" and so Connors presented her with a fancily decorated cake. While Copeland tried to figure out how the little cake could be split 350 ways, someone in the crowd hollered "Speech, speech!"

"Hell, no," hollered someone else, "don't get her started."

Copeland said she thought that was a good one and said that the folks from Colonial Church should start serving. Noises of dishing up and eating commenced.

Back in the office, Copeland said she was very pleased that 15 churches have responded to her idea. The lunch line has been offered about 40 times since Visitation Church stepped forward in early October. First Baptist Church, for instance, has provided lunch six times. For three years before the program, they'd lugged over a big kettle of soup every Wednesday.

"Three fellows always brought it, nicest guys you'd ever want to meet," Copeland said. She said that she wants to operate the lunch line every day, all year long, not only at Branch II, but also at Branch III. That means there are lots of open dates for which no churches have stepped forward. "So we need more churches to participate."

Churches wishing to step forward can organize, pay for the food and prepare it in any way they wish. Copeland, for instance, attends St. Alphonsus Catholic Church in Brooklyn Center. St. Alphonsus doesn't have a kitchen, so they buy food and prepare it in a kitchen at Church of the Master nearby. The important thing is that groups bring home-cooked food — chili, soup, stew, casseroles, sandwiches, milk, fresh fruit — to serve 350 people. They also should serve the food themselves so they can meet the people they're serving it to.

"The important thing," said Copeland as she picked up a telephone, "is to bring sunshine into these people's lives, a ray of hope — to let them know that people think enough of them to come down here and serve them."

— D.W.

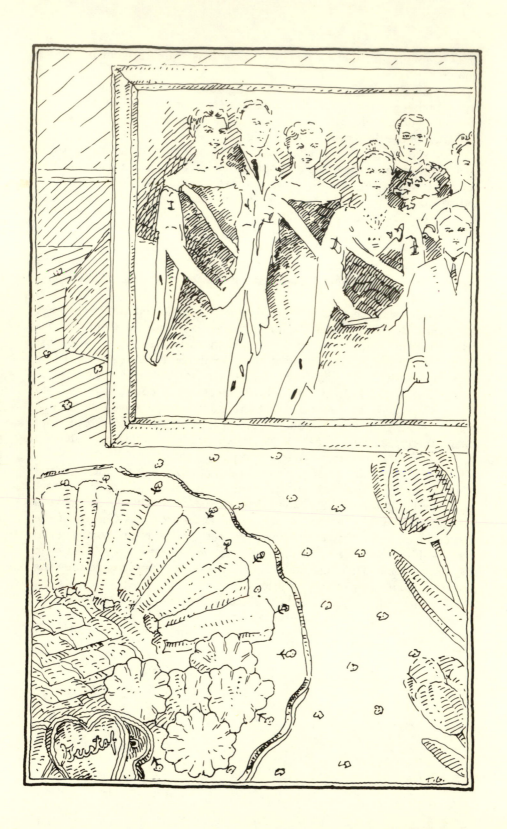

Gunhild and Hilding Anderson
Entertaining the Swedish Royalty

Minneapolis, Minnesota
1982

IT'S WEDNESDAY afternoon, five days before the Swedish king and queen will be visiting this stucco bungalow in south Minneapolis. The pepparkakor and sandbakelser are baked; the cans of Folgers are in the cupboard; the floors are clean enough for a king to eat off (not that he'll be asked to do so), and the Swedish crystal is sparkling after a bath in vinegar and water.

But Gunhild Anderson is scurrying and worrying.

Her head buzzes with questions, which she shoots at her husband, Hilding, and anyone else who will listen:

Should we stick with the decision to use the rose-patterned china rather than the cups with the little violets? Will blue-and-white towels be nice in the bathroom? Would the king like a little orange juice? Is the garage clean enough? Is there any chance the queen will get upstairs and see all the junk stashed up there? Do we know how to curtsy? Should we leave the stack of magazines in the TV room so it looks homey? Will the king and queen be comfortable on the love seat? Would it do any good to scrub the sidewalk?

Then, with a wring of her hands, she goes on to bigger issues:

What can we do to make ourselves better by Monday? Is there still time to tear out the interior of the house and start over?

She amuses even herself at her need to have everything *perfect* for the half-hour visit by King Carl XVI Gustaf and Queen Silvia, but this is a *big* deal, you understand. The royal couple asked to visit the home of Swedish immigrants — regular people, please; not the rich or famous — and the Andersons were chosen for the honor. They both came to America in 1926; he was 20 and she was 16. They met for the first time the next year in Minneapolis. He drove a milk truck for a living, and they've lived in the same house at 5020 16th Av. S. since 1948.

Their names and those of other couples were submitted to the Swedish consulate months ago. When the word came last month that the Andersons were picked, cleaning inside and out began in earnest. Exercising the restraint their nationality is known for, the Andersons decided not to go over-board. They wouldn't buy anything new for the house, and they wouldn't shop for a fancy home on Lake Minnetonka.

"We're not going to put on the dog," Gunhild says. "We're just using what we have for regular company."

They did buy one new thing: an indoor-outdoor carpet for the front porch. However, they learned it couldn't be installed unless the temperature rose above 50 degrees, so the new brown one is in the basement and the old green one is the rug on which the royal shoes will tread.

"I'll take the king downstairs if he wants to see the new carpeting," Hilding kids.

"Oh, Hilding," Gunhild says. "Don't even joke about that. He just might want to. He's just the plainest, nicest person, and the queen, she's so wonderful. They're wonderful people."

She has been infatuated with Swedish royalty all her life. The current king's grandfather, Gustaf VI Adolf, happened to be on the same ship when she immigrated to America. He and his wife paid a visit to the third-class deck, where Gunhild was a passenger, and they stayed for dinner and danc-ing. Gunhild gawked.

She has thought the present king charming all his life: "He was just an adorable baby. Every time you got a magazine from Sweden and saw the little prince, you just went crazy." A plate with his engagement picture is hung on a wall near the bedrooms, and books about the royal family are on her coffee table all the time, not just when royalty happens to be dropping in.

Some of the pressure on Gunhild was removed when members of the Idun Guild at the American Swedish Institute offered to make the cookies for the visit. The guild is in full gear at the ovens anyway because the institute is having a big holiday bazaar Nov. 20. Gunhild and her friend, Daisy Samuelson, made at least 90 dozen pepparkakor, spicy little cookies shaped like hearts. Her friends in the guild provided the syltkakor and the brysselkex and eight other kinds of cookies, all beautiful and delicious, she said.

This reporter personally can vouch for four kinds. "Please have one," Gunhild said. "The king is not going to eat all these." One became two, and two became four. Not knowing if mere royal cookies would be wonderful enough for the press, she also provided drom (two dots over the o) tarta (one dot over the first a), a delight of cocoa and eggs and sugar and butter. She told how to make it, something about beating the daylight out of it.

But anyway, the Andersons have strict instructions to just sit and chat with the royal couple. There will be no jumping up and down to serve them. So the Andersons are bringing in a one-day supply of servants: their daughter, Maureen Milbrath; her husband, Bill, and the grandchildren, 27-year-old Michael and 25-year-old Patricia.

The Milbraths will hang up coats (not even the king's can be put on the new dry-clean-only, cream-colored bedspread), and they'll bring in Swedish coffee bread on the Andersons' Swedish brass tray and cookies on the big hammered-aluminum tray, graced with a doily.

Meanwhile, Gunhild and Hilding hope to be telling the king and queen about their lives in America and their seven visits to Sweden. Hilding especially wants to talk about last Christmas morning in his native village of Matfors, where his parents are buried. Their daughter arranged by mail to have a horse and buggy take the Andersons to 6 a.m. services, and they got to sit in the first pew of the church. "Yah, I pretty near cried," Hilding remembers.

With the royal couple in the house Monday will be the Swedish ambassador and his wife, his majesty's press secretary and the press counselor. Everyone else in the royal contingent and press corps will be out back in the Anderson garage. Good strong coffee, of course, will be provided there, and maybe a few cookies too.

The Andersons' neighbors are being encouraged to fly American and Swedish flags for the visit. They may watch the arrival and departure from behind the ropes that security people put up. The neighborhood can count on a clean street; Alderman Walter Rockenstein has promised a street crew by Monday.

So things are pretty well lined up. Of course, Gunhild will scrub the kitchen floor one more time, and someone will *have* to decide if she should wear the blue flowered dress or the brown velvet. She'll put out the nice new bar of Dove and a new roll of white toilet paper in the bathroom and light the candles in the living room and dining room. Then wait and worry some more and hope for the best.

Hilding said, "You see, never in our wildest dreams did we think we could have the king and queen come visit."

"No, no," she said. "We come from plain, ordinary working people. His father was a farmer, mine was a carpenter. No way could we have had this experience home in Sweden. No way."

Hilding added, "We certainly hope it turns out all right, that we don't make a boo-boo."

—P.M.

Everything went fine. The Andersons don't think they made a boo-boo.

Index

Chaplain, 203-206
Christmas, 71-72
Clergy, 1-3, 203-206, 217-222
Clock repair, 195-198
Coffey, Jeanne, 4-7
Coffey, Richard, 4-7
Comeau, Florence, 66-67
Contest winner, 171-173
Copeland, Mary Jo, 231-233
Corrigan, Greg, 200
Curtis Hotel, 144

D

Deaf interpreter, 158-160
Department store, 126-131
Detours, 199-202
Dieleman family, 27
Dress shop, 144-147
Dubow Family Scholarship, 34-36
Dubow, Irvine, 34-36
Dubow, Lillian, 34-36
Dunfey Corp., 65

E

Effie, Minn., 138-143

F

Family reunion, 174-177
Farmer, Debi, 9-11
Ferrari, Joyce, 133, 136
Fredrickson family, 163-165
"From the Mountains to the Prairies: Selected Poems
    for Everyone's Enjoyment," 30-33
Funeral director, 95-98

G

Ganley, Jerry, 8-11
Ganley, Mick, 8-11
Geiger, Harold Emery, 30-33
Geltz, Jeff, 66
Gilgosch, Ag, 73-76
Gilgosch, Al, 73-76
Graff, Robert S., 133-137
Gumshoe, 191-193

H

Handicapped, 65-69
Hanke, Ann, 68
Hanson, Don (Sauk Centre), 60-64
Hanson, Don (Kenyon), 96-98

Hanson, George, 95-98
Harris, Elizabeth, 8-11
Helgeson, Bill, 155-157
Hennepin County Historical Museum, 183-188
Her, Dang, 55
Highway 12, 199-202
Hinckley, Minn., 4-7
Hmong, 53-56
Hoff, Albert Charles, 134
Holland, 25-29
Hospital, 203-206
House of Breakfast Par Excellence, 149-152
Hulst, The Netherlands, 27

I

Ingebretsen family, 39-43
Ingebretsen's Scandinavian Center, 39-43
Iron Range, 44-46

J

Jail, 21-23
James, Edith, 17-20
Jewelers Exchange, 195-198
Jews, 34-36, 126-131
Jitrnice, 89-93
Johnson, Edward Earl, 11
Johnson, Robert Ed, 11
Jones, Pat Dunn, 52
Judge, 133-137

K

Kaplan Brothers Department Store, 126-131
Kaplan, Jacob, 126-131
Kaplan, Joseph, 126-131
Kaplan, Steve, 126-130
Kent, Mary Claire, 105-111
Kenyon, Minn., 95-98
Kirk's Mobil, 99-104
Knapp, Wis., 200-201

L

Lake Nokomis, 30-33
Lakeville, Minn., 163-165
Lanesboro, Minn., 209-212
Lang, Dennis, 134
Latvia, 166-169
Leu, Paula, 178-182
Lewis, Sinclair, 59-64
Lind, Donna, 183-188
Lindstrand, Marge, 13-14

Peterson, Marilyn, 51-52
Peterson, Mina, 13-15
Peterson, Morrie, 112-116
Peterson, Winnie, 112-116
Pianist, 77-82
Pie Lady of Winthrop, 13-15
Pine County Historical Society, 5
Pink Flamingo (award), 77, 81
Piper, Jaffray & Hopwood, Inc., 86-88
Pitzen family, 138-143
Plymouth cars, 171-173
Poet, 30-33
Pollinger, Heinz, 66
Powder room attendant, 213-216
Priest, 1-3
Private investigator, 191-193

Q
Quie, Al, 138

R
Reed, Agnes, 144-147
Robbinsdale, Minn., 203-206
Rodeo, 138-143
Rollingstone, Minn., 119-125
Roseberry, Rick, 191-193
Roundtree, Hank, 101-103

S
St. Nicholas, 71-72
St. Paul, Minn., 53-56, 73-76
Sauk Centre, Minn., 59-64
Sausage, 39-43, 89-93
Sazenski, Felix Joseph, 135
Scandinavian specialty shop, 39-43
Schell, Jamie, 119-125
Schneider, Debby, 171-173
Scholarships, 34-36
Schroeder, Alina, 158-160
Schuelke, Richard Paul, 134, 136
Scott, Barb, 226
Scott, Jim , 226-228
Service station, 99-104
Sheboygan, Wis., 85
Ships, 112-116
Singers, 77-82, 105-111
Slavery, 174
Snider, Lou, 77-82
Sowden, Bill, 51-52
Sparrow, Diane Frandrup, 49-52

Michael A. Carroll/book designer
Brian A. Cravens/composition analyst
Todd Grande/illustrator
Linda James/indexer and researcher
Dorothy Meyer/keyboarder
Ingrid Sundstrom/book editor